LEADING BEAUTIFULLY

Leading Beautifully provides a new dimension to understanding effective leadership. Drawing from lessons in the arts and the humanities, English and Ehrich explore how educational decision-making in schools can be informed by identity, personal competence, and an understanding of the field's intellectual foundations. Based on in-depth interviews of artists and educational leaders, this book provides insight into the inner world of successful leaders who have developed competencies and understandings that extend beyond the standard leadership tool box. This exciting new book explores the theory and practice of leadership connoisseurship as a human-centered endeavor and as an antidote to mechanistic, business-oriented practices. The authors' well-grounded reconsideration of educational leadership will enliven and enhance any educational leader's practice.

Fenwick W. English is the R. Wendell Eaves Senior Distinguished Professor of Educational Leadership at the University of North Carolina at Chapel Hill, USA.

Lisa Catherine Ehrich is Associate Professor of Education at Queensland University of Technology, Australia.

LEADING BEAUTIFULLY

Educational Leadership as Connoisseurship

*Fenwick W. English and
Lisa Catherine Ehrich*

Routledge
Taylor & Francis Group

NEW YORK AND LONDON

First published 2016
by Routledge
711 Third Avenue, New York, NY 10017

and by Routledge
2 Park Square, Milton Park, Abingdon, Oxon, OX14 4RN

Routledge is an imprint of the Taylor & Francis Group, an informa business

© 2016 Taylor & Francis

Library of Congress Cataloging in Publication Data
English, Fenwick W.
Leading beautifully : educational leadership as connoisseurship /
Fenwick W. English, Lisa Catherine Ehrich.
pages cm
Includes bibliographical references and index.
1. Educational leadership. 2. School management and organization.
3. School administrators. I. Ehrich, Lisa Catherine. II. Title.
LB2806.E566 2016
371.2—dc23
2015025835

ISBN: 978-1-138-01678-1 (hbk)
ISBN: 978-1-138-01679-8 (pbk)
ISBN: 978-1-315-78058-0 (ebk)

Typeset in Bembo
by Florence Production Ltd, Stoodleigh, Devon, UK

Printed and bound in the United States of America by Publishers Graphics, LLC on sustainably sourced paper.

This book is respectfully and lovingly dedicated to our
first mentors and friends in the world, our parents,
Phyllis and Melvin English and Gwen and Max Ehrich.
We continue to be inspired and humbled by your love,
patience and belief in us. We cherish that legacy.

CONTENTS

ILLUSTRATIONS

Figures

Photographs

Tables

PREFACE

You're interested in art because you're more interested in life. Art helps you actually get closer to life because there are so many things in life that you can't look at too closely, but art gives you a way not only to recognize beauty but to recognize pain. Art was invented as a way to face really difficult things with a sense that in facing them, you've already started the healing process.

(Peter Sellars in Alexandra Wolfe, 2015, C11)

The purpose of the book is to reveal the many dimensions of the concept of *connoisseurship* and how they relate to and may enhance our understanding of leading and leadership. The co-authors and co-researchers are largely products of the current research practices and texts in educational leadership. Between the two co-authors we've written over 40 books in leadership and ancillary areas. But by no means did we ever feel we had exhausted our understanding of leadership. In fact, we felt that not only our own texts but most of the extant ones in our field also fell considerably short in coming to grips with a very complex phenomenon of human interaction, universal in nature but context specific in application.

The research behind the book began with interviews of artists to gain a better appreciation of how artists come to their own understanding of leadership and the constraints they face in practicing their craft. We deliberately avoided starting with educational leaders. We were cognizant of Marcel Proust's adage that, "The voyage of discovery lies not in finding new landscapes . . . but in having new eyes" (Conord & Conord, 2002, p. 171). It was our purpose in starting outside of schools to try to acquire "new eyes" when coming back to a landscape with which we believed ourselves to be fairly intimate. Our journey was rewarding. We began to see leadership differently and the practitioners in the schools in new ways. This book is an attempt to capture our discovery and to share with readers what we saw and learned. We are grateful to the artists who shared with us their work and stories, and to the educational leaders in Australia and America who allowed us to learn from them their continua on their own journeys towards connoisseurship.

The intended audience for our book are educational practitioners, professors, policy developers and researchers who are similarly interested in understanding more of the process of leading. We see this work as part of an ongoing conversation which we have enjoyed for over four decades with colleagues all over the world. As we wrote this book snippets and echoes of those conversations were remembered, some with great clarity because of their incisiveness and intensity. We hope this effort continues to provoke colleagues in our field to reconsider some rather fundamental notions of what constitutes leading and how one should conduct research about it. The content of the book is as follows:

In Chapter 1 we explore the knowledge base for connoisseurship and the 10 dimensions which comprise it. We provide real life examples of leaders that have met those dimensions and thus qualify to be considered connoisseurs. We present portraits of connoisseurs such as Hildegard of Bingen, Leonardo da Vinci and Bernard Berenson.

In Chapter 2 we provide a classification of types of connoisseurs and indicate that there are three types. The first are connoisseurs of leaders, the second are connoisseurs of leadership performance, and the last are those persons who are both connoisseurs of leaders and connoisseurs of leadership performance. In the first category we placed L. Mestrius Plutarch, Niccolò Machiavelli, Giorgio Vasari and Edward Said. In the category of connoisseurs of leadership performance we placed Saint Mary MacKillop of Australia and Frida Kahlo of Mexico. In the last category we identified Nelson Mandela, Paul Keating and Winston Churchill.

In Chapter 3 we highlight educational connoisseurs and their backgrounds and accomplishments. These include Paulo Freire of Brazil, Maria Montessori of Italy, Tsunesaburō Makiguchi of Japan, John Dewey of the United States and Jacob Riis of Denmark and the United States.

In Chapter 4 the conceptual frame of the seven ways that the arts can enhance education and educational leadership from the work of Elliot Eisner are discussed. Of critical importance is the development of the connoisseur's *discerning eye*. The chapter presents empirical work that reports on our study of artists and leaders.

In Chapter 5 we present four portraits: a sculptor, an actor/director, a choreographer, and a visual artist, and we consider these in terms of our 10 dimensions of connoisseurship.

In Chapter 6 we present six portraits of educational leaders on the continuum of connoisseurship, two from Australia and four from the United States. They include principals, a director, a consultant and two supervisors of school principals.

In Chapter 7, 20 dimensions of connoisseurship are applied to connoisseurs and to the views of *managerialism*, the dominant ideology of leadership in the corporate and public sectors today and how they differ critically in their approach to leading and leadership.

In Chapter 8 all of the strands and dimensions of connoisseurship are integrated and linked. The idea of "leading beautifully" is compared to the conventional notion of "leading effectively." The latter notion is shown to be minimalist in application.

Finally, in the Epilogue, the five major lessons learned in the journey of the book are presented.

The unique structure of each chapter is that there is a brief overview of what each one is about followed by a general chapter introduction. At the end of each chapter key terms are defined and discussed along with the policy and practice implications regarding the chapter's content and critical themes. This feature will help the reader better understand the meaning and complexities of connoisseurship as well as translate them into policy and practice.

Connoisseurship is sometimes presented as a realized capacity of only a very minute part of any population of artists or in this case leaders and educational leaders. The book shows that connoisseurs are not elite, but rather that all humans are on a continuum leading to connoisseurship. The four stages of connoisseurship are identified, illustrating major developmental points on that continuum. That only some attain that status is testimony to their fields, the context and their skills and discipline in pursuing heightened areas of knowledge and competence. Experience, persistence and the ability to confront ambiguity and dissonance in one's environment are crucial mitigating factors. In the end leadership is about performance and it is about *leading beautifully*.

References

Conord, B. & Conord, J. (2002). *Costa Rica*. Edison, NJ: Hunter Publishing.

Wolfe, A. (2015, March 21–22). Weekend confidential: Peter Sellars. *Review: The Wall Street Journal*, C11.

ACKNOWLEDGMENTS

While authors may write alone, they do not live alone. Lives are lived in context and involve interactions with significant others. The authors wish to acknowledge family, friends and professional colleagues who influenced and supported them in the crafting of this book. Fenwick English wishes to thank the School of Education at the University of North Carolina at Chapel Hill for its support and especially his Dean, Dr. William McDiarmid, who provided for course relief in the spring of 2014 so he could work in Australia. Lisa Catherine Ehrich wishes to thank her institution, the Queensland University of Technology in Brisbane, Australia, and especially her Head of School, Professor Suzanne Carrington and Dean of the Faculty of Education, Professor Wendy Patton, for supporting three months' professional development leave in 2011 to enable her to work with Fenwick English at the University of North Carolina at Chapel Hill. It was during this leave that the ideas for the book first took shape.

Professor English acknowledges the continued support for his work among his Chapel Hill educational leadership colleagues and those who have worked with him nationally and internationally over the years. He also thanks his family, especially Betty Steffy-English, for her encouragement and support. He also wishes to thank Val Klenowski, Suzanne Carrington and Dean Wendy Patton for his appointment as Adjunct Professor in the Faculty of Education at Queensland University of Technology. Associate Professor Ehrich wishes to thank members of her family—Gwen, Michelle, Kris-Ann, John, Paul and Caleb Joseph. She also wishes to thank friends and colleagues who have shown an interest in her and her work over the years. Both authors wish to thank friend and colleague, Megan Kimber, for locating research materials that proved invaluable for the book; Chris Steffy for his insightful comments on early drafts; and QUT's excellent library staff.

Finally, the authors wish to thank all of the persons interviewed in the study of leadership and connoisseurship and who took time to review and respond to interview notes and queries. We also wish to thank the anonymous reviewers of several papers accepted for presentation on our work at UCEA (University Council of Educational Administration) and AERA (American Educational Research Association).

1

CONNOISSEURSHIP REVEALED

Most of us suffer from an illusion that might be called the completeness of perception. We think that because we have pointed our eyes at something we see what is there to be seen. But we are profoundly mistaken. We take in a scene holistically without realizing how partially we are seeing it, how schematic our perceptions generally are. For a truly intelligent eye, we need to get beyond the limits of experiential intelligence. To do that, we need to understand these limits better.

(Perkins, 1994, p. 24)

WHAT THIS CHAPTER IS ABOUT

Connoisseurship is an unusual term to describe leaders or leadership in educational administration or in the leadership genre writ large. Partly the reason is that in much of leadership studies, the practice of management has subsumed or erased the artistic and/or so-called non-scientific aspects of leadership such as the role of emotion, intuition, morality and ethics. This chapter establishes the basis for considering connoisseurship as a useful term to re-examine the nature of leadership in general and educational leadership in particular.

Specifically this chapter addresses the following points:

- The idea of concept of connoisseurship and the development of "the discerning eye."
- The role of tacit knowledge as the basis of connoisseurship.
- The conceptual and theoretical base of the study of connoisseurship in this book.

- Some historical examples of connoisseurship in Hildegard of Bingen and Leonardo da Vinci.
- The 10 essential dimensions of connoisseurship based on the study which forms the base of this book.
- A test case of the 10 dimensions of connoisseurship in the life of Bernard Berenson.

Introduction

There's something visible and invisible about connoisseurship. A common metaphor is that of an iceberg. You know it when you encounter a connoisseur. That person is visible. The knowledge he/she possesses is obvious almost immediately. There are insights and nuances that rarely escape their recognition. What is known by a connoisseur is huge. The scope of their view, knowledge and reservoir of information dwarfs that of most other persons. A connoisseur has a command not only of the facts, but of their implications. A connoisseur seems to have this sixth sense, this uncanny ability to comprehend and understand things.

For example, Ernest Samuels (1979) the biographer of the legendary Italian Renaissance art connoisseur Bernard Berenson (1865–1959) wrote of him:

> For all his avowals of science, it had in fact become increasingly clear to Berenson from his own practice that the ultimate authority for an attribution must be the "properly trained eye" intently focused on the work of art itself. It is this informed and educated "seeing" that almost from the beginning of his study had actually been a preoccupation; all mechanical tests were in truth subordinate to it.
>
> (pp. 375–376)

And this notion of "informed seeing . . . became less the product of scientific investigation than of critical intuition" (p. 376).

The Role of Tacit Knowledge as the Basis of Connoisseurship

Famed British physical chemist Michael Polanyi who engaged in research regarding thermodynamics, X-ray analysis and reaction kinetics explained how scientists also developed such a sixth sense about their work, and that "the grounds of both science and art were neither objective nor subjective, but personal" (Prosch, 1986, p. 262). Polanyi (1891–1976) asserted that the simple reading of scientific instruments, which is objective in one sense, becomes subjective when a scientist attaches meaning to the data produced from the instruments. Meanings often exceed and go far beyond the process of quantification and measurement. This extension by the scientist Polanyi called "tacit coefficients" and as Prosch (1986) comments, "It, too, is the product of unspecifiable skills and is not purely detached and objective 'information' that it is usually assumed to be" (p. 88). Polanyi (1967) summed it up succinctly, "I shall consider human knowledge by starting from the fact that we can know more than we can tell" (p. 4).

But connoisseurship has an invisible side to most external viewers. This is the iceberg below the water line. The secret of understanding a connoisseur is to grasp that what they see more completely than others is not "out there" but "in there," that is, the connoisseur sees the iceberg below the water line because what is there to be seen abides in the mind itself. Polanyi (1967) called this *tacit knowledge* and explained it this way:

> Our own body is the only thing in the world which we normally never experience as an object, but experience always in terms of the world to which we are attending from our body. It is by making this intelligent use of our body that we feel it to be our body, and not a thing outside.
>
> (p. 16)

Therefore, the connoisseur is not some sort of genetic freak of nature but simply a person who acquires the mental discipline and predispositions to perceive what is before all of us which we don't see.

The connoisseur has created what Polanyi (1967) has called an "indwelling," which means that a human being is engaged in the interiorization of knowledge, "not by looking at things, but by dwelling in them" (p. 18). At first blush this explanation may strike the reader as some sort of exotic mysticism. But Polanyi insists that it is employed every day in scientific problem solving because to state a problem well is to "see something that is hidden. It is to have an intimation of the coherence of hitherto not comprehended particulars. The problem is good if this intimation is true; it is original if no one else can see the possibilities of the comprehension that we are anticipating" (Polanyi, 1967, pp. 21–22).

But to see a problem in this way requires our use of the creation of the "discerning eye," that is, the ability to engage in "indwelling" of what we see and the result is where the iceberg below the water line is simply the tacit knowledge where we know more than we can explain.

> The most striking feature of our own existence is our sentience. The laws of physics and chemistry include no conception of sentience, and any system wholly determined by these laws must be insentient. It may be in the interest of science to turn a blind eye on this central fact of the universe, but it is certainly not in the interest of truth.
>
> (Polanyi, 1967, pp. 37–38)

This insight from Polanyi was behind the classic story told by the Greek philosopher Plato in his famous *Allegory of the Cave* penned between 300 and 400 BCE. In this vintage narrative Plato tells the tale of men who lived as prisoners chained to a wall in a cave. The men could not see outdoors. All they could see were the shadows on the cave's wall from the sun at the cave's entrance. These shadows were cast from material objects traveling across the cave's opening.

When the men were eventually freed and ventured outside the cave they saw the material objects and living things and came to understand that the shadows on the cave's wall were not reality at all, but were caused by the interaction between the sun and the objects under its rays. Plato used this allegory to posit that the reality of the material objects of the world were simply the equivalent of shadows and that the actual world consisted of universal objects and ideas. Thus, reality was not a specific thing, but a universal idea behind that specific thing. This "reality of forms" were the universals that were the repository of true knowledge and thus understanding. They were "the truth" behind perception. They were the "indwelling" cited by Polanyi.

All of these descriptions of being a *connoisseur* are derived from the French word *connoistre* which means *to know* (Barnhart, 1995, p. 153) and comes from the Latin word *cognosco* (or *cognoscere*) which has a much more inclusive understanding than *connoistre*. In Latin *cognosco* means

> to become acquainted with on all sides (by the senses or mentally), to examine, investigate, perceive, see, understand, learn and in the tempp. Perff (cf. nosco), to know, have knowledge of (very freq. in all periods and species of composition).
>
> (Andrews, 1854, p. 299)

A connoisseur from the Latin perspective is not only an expert, but one who "has knowledge of all species and periods." Such a person's judgment is much more highly prized and authoritative and indeed one of the other meanings of *cognosco* is "to examine a case in law, to investigate judicially" (Andrews, 1854, p. 299).

A connoisseur is someone therefore who has an extended knowledge base which is more inclusive than most others and is able to relate and connect aspects of this knowledge to particular cases and examples beyond the scope of most others. This capacity propels him/her to a position of authority and enables that person to render judgments regarding the propriety, legality, authenticity, correctness of objects and issues which require expert opinion to resolve.

We now turn to some historical examples of connoisseurs in different fields to highlight the lives of the connoisseur. Connoisseurship is situated within context, culture and time. Our discernment of connoisseurship lies in the approach of Wittgenstein's philosophical investigations where he engaged in "an album of sketches made at different points in a long and involved journey" (Pears, 1970,

p. 190). We also share his sentiment of "strong feeling that the great danger to which modern thought is exposed is domination by science, and the consequent distortion of the mind's view of itself" (Pears, 1970, p. 197) for it is within the mind that connoisseurship begins and ends.

Our Approach to the Study of Connoisseurship in Leadership

The approach we have taken in understanding the nature of leadership connoisseurship has been influenced by gestalt psychology generally and has utilized methodological insights from both phenomenology and portraiture.

Gestalt psychology represents a perspective of perception in which the "whole form" to be perceived is presented and from this whole form the parts or patterns are subsequently detailed. An important tenet of gestalt psychology is that "the whole is different from the sum of its parts acting in isolation" (Gordon, 2004, p. 18). An example is that a melody is more than simply the notes that form it; it is experienced as a whole (Schroeder, 2007). In other words, the individual notes mean little on their own. The melody is understood as a total experience where each of the notes are played and ordered in a particular way.

Gestalt psychology was first formulated in 1890 by Christian von Ehrenfels and explored further by Max Wertheimer, Wolfgang Köhler and Kurt Koffka (Gordon, 2004). As a theory of mind, it posits that the brain approaches objects in their entirety before differentiating them into smaller pieces. This was certainly how we approached the notion of connoisseurship.

Gestalt psychology emerged at the end of the 19th Century as a reaction to both structuralism and behaviorism, both of which were dominant approaches to psychology. Structuralism, following the work of Wundt, maintained that subjective experiences could be studied if they were broken down into more simple and basic experiences or sensations, while a key goal of behaviorism is the search for objectivity and objective behavior thus denying any subjective experiences. Gestalt psychologists, then, rejected these two perspectives because of the former's "mosaic view of perception" (Gordon, 2004, p. 12) and its atomistic and mechanistic view, and the latter's focus on objectivity (Gordon, 2004).

Around the same time in history, the writings of Husserl, founding father of *phenomenology*, emerged. Husserl devised both a philosophical phenomenology and phenomenological psychology (Husserl, 1927/1971). Like gestalt psychology, phenomenological psychology at the turn of the 19th Century also rejected the dominance of behaviorism in psychology characterized by its focus on measurement rather than meaning. Another point of commonality between these two approaches to psychology is the idea that psychological phenomena should be described as they appear within experience "undistorted by their a priori assumptions about their nature" (Schroeder, 2007, p. 296). In other words, phenomenology is a turning towards "the things themselves" (Husserl, 1900/1970, p. 252) so that a person's experience can be placed at the center of phenomenological investigations (Merleau-Ponty, 1962) and be uncontaminated by theory or pre-existing knowledge.

According to Husserl (1900/1970), phenomenology can be described as the study or description of phenomena as one experiences them. It is also a "study of essences" (Merleau-Ponty, 1962, p. vii) and these essences reveal the nature of a phenomenon (van Manen, 1984, 1990). Phenomenology, then, seeks to explore the "isness" of a phenomenon or, in other words, what makes a thing what it is "and without which it could not be what it is" (van Manen, 1984, p. 1). van Manen (1984) says that a phenomenological inquiry

> is not unlike an artistic endeavour, a creative attempt to somehow capture a certain phenomenon of life in a linguistic description that is both holistic and analytic, evocative and precise, unique and universal, powerful and eloquent.
>
> (p. 6)

In exploring the nature of connoisseurship, we were particularly influenced by insights provided by van Manen. van Manen (1984) explores what it means to be human as he seeks to understand "the nature of lived experience itself" (p. 3). We believe that leadership is a human-centered phenomenon and that leader connoisseurship is a type of human activity worthy of investigation. Hence, we were attracted to van Manen's work on how to undertake phenomenological research. He says that it requires researchers to be sensitive and open to new possibilities and understandings about the nature of a phenomenon. Researchers also need to be "attentive to other voices, to subtle significations in the way that things and others speak to us" (van Manen, 2006, p. 713). van Manen (2007) likens the work of phenomenologists to that of poets since poets "direct the gaze towards regions where meaning originates, wells up, percolates through the porous membranes of past sedimentations—and then infuses us, permeates us, infects us, touches us, stirs us, exercises a formative effect" (p. 11).

van Manen's (2007) ideas regarding attentiveness to others, being open to the subtleties inherent in experience, and poetizing resonated with us as we planned a research project that enlisted ideas of artists and leaders. Our aim was to be fully aware of the finely graded and nuanced understandings we were observing, hearing and sensing. Later in this chapter we discuss the research ideas we adopted from van Manen that helped us to arrive at our understanding of the essence of connoisseurship.

Another perspective we referenced in our work was that of Roman Ingarden (1893–1970) and his work on phenomenological aesthetics (1989). In this treatise he captured a dynamic tension between the artist and the observer when he noted that the artist becomes an observer of his own emerging work, but even then it is not completely passive apprehension but an active, receptive behavior. On the other side, the observer too does not behave in a completely passive or receptive way, but being temporarily disposed to the reception and recreation of the work itself, is also not only activity, but in a certain sense at least creative.

(Ingarden, 1989, p. 189)

We found in our interviews of artists and educational leaders this dynamic tension in connoisseurship. More will be said about this in a later chapter.

The final approach that influenced us in our work was *portraiture*, a qualitative method that seeks to "capture the richness, complexity and dimensionality of human experience in social and cultural context, conveying the perspectives of the people who are negotiating those experiences" (Lawrence-Lightfoot & Davis, 1997, p. 3). To help illuminate the concept of connoisseurship, we have included portraits of artists and leaders in our study and these portraits appear in subsequent chapters. The reason we decided to include portraits was to provide a rich narrative that endeavored to capture connoisseurship in its complexity and wholeness.

An additional thought as we begin our journey on connoisseurship is that most human beings have the capacity to become connoisseurs, but that our own research and readings in the literature strongly suggest that it takes years of hard work, study and discipline to expand one's vision and to begin to extend the awareness of one's senses, that is, to expand the awareness of the body to include a larger sensory repertoire via the process of Polanyi's (1967) "indwelling."

Some Historical Examples of Connoisseurship and the Discerning Eye

We begin examining the nature of connoisseurship in an undifferentiated fashion and then move to engaging in a finer discrimination based on our research.

Portrait 1: Hildegard of Bingen: A Female Connoisseur Who Became a Saint

Hildegard of Bingen (1098–1179) is considered a remarkable woman for her time; and remarkable because she was accomplished in so many ways. She was a writer of books on a variety of different topics, composer of over 70 songs of sacred music, speaker/preacher, visual artist, celebrity, and visionary. She had the ears of popes and other religious leaders, kings and emperors (Logan, 2002). We consider her a *connoisseur* for her talent as an artist who traversed many media and for her preachings and writings that had an enormous influence during her time. For a woman in a male-dominated institution such as the church to have been received with a deep reverence and respect was an enormous achievement in 12th Century Europe. This was particularly the case as Benedictine nuns were not allowed to leave their cloister without permission, nor were they allowed to preach. Through Hildegard's preachings and teaching, she interacted with the outside world (Atherton, 2001). As McVicker (2011) states, Hildegard "was sought for her wisdom by popes, rulers, clergy and lay people not only for her mystical abilities and wisdom, but also for her diplomacy and political wisdom. Her correspondence was widespread, reaching many in government and religious life" (p. 6).

Her story begins when, as a young girl, her parents entrusted her into the care of a holy woman called Jutta. She was taught to read the holy books by Jutta (McVicker, 2011) and together they lived in a Benedictine monastery in St Disibod, Germany. Hildegard remained under Jutta's tutelage for some 30 years (Fox, 2012). Around the age of 14, Hildegard became a nun. When Jutta died in 1136, Hildegard became head of the religious community of nuns. She and her community of nuns later moved to Rupertsberg (near Bingen) where they founded a monastery (Logan, 2002). As Hildegard's fame grew, more and more women joined her order (McVicker, 2011).

Hildegard claimed to have had visions since she was a young child yet it was not until later adulthood that God ordained her to speak and write about these visions (Fox, 2012). Her first book was *Scivias* ("Know the Ways"). This book also contains paintings and opera. Her second book, *Liber Vitae Meritorum* ("Books of the Rewards of Life") was concerned with morality and ways to overcome vices. Her third visionary book was called *Liber Divinorum Operum* ("Book of Divine Works") and it explores 10 of her visions illuminating creation and salvation (Fox, 2012, pp. 6–7). Other writings included two medical treatises, *Physica* and *Causae et Curae* ("Causes and Cures"). The latter of these medical books was the first book to focus on physiological and psychological health problems from a woman's point of view (Larrington, 1995, p. 201). In addition to these books, Hildegard wrote a book that invented a new language. She was also an avid letter writer and she penned over 300 letters during her life.

Hildegard was not afraid to speak her mind truthfully and her message to members of the clergy was one of "repent and reform." She didn't care who she offended (Logan, 2002). According to Fox (2012), Hildegard was a "mover and a shaker." He says her message is as critical today as it was back then. For example, she stood up to corruption and patriarchy as she cautioned against hypocrisy and the unjust actions of the clergy.

She taught about wisdom and this was a big part of her book, *Scivias*. As Fox (2012, p. 87) said, wisdom for Hildegard could not only be found in all creative works but could be best understood through compassion. Fox (2012) said that, for her, "relation, not thing-ness, is the essence of all that exists. Compassion is about relation—about sharing joy, sharing grief, and working to relieve one another's pain" (p. 77).

Hildegard warned of the "domination of the rational masculine even while she praise[d] the use of rationality and intellect. In short, she takes us to a place where the Divine Feminine is welcomed once again" (Fox, 2012, p. xvii). Writers have said that Hildegard, as a Rhineland mystic, was influenced by Celtic theology which includes an appreciation of the Divine Mother, a joy-filled spirituality, and a focus on creativity and birthing (Fox, 2012, p. 65).

Hildegard had strong views about the earth and the need to preserve it. She advocated a type of creativity which she called "greening power" which meant that we should respect Mother Earth and our environment (Fox, 2012, p. xv). She saw that human beings are important parts of nature (Atherton, 2001).

The nature and experience of Hildegard's visions interested her contemporaries and continue to interest people today. She said:

> Since I was an infant, I had this visionary gift in my soul, and I have it to this very day. In these visions my spirit is raised by God up to the heavens and into the winds, and it meets a wide range of people, even those far distant. Since this is the way that I see, my sight is dependent on moving clouds and other conditions. No, I do not hear what I hear with bodily ears nor with the feelings of my heart not with my five senses. I see them in my spirit with my eyes wide open. Never do I experience a trancelike state in my visions. I am fully awake and see visions both day and night. Still, my body experiences such pain that I feel I might die.
>
> (Hildegard in Logan, 2002, p. 180)

She goes on to say:

> It is like looking into the heavens when there is but a light cloud on a starless night. I see in this light the things that I speak of and I hear the responses that I give to those seeking my advice.
>
> (Hildegard in Logan, 2002, p. 180)

According to Logan, there are a number of ways of viewing Hildegard's visions. For those who believe in God and believe that God talks through others, then Hildegard's visions may be credible. Two other propositions are put forward by Logan. Firstly, Hildegard may have fabricated the visions for personal reasons. However, he dismisses this based on what is known about the type of person Hildegard appears to be through her life and teachings. Secondly, he puts forward what he sees as a more plausible explanation and that is her visions seem to be related to migraine episodes since migraines affect not only vision but sometimes can be experienced as lightning type flashes across the eyes. Logan cites the work of Oliver Sacks, who said that Hildegard's visions were "indisputably migrainous" (in Logan, 2002, p. 182). Logan (2002, p. 182) says:

that her visions may be explained in neuro-psychological ways should not diminish the importance of their content. In such a state with unusual visual experiences occurring, Hildegard might quite understandably have thought them experiences from God, and that consequently, what she was thinking while having such experiences came directly from God.

(p. 182)

In 2012, Hildegard of Bingen was declared a saint by the Roman Catholic church and a Doctor of the Church. A Doctor of the Church is given to persons for their influential writings and teachings (Maddocks, 2013). Others in history who have received this award are St Thomas Aquinas, St Augustine and Catherine of Siena (Maddocks, 2013). Fox (2012) finds this ironic as Hildegard was so outspoken about lazy and corrupt church leaders and much of what she advocated (i.e. the importance of a voice for women, following one's conscience rather than blind obedience to the patriarchal tradition of the church) seems to be at odds with church teaching.

Regardless of the speculation regarding the source of Hildegard's visions, her insights and wisdom gained her fame and influence in a time when few women were considered as sources of connoisseurship.

Portrait 2: Leonardo da Vinci: Polymath, Painter, Visionary

Leonardo da Vinci (1452–1519) was the connoisseur par excellence. He was described as "a genius who ignored the boundaries of the various disciplines and roamed freely through the immense realms of knowledge" (Galluzzi, 1987, p. 41). He had a sophisticated "discerning eye" across many disciplines and a "power of seeing, feeling and rendering" (Berenson, 1968b, p. 33). Like Hildegard some centuries before him, he was a visionary who had an acute ability to "see," although the nature of his visions was quite different. While Hildegard's visions were of a theological and mystical nature, Leonardo's "prophetic tone" (Galluzzi, 1987, p. 44) put much store in technology as the enabler of humanity. As Galluzzi (1987) states, Leonardo "had a faith in the development—through technology—of un-heard powers in man (to fly like a bird; to live underwater like a fish)" (p. 44). It was his compelling urge to know and understand that led him to embark upon a lifetime of discovery and innovation.

Leonardo's inventions were legendary and recorded in his copious drawings. From those drawings and plans he has been hailed as "the father of the airplane, the helicopter, the parachute, the submarine, the automobile, and now even the bicycle" (Pedretti, 1987, p. 1). While Leonardo is renowned for his legendary talents, most of his energy and time was spent on "activities of a technological nature" (Galluzzi, 1987, p. 41). By this, Galluzzi refers to Leonardo's quest for innovation and discovery through his work as an engineer who created military technology and designed machines and mechanical devices. He also created technical solutions to practical problems posed by his patrons. One of these solutions was a system for providing hot water for the Duchess Isabella of Aragon's bath (Pedretti, in Galluzzi, 1987, pp. 44–47). Whether he was working as an artist or as a scientist, Leonardo's quest for knowledge was insatiable and he went about it by observing, comparing and analysing the natural world (Clark, 1958, p. 14).

Leonardo recognized the importance of observation and devoted hours to exploring nature, watching the fall of the light and shadow, and the movement of the human body (King, 2012, p. 330). So that he could excel at painting muscles and joints of human beings, he dissected corpses in his quest to delve deeply into these features of men (King, 2012, p. 33). Unlike most of his contemporaries, he devoted considerable time to the study of anatomy and his superior drawings of the body reflected his sophisticated understandings of proportion and perspective (Field, 2002).

On describing Leonardo, Berenson (1968b, p. 32) said:

> that all artistic occupations whatsoever were in his career but moments snatched from the pursuit of theoretical and practical knowledge. It would seem as if there were scarcely a field of modern science but he either foresaw it in vision or clearly anticipated it.

To understand a bit more about this "truly marvelous and celestial" (Vasari, 1568/1996, p. 625) person, there is a need to consider his early life.

Leonardo was born in a small town near Vinci in 1452 to a peasant woman and a Florentine notary. He was raised by his mother for the first years of his life and then lived in the house of his father and grandfather. According to King (2012, p. 21), Leonardo did not appear to experience any disadvantage due to illegitimacy except that he was barred from the university and legal profession. However, this worked in Leonardo's favor as he was able to explore freely a range of creative and scientific pursuits.

It is likely that Leonardo attended elementary school from the ages of 6–11 where he learned to read and write. After that he attended an abacus school where the focus of the teaching was on mathematics and some literature. It was at the abacus school that Leonardo excelled in geometry although he struggled with Latin and Italian (King, 2012). In his teens, Leonardo was apprenticed to Andrea del Verrocchio, a Florentine goldsmith, sculptor and painter, who was employed by the Medici family at the time Leonardo studied under his tutelage (King, 2012, pp. 24–25). There he lived for about 10 years learning the skills of painting and sculpture and assisting his master on several key works. According to King (2012, p. 29), Verrocchio was an intelligent person with many interests including geometry, music, the sciences and literature, and it is likely that he was a mentor to Leonardo and helped to shape his insatiable appetite for learning across a range of endeavors. Verrocchio's links to the Medici also paved the way for Leonardo to make his mark as an artist. When he was in his 20s, he scored several important commissions that established him as a successful painter. Yet, as King (2012, p. 32) says, a number of these commissions were not completed due to a range of factors, including a quest for perfection, a loss of interest, and other distractions. King (2012) put it thus that Leonardo

> was frustrated by the extremely high standard he set for himself in his quest for a new visual language. He looked much more closely at the world than his contemporaries, wishing to integrate its features more naturalistically into his art.
>
> (p. 32)

Around the early 1480s, Leonardo left Florence to work in the court of Lodovico Sforza where he undertook a variety of activities such as painting, designing artillery, planning for and creating a large sculpture of the Duke's father sitting on a horse, in addition to various engineering projects. He also undertook a number of commissions, one of which was the painting of "The Last Supper." He lived in Milan for almost two decades but made a hasty departure after Sforza was overthrown by the French (Field, 2002). Leonardo returned to Florence where he continued with commissions and was employed as an architect and engineer. During his last years he did not undertake much painting but instead devoted his time to drawing machines and other inventions (Field, 2002).

In recent times, because of the writings of art connoisseurs such as Berenson (1968b) and Kenneth Clark (1958), Leonardo's genius as a painter has received more recognition (Field, 2002). However, painting was not a priority and this is evident in the small output of paintings (compared to his contemporaries such as Michelangelo and Raphael) Leonardo produced during his life. Berenson (1968b) sums it up well when he says:

> Painting, then, was to Leonardo so little of a pre-occupation that we must regard it as merely a mode of expression used at moments by a man of universal genius, who recurred to it only when he had no more absorbing occupation, and only when it could express what nothing else could, the highest spiritual through the highest material significance.
>
> (p. 32)

Ironically, two of the most famous paintings in the world were painted by Leonardo: "The Mona Lisa" (hanging in the Louvre, Paris) and the fresco, "The Last Supper" painted inside the church of Santa Maria delle Grazie (Milan) (Field, 2002). Berenson's great praise for Leonardo is captured in the following quote where he is describing one of Leonardo's finest paintings, "The Virgin of the Rocks." He says:

> no one has succeeded in conveying by means of light and shade a more penetrating feeling of mystery and awe than he in his "Virgin of the Rocks". Add to this a feeling for beauty and significance that have scarcely ever been approached. Where again youth so poignantly attractive, manhood so potently virile, old age so dignified and possessed of the world's secrets?
>
> (Berenson, 1968b, p. 31)

In the history of humankind, it is probably true to say that Leonardo da Vinci was not only the consummate artist and scientist but also one of the greatest connoisseurs who ever lived.

The 10 Dimensions of Connoisseurship

The idea of leadership connoisseurship initially emerged from a sequentially staged study of artists and leaders conducted in Australia and America over 18 months. While both co-authors are professors of educational leadership, a deliberate decision was made by us *not* to start with school leaders because the field has so long been dominated by social science concepts and methods that probing any new dimension not previously discussed in the literature would be highly unlikely.

Many thoughtful researchers in educational leadership also have reflected and commented upon this state of affairs. For example, over 20 years ago William Foster (1986) noted, "The scientific study of leadership has essentially faltered, partly because the wrong phenomenon has been studied and partly because the functionalist paradigm that houses the studies has gone bankrupt" (p. 3).

Similarly one of the co-authors and co-researchers of this book observed:

> The social sciences have all but petered out in telling us anything new or different about leadership. Leadership studies must move beyond the sciences and recognize that effective leading is about drama and performance—artistry! Artistry involves the whole human, not simply the head, but the heart. Human action contains vision, emotion, and belief embodied in artful performance.
>
> (English, 2008, p. 166)

Dantley and Green (2012) also commented, "For all kinds of societal and demographic reasons, educational leadership is under a mandate to reimagine itself" (p. 3).

Our work on leadership connoisseurship is an attempt to reimagine the field of educational leadership. As discussed earlier in this chapter, we utilized insights from gestalt psychology, phenomenology and portraiture to achieve this.

In particular, the phenomenological ideas of van Manen (1984, 1990) were very useful as we began our journey to discover new interpretive possibilities of leadership.

van Manen (1990) adumbrates several relevant forms of data that are suitable for phenomenological studies and these include using personal experience as a starting point, referring to the etymological sources of a phenomenon, obtaining experiential descriptions from others through interview and observation, referring to phenomenological texts, and locating experiential descriptions in literature and art, including biographies, journals and poetry. In this study, we utilized all of these sources to help us unravel the essential elements or essence of connoisseurship. For example, we were guided by the etymology of connoisseurship as connoisseurship refers to an ability to know, to see, to discern. We reflected upon our own understandings of connoisseurship represented in art forms such as dance, theater and music. We were influenced greatly by autobiographies and biographies of connoisseurs from fields such as art, leadership and politics, and these biographies became important focal points around which we were able to expand our understanding of connoisseurship. The use of biography in this fashion has been previously employed with other major writers in leadership such as James Barber's (1985) *The Presidential Character: Predicting Performance in the White House* and Howard Gardner's (1995) *Leading Minds: An Anatomy of Leadership*.

Our preliminary interviews with artists from a variety of fields also enabled us to gain a deeper understanding and knowledge of connoisseurship through the telling of their personal experiences and reflections on creating art. Based on these data, we then engaged in the phenomenological process of "imaginative variation" that involves "discover[ing] aspects of or qualities that make a phenomenon [i.e. connoisseurship] what it is and without which the phenomenon could not be what it is" (van Manen, 1990, p. 107). The outcome of our exploration led us to identify 10 essential components or dimensions of connoisseurship. These are explained briefly below.

1. *Knowledgeable perception.* What Polanyi (1967) called "indwelling," Eisner (1979) labeled "sensory memory" (p. 193). This dimension enables the connoisseur to be able to recall from his/her memory the qualities of other particular objects, concepts, theories or ideas so as to make a comparison of one object, concept, theory or idea with others and even move to classes of objects. This ability enables a connoisseur to compare and contrast and to make qualitative judgments involving very fine-grained distinctions regarding quality and worth.

Polanyi also cited that a connoisseur was one who recognized that "a grasp of realities that are always expected to contain more than the logical implications we can milk from any possible explicitly formalized concepts of them" (Prosch, 1986, p. 84). What this means is that reality is more than a simple perception of it. "Stravinsky said that the key to creativity is observation: noticing the possibilities right in front of your nose" (in Kapilow, 2011, p. 66).

2. *Experience.* It stands to reason that first dimension, *knowledgeable perception*, takes time to develop. It many cases it takes years to enable one to both observe and understand "what is significant about one set of practices or another" (Eisner, 1979, p. 193). As Eisner indicates, length of time or frequency of involvement in an activity may not necessarily indicate connoisseurship. It is the quality of the experience and how the person chooses to hone his or her skills and insights into a fine-tuned set of measurements which serve as the qualitative index for the subtle interplay of dimensions that connotes connoisseurship.

3. *Competence.* Basically the acquisition of competence is the ability to engage or perform at some sort of minimal level of activity to duplicate or replicate the processes or outcomes which comprise the essence of the activity or process being judged but leaders must be technically proficient and demonstrate artistry and emotional and kinesthetic knowledge. Demonstration of competence involves leaders using not only their heads (or cognitive knowledge) but also their hearts, hands and bodies (or kinesthetic knowledge) in working with and alongside others (Palus, 2002). Kinesthetic knowledge in the realm of competence is important. This is more than merely an awareness of body language; it refers to leaders' sensitivity to movement and space, and to their presence and others' presence in the world (Ropo & Parviainen, 2001).

Similarly for artists, competence goes beyond technique and embraces passion and emotion. Of music, Daniel Barenboim (2008) says:

> intellect and emotion go hand in hand, both for the composer and for the performer. Rational and emotional perception are not only in conflict with one another; rather each guides the other in order to achieve equilibrium of understanding in which the intellect determines the validity of the intuitive reaction and the emotional element provides the rational with a dimension of feeling that renders the whole human.
>
> (pp. 46–47)

4. *Framing.* Connoisseurship involves an understanding of how an act, process or interaction represents a choice of how, where and when to represent or display it. Eisner (1979) says that connoisseurship requires "an ability not only to perceive the subtle particularities of educational life but also to recognize the way those particulars form a part of the structure" (p. 195). Choice is part and parcel of connoisseurship and how to place an activity into a context is as important as the outcome and, in fact, defines and shapes that outcome. The frame is the beginning and the end of an artistic or leadership situation. Stravinsky, the 20th Century Russian composer, once wrote:

> The more art is controlled, limited, worked over, the more it is free. My freedom thus consists in my moving about within the narrow frame that

I have assigned myself for each of my undertakings. I shall go even further: my freedom will be so much the greater and more meaningful the more narrowly I limit my field of action and the more I surround myself with obstacles. The more constraints one imposes the more one frees oneself of the chains that shackle the spirit.

(Stravinsky in Kapilow, 2011, p. 37)

5. *Desire.* A connoisseur is driven to understand and to develop a set of finely tuned capacities to engage in the increasingly complex and different gradations of a process, act or interaction which comprise his or her area of expertise. There is nothing "neutral" about this desire. The motivation for such a desire is complex and not always altruistic. A good example that fits here is the painter, Lucian Freud, hailed as one of the most famous 20th and 21st Century figurative artists for whom "painting was the obsessive centre of his life" (Greig, 2013, p. 10). Freud himself said:

it is the only point of getting up every morning: to paint, to make something good, to make something even better than before, not to give up, to compete, to be ambitious . . . All I ever really want to do is to paint. I am very selfish about it.

(Freud in Greig, 2013, p. 129)

Hence, connoisseurs have a strong desire to create or pursue knowledge and they will not rest until they achieve it. Why they want to develop the capacity may be selfish, as in the case of Lucian Freud; it may be a form of acquiring property or power, it may be to achieve perfection or at least come closer to it, it may be to benefit human kind, i.e. to release human potential or be of service to a set of clients or persons in need of such services. Sinclair (2005, p. 403) adds that leadership as bodily practice also has the advantage of helping leaders to "foster a capacity to read, register and feel compassion [for others]" (p. 403) as well as providing a "capacity for openness and learning" (p. 404). Yet for narcissistic leaders, selfish and self-serving motives drive their behaviors (Rosenthal & Pittinsky, 2006). The challenge for good leaders, then, is "shifting between different modes of attention" (Palus, 2002, p. 12) by not being stuck in a rational mode when making decisions but calling upon other modes of perception such as intuition, emotions and kinesthetic understandings. These dimensions will be explored in greater detail in the ensuing chapters.

6. *Understanding of practice.* Our data and the literature reviewed underscore not only a deep understanding of the connection between practice and theory, but within leadership the importance of critical interaction among those involved in the leadership connection between leaders and situational followers. The term *practice* refers "to the co-ordinated activities of individuals and groups in doing

their 'real work' as it is informed by a particular organizational or group context" (Cook & Brown, 1999, pp. 386–387). It is group context that gives meaning to the action (the doing) of practice.

For example, Gupta (2012) stressed the importance of the role of interpersonal relationships in artistic development and used the three dimensions to explain extraordinary artistic work. These were an interactive confluence of an *individual's talents* (called personal capacities); a *field* which consists of a specific institution and its history, including members of that institution who subsequently render judgments about a creative work, and a *domain* which is principally the medium in which an artist works. We were concerned with how artistic leaders develop connoisseurship. Gupta's work on Picasso stresses the importance of interpersonal relationships as crucial in determining the merits of creativity and how such determinations work within extant socio-cultural beliefs and practices. A quick transfer to educational leadership was hinted at in a study of reputationally successful school superintendents in Ohio by Nestor-Baker and Hoy (2001), which revealed that "those who can be considered as expert performers—have larger amounts of if-then scenarios to draw on in navigating the superintendency, allowing them a seemingly intuitive orientation to the tasks at hand" (p. 123).

7. *Aesthetic vision.* This dimension "couples imagination with agency" (Dimension 5, Desire) and is rooted in "the appreciation of difference and the appropriation and negotiation of such differences as sources of the self" (Bates, 2006, p. 218) (Dimension 10, Identity). Aesthetic vision is essential to any moral purpose of education and it serves as a function to move beyond mere technical rationality where the only thing that matters is test score gains. The work of artists involves juxtaposing and critiquing existing notions of contemporary practice. Aesthetic vision involves an understanding of the importance of critiquing the kind of rationality that is now dominant in educational leadership with the exclusive focus on economic efficiency and the narrowest type of cost–benefit calculation in which the moral purpose of schooling has been erased. The result is a "society . . . devoid of spirit, substantive values, emotion and authentic self-expression. As these represent the source of morality, ethics, culture, art and aesthetics, a society without them can be very ugly indeed" (Milley, 2006, p. 83). Gablik (1993) put it this way:

> To see beyond the individual's perspective is to engage with the world from a participating consciousness rather than an observing one. The model of distanced, objective knowing, removed from moral and social responsibility, has been the animating motif of both science and art in the modern world. As a way of thinking, it is now proving to be something of an evolutionary dead end.
>
> (p. 307)

8. *Cultural awareness and reflexivity*. Connoisseurship involves an ability to step outside the cultural conditioning of one's own background and to see anew or with different eyes. This is because the connoisseur understands that "with the aid of culture we learn how to create ourselves" (Eisner, 2002, p. 32). The connoisseur is aware of how his/her own thinking and perception are anchored in both conscious and unconscious conditioning. The connoisseur both trusts and distrusts his/her own perceptions and is always in a state of where such perceptions are put to the test. Connoisseurs are aware of differences in power within specific fields. Bourdieu (1993) notes that a literary or artistic field is contained within a field of power and within it a certain form of hierarchization. The field is the focal point of consistent struggle for domination and legitimacy. Connoisseurship involves the ability to transcend the binary of objectivity/subjectivity. In short, there is no such thing as a "fresh eye" as everything is viewed from the lens of culture.

Another example of cultural awareness and reflexivity is found in the ideas of Dreyfus who invites us to consider J.S. Bach's connoisseurship "as the result of a musicality that devises and revises thoughts against a resilient backdrop of conventions and constraints" (in Said, 2006, p. 129). Dreyfus goes on to say that Bach had an inclination "to regard certain laws as binding and others as breakable . . . [he] accept[ed] certain limits as inviolate and others as restrictive . . . and judge[d] certain techniques productive and others fruitless" (Dreyfus in Said, 2006, p. 128).

9. *Discipline*. Discipline involves working hard and showing great dedication to mastering one's art or profession. In writing about J.S. Bach, Gaines (2006) says, "He had an almost obsessively stubborn insistence on mastering the most difficult forms and ideas in the music of his time, and he worked with constant, riveted concentration. No composer has ever been more diligent" (p. 231). Bach saw himself as a dedicated craftsman fulfilling his work in the service of patrons and listeners (Kapilow, 2011, p. 26). Discipline also refers to an understanding that work is defined by rules and expectations. It is learning about the forms which govern thought, why some ideas are considered worthwhile and others simply not, and grasping the importance of structure. There are all kinds of structures and ways of understanding structure, in art, music, literature and leadership.

10. *Identity*. A strong sense of personal identity is essential for the connoisseur. The connoisseur has to understand himself/herself and feel comfortable with himself/herself. He/she has to know what is motivational, what is worthwhile, and what is not. Elie (2012) puts it well:

> An artist must be strong enough to feel independent of everything that has been done, and of everything he [*sic*] has learned, and he must convince himself/herself that to "feel" independent of any routine or tradition is his

main duty or purpose. He goes the wrong way who does not question himself or listen to the "voice" of his artistic nature . . . What does matter is what we feel, and is what we have to express.

(pp. 81–82)

The personal identity of a leader is of the utmost importance because as Shamir, Dayan-Horesh and Adler (2005) observe:

> It is likely that in order to lead, people must perceive themselves as leaders or at least believe they have a right and an ability to play a leadership role. In other words, to lead, people need to justify to themselves, as well as to others, not only their social position, but also their sense of self-confidence and self-efficacy, and knowing better than others where to go or what to do. Furthermore, leadership is a highly involving role in the sense that the role and the self are relatively undifferentiated. In other words, leaders are persons for whom the identity of a leader is a central and important part of their self-concepts.

(p. 15)

Identity is also crucial to connoisseurship because, as Eisner (1998) states, "criticism provides connoisseurship with a public face" (p. 85).

Table 1.1 provides a summary of the dimensions of connoisseurship and includes illustrations of how both artists and leaders would display connoisseurship.

An Application of the 10 Dimensions of Connoisseurship: The Life of Bernard Berenson

In this section we take an acknowledged and celebrated connoisseur and show how the 10 dimensions of connoisseurship relate to his life. We have already mentioned Bernard Berenson, who was considered one of the most influential and celebrated connoisseurs of Italian Renaissance art during the turn of the century and first half of the 20th Century. He was an art critic, art historian, and writer of several seminal books that established his reputation as an expert in his field. Four of his fundamental books were: *Venetian Painting in America* (1916), *The Study and Criticism of Italian Art* (1916), *Essays in the Study of Sienese Painting* (1918) and *Studies in Medieval Painting* (1930). These were known as "the four gospels" (*Dictionary of Art Historians*, 1964).

His approach to connoisseurship was referred to as "scientific." He used his discerning eye to categorize paintings according to how an artist approached surface texture, and the volume and weight given to figures in the painting. On describing his approach, Hughes (1979) says he used:

TABLE 1.1 Dimensions of connoisseurship: how artists and educational leaders display connoisseurship

Dimensions of connoisseurship	How artists display connoisseurship	How educational leaders display connoisseurship
1. Knowledgeable perception	Able to recall significant distinctions from acknowledged master works	Able to recall similar contextual differences and connecting them to a range of past successful decisions
2. Experience	Able to reflect, interpret and assimilate a wealth of experiences and come to finely tuned assessments	Able to reflect, interpret and assimilate a wealth of experiences and come to quality decisions
3. Competence	Demonstrate not only a solid background and experience in an artistic field but also utilize aesthetic qualities (intuition) and sensibilities when making judgments	Demonstrate a solid background and experience in leadership but also utilize aesthetic qualities (intuition) and sensibilities when making decisions
4. Framing	Understanding of the limitations of an artistic work is part and parcel of the work itself	Understanding the nature of bounded decision-making is inherent within working within an institutional or organizational setting
5. Desire	Passion to improve oneself, one's understanding and overall practice in the field	Passion to improve oneself, one's understanding and overall practice in the field
6. Understanding of practice	Underpinned by informed judgments made within an artistic discipline	Underpinning by informed judgments made within a professional context of practice
7. Aesthetic vision	Recognition that art both reflects and critiques social life and art's role is to provoke, inspire and re-envision	Recognition that educational leadership is a moral, humanistic and aesthetic endeavor
8. Cultural awareness and reflexivity	Expert knowledge is located within and determined by the broader culture and context	Expert knowledge is located within and determined by broader culture and context
9. Discipline	Exists within a particular arts-based discipline, i.e. painting, dance, sculpture, etc., that has its own traditions, history, rules, theories, and corpus of knowledge	Exists within the discipline of educational leadership that has its own traditions, rules, theories and corpus of knowledge
10. Identity	The identity of the artist connoisseur is introspective, personal and subjective and central to what he/she brings to the field	The identity of the leader connoisseur is introspective, personal and subjective and central to what he/she brings to his/her work

a system of discrimination based not on any special power of argument, still less on the iconographical or social meanings of art, but on meticulous observation of detail, sensitivity to style, and exhaustive comparison based on a retentive visual memory.

(p. 6)

His way of attributing was deemed novel as he insisted "that no matter what the documents [i.e. the painting itself] said, the primary evidence on which one judged the authorship and date of a work of art was the work itself" (Hughes, 1979, p. 7). As well as being a connoisseur, much sought after by museums and private collectors for authenticating Italian old masters, he was an astute business person. For over 25 years he had a secret partnership with a dealer called Duveen. During that time he received hefty commissions from Duveen for authenticating pieces of art and it was Berenson's authority that enabled pictures to be validated, purchased or sold (*Dictionary of Art Historians*, 1964). Yet, he was criticized for this conflict of interest and accusations of "impartiality" were charged against him (*Encyclopedia of Art Education*, n.d.). Despite these criticisms, "his way of seeing, presented in his books, codified in his attributions, and institutionalized in the many important American collections he helped to build, goes on shaping the American understanding of art today" (Cohen, 2013, inside cover). The first dimension we consider is knowledgeable perception.

Knowledgeable Perception

There is no question that Berenson had a sophisticated "knowledgeable perception." Robert Hughes, the well-known art critic wrote:

> Berenson's perceptions about art were not easy to debate. Intuitions rarely are; they do not partake of the nature of the argument, and Berenson staked his entire career on the superiority of his eye, backed up by an incomparable memory bank.

(Hughes, 1979, pp. 13–14)

Cohen (2013) also writes that Berenson

> had an encyclopedic visual memory, and he mastered the careers and paintings of hundreds upon hundreds of Italian painters. His gift for discerning the artistic personalities of different painters and for naming their qualities with a few choice phrases mean that, when his readers encountered the works of these artists, the pictures seemed to come forward.

(p. 3)

An example of this can be seen in the following paragraph where Berenson compares and contrasts several Italian Renaissance painters. He says (1968a):

> And yet, if we may not place Correggio alongside Raphael and Michelangelo, Giorgione and Titian, it is not merely that on this or that count he is inferior to them for specific artistic reasons. The cause of his inferiority lies elsewhere, in the nature of all the highest values, whereby everything, whether in art or in life, must be tested. He is too sensuous, and therefore limited; and the highest human values are derived from the perfect harmony of sense and intellect, such a harmony as since the most noble days of Greece has never again appeared in perfection, not even in Giorgione or Raphael.
>
> (p. 102)

Experience

As we discussed earlier in this chapter, it takes years and experience to develop knowledgeable perception. Important influences on Berenson that enabled him to become a connoisseur were:

• University years and exposure to ideas from professors and wide reading.
• Key writers whose work influenced his thinking (Murillo, Pater).
• Travel abroad (funded by wealthy benefactors) and immersion in art.
• Relationships with women (sister, wife, lovers).
• Relationships with business associates.
• Opportunities that presented themselves; meetings with others.

Competence

As identified earlier, Berenson was one of the most influential art connoisseurs of his generation. As Cohen (2013) argues, "his contemporaries thought of him as one of the greatest perceivers of paintings, a man whose sensitivity to art had seldom being surpassed" (p. 4). His contemporaries were not only the wealthy with whom he did business, but also the educated and those who dwelled in museums and institutions of art.

Framing

Berenson was able to discern coherence in works of art by looking for patterns of similarity that had not been associated before. He would organize, classify and interpret works of art and put these in groups. In this way, each painter could be seen as working within a broader context, influenced by his or her teachers, and influencing his or her pupils, and collaborating with friends (Cohen, 2013, p. 97).

Desire

According to Cohen (2013, p. 12) Berenson "had a lively curiosity." He also had a burning desire to "dedicate his entire activity, his entire life to connoisseurship" (Cohen, 2013, p. 70). Berenson came from a poor yet educated Lithuanian Jewish family and emigrated to the United States when he was 10 years of age. He was an avid reader and spent great lengths of time in the Boston public library. He excelled at school and matriculated from Boston University. He was able to attend Harvard University through the financial support of a wealthy friend. This was the first of many times when he was the object of patronage. Wealthy art collector, Isabella Stewart Gardner, was one of a number of benefactors who recognized his great abilities and talents and sponsored his European training.

Ernest Samuels, biographer of Berenson, said that Berenson's "passion to share his ecstatic feelings came from a deep-seated drive for self-assertion and intellectual domination" (in Cohen, 2013, p. 97).

Understanding of Practice

Understanding of theory and practice nexus refers to a connoisseur's ability to understand the intellectual ideas behind the practice of what he or she is discerning. Berenson as an art historian had an extensive knowledge of the history of art and its intellectual tradition. In his essay, "The Decline of Art" (1968a), he says "it has been my aim to sketch a theory of the arts, particularly of the figure arts, and especially of those arts as manifested in painting" (p. 103). In this essay, he explains his theory of art which is concerned with the "effect of life-enhancement." He goes on to say that in figure painting:

> the principal if not sole sources of life-enhancement are TACTILE VALUES, MOVEMENT, and SPACE-COMPOSITION, by which I mean ideated sensations of contact, of texture of weight, of support, of energy, and of union with one's surroundings. Let any of these sources fail, and by that much the art is diminished.
>
> (Berenson, 1968a, p. 103, capitals in original)

He applied his theoretical concepts to illuminate the work of artists in his two volumes on *The Italian Painters of the Renaissance* (Berenson, 1968a, 1968b).

Aesthetic Vision

For Berenson, "looking at a painting . . . was an experience both sensual and spiritual" (Cohen, 2013, p. 84). He (1968a) said:

> We must look and look and look till we live the painting and for a fleeting moment become identified with it. If we do not succeed in loving what

through the ages has been loved, it is useless to lie ourselves into believing that we do. A good rough test is whether we feel that it is reconciling us with life. No artifact is a work of art if it does not help to humanize us. Without art, visual, verbal and musical, our world would have remained a jungle.

(p. xi)

On discussing Berenson, Cohen (2013, p. 104) said:

The thought that one could be in an active relationship with paintings, and that having one's own private and profound experiences of them was not just for the rich or gifted but a natural capacity of the human mind and therefore available to everybody, became identified with Berenson.

(p. 104)

We also find the active involvement of an observer in Ingarden's (1989) comment that:

It is the whole man [*sic*] endowed with defined mental and bodily powers, which during the process undergo certain characteristic changes which will differ, depending upon how the encounter is taking place and upon the shape of the work of art, or the relevant aesthetic objective, that is being created. If this process leads to the creation of a true and honest work of art, then both this process and the manifest face of the work leaves a permanent mark in the artist's soul. To some extent, the same happens when the observer encounters a great work of art, an encounter which produces the constitution of a highly valuable aesthetic object. He [*sic*], too, then undergoes a permanent and significant change.

(p. 190)

Cultural Awareness and Reflexivity

Berenson's story is one of transformation; he came from a poor Jewish immigrant background but, over his lifetime, transformed himself into a legendary connoisseur and intellectual. He learned early in his life how critical it was to read and reading became one of the key ways in which he not only developed an immense store of knowledge about art (Cohen, 2013), but it also helped him to see, understand and experience the world anew, and become culturally aware and reflexive.

According to Hughes (1979, p. 2) Berenson was acutely aware of his Jewish background and, for this reason, he "dissembled his own Jewishness." This was so that he could be accepted by his contemporaries who had contempt for Jews and to enable a smoother pathway for achieving his ambition of a life dedicated to connoisseurship (Hughes, 1979, p. 8).

Berenson's significant contribution to art attribution was to apply Morelli's system of scientific identification to paintings where he was able to categorize paintings into groups and distinguish between them and others based on a range of qualities. This had not been done before (Hughes, 1979). Berenson once wrote, "My career has followed from my being regarded (even by my worst enemies) as the safest attributor of Italian paintings" (in Cohen, 2013, p. 157).

Discipline

Discipline was evident in his prolific output (books, essays, etc.) during a lifetime dedicated to art. For example, Cohen (2013, p. 133) says that Berenson labored for many years when he was writing his book *The Drawings of the Florentine Painters*, which is considered to be among his best and is used today by art historians and galleries.

Identity

Cohen (2013, p. 6) claims that Berenson's life was a struggle between "scholarship and commerce." He was an intellectual and his books were well respected by art historians and museum curators yet he wanted a life of wealth and had a great desire for beauty. Cohen (2013) says his life was one where he "had to reconcile tendencies that often conflicted: his passion for looking at art, his desire to be wealthy and independent, his hope to write seriously, and his grave self-doubts" (p. 37). Anne Truitt (1982), an artist, discusses how artists have to balance what they do between engaging in their practice in which they are required to produce their work out of themselves, attend to its implications, and then to "present themselves turned inside out to the public gaze" (p. 24).

We contend that this is precisely the task facing educational leaders. While leaders may be benchmarked to functional skill lists, the real work of their roles is to turn themselves inside out and to present their schools to the public gaze. What is blatantly missing in all of the government sanctioned lists of leadership tasks and competencies is the matter of the leader's identity. This is the proverbial 500 pound gorilla in the center of the room that nobody wants to talk about or acknowledge. Who really is this person called "educational leader"? While we know that such persons have hearts, minds and souls, we never talk about it.

Summary

Connoisseurship is a term most often heard in artistic fields. That it is connected to deep knowledge and part of the expected repertoire of acknowledged experts within a field is well established. Michael Polanyi (1967) also used the term in the sciences to describe how scientists make sense of the data produced in the quantification of their work, that is, that they understood more than they could sometimes express in any objective terms.

It is with the research reported in this book that the co-authors first employed the term in coming to understand facets of educational leadership from their interviews of artists and educators (Ehrich & English, 2013). Connoisseurship has been described by a variety of writers. Interview data and sources from selected writers have been used to construct a preliminary sketch of the dimensions of connoisseurship in order to more clearly understand its application in practice and to aid in recognition of it, which it is hoped will lead to improved preparation practices for school leaders.

IMPLICATIONS FOR POLICY AND PRACTICE

Connoisseurship as a Concept Fills a Void in Leadership Studies by Restoring and Legitimizing the Non-Rational Aspects of Leadership Performance

The legacy of leadership and policy studies is one anchored in behaviorism and structural functionalism which de-legitimizes the non-rational aspects of performance such as emotion, intuition, ethics and caring as the proper way to view leadership and to conduct research on how to improve it. The full human being as leader is left to be only half-human and always shaped by the tenets of rationalism and efficiency, which is why the field of economics and business has become dominant in shaping ideas of how to improve leadership and school system management. This trend has led to the increasing bureaucratization of education and to the wide application of corporate models of management in education. At the moment artistic fields are often viewed as not only irrelevant to improving managerial practice but as having little legitimacy as a source of contestation for rival perspectives to compete for public funding and policy alternatives. The idea of connoisseurship re-establishes these fields from, if not a rival perspective, at least one which is a working dyad in improving leadership performance. The perspective advanced in this book is that connoisseurship is not a binary to rational choice theory and economics domination, but restoring the full range of human insight and competence to what has been an extremely narrow vision of leadership itself.

Key Chapter Ideas

• Connoisseur

A *connoisseur* is an expert, one who has an extended knowledge base, uncommon insights, and a comprehensive grasp of a field of studies or a human activity which is deeper and richer than most. The capacity of the connoisseur is centered on the notion of "indwelling" or a complex sensory memory that enables a person to move beyond classes of objects and render very fine-grain judgments in the area of his/her expertise.

• Tacit Knowledge/*The Discerning Eye*

Tacit knowledge is information which is extensive but not always grasped consciously by an individual who has a way of seeing hidden meanings or relationships often missed by others. The capability of such a comprehensive perspective is sometimes referred to as *the discerning eye*.

• Phenomenology

Phenomenology can be described as the study or description of phenomena as one experiences them (Husserl, 1900/1970). It seeks to explore the "isness" of an object or what makes it what it is (van Manen, 1984).

• Portraiture

Portraiture is a method of qualitative research that attempts to sketch out the meaning of humans and their actions within their context or sphere of experience as a participant observer of them (see Lawrence-Lightfoot & Davis, 1997).

References

Andrews, E.A. (1854). *Copious and critical Latin-English lexicon, founded on the larger Latin-German lexicon of Dr. William Freund.* New York: Harper & Brothers, Publishers.

Atherton, M. (2001). Introduction (M. Atherton, Trans.). In *Hildegard of Bingen: Selected writings* (pp. ix–xliii). London: Penguin.

Barber, J.D. (1985). *The presidential character: Predicting performance in the White House* (3rd ed.). Englewood Cliffs, NJ: Prentice-Hall.

Barenboim, D. (2008). *Everything is connected: The power of music.* Great Britain: Phoenix.

Barnhart, R.K. (1995). *The Barnhart concise dictionary of etymology.* New York: HarperCollins.

Bates, R. (2006). Towards an aesthetics for education administration. In E. Samier & R. Bates (Eds.), *Aesthetic dimensions of educational administration and leadership* (pp. 205–220). London: Routledge.

Berenson, B. (1968a). *The Italian painters of the Renaissance: The Venetian painters, the North Italian painters. Vol. 1.* London: Phaidon.

Berenson, B. (1968b). *The Italian painters of the Renaissance: Florentine and central Italian schools. Vol. 2.* London: Phaidon.

Bourdieu, P. (1993). *The field of cultural production.* New York: Columbia University Press.

Clark, K. (1958). *Leonardo Da Vinci: An account of his development as an artist.* Harmondsworth: Penguin Books.

Cohen, R. (2013). *Bernard Berenson: A life in the picture trade.* New Haven: Yale University Press.

Cook, S.D.N. & Brown, J.S. (1999). Bridging epistemologies: The generative dance between organizational knowledge and organizational knowing. *Organization Science, 10*(4), 381–400.

Dantley, M. & Green, T. (2012, May). *Rupturing notions of leadership for social justice: Reconstructing a discourse of accountability through a radical, prophetic, and historical imagination.* Paper presented at the Fifth Annual Duquesne Educational Leadership Symposium, Pittsburgh, Pennsylvania.

Dictionary of Art Historians (1964). Bernard Berenson. A biographical dictionary of historic scholars: Museum professionals and academic historians of art. Retrieved from http://www.dictionaryofarthistorians.org/berensonb.html.

Ehrich, L.C. & English, F.W. (2013). Leadership as dance: A consideration of the applicability of the "mother" of all arts as the basis for establishing connoisseurship. *International Journal of Leadership in Education, 16*(4), 454–481.

Eisner, E. (1979). *The educational imagination: On the design and evaluation of school programs.* New York and London: Macmillan Publishing Co. and Collier Macmillan Publishers.

Eisner, E. (1998). *The enlightened eye: Qualitative inquiry and the enhancement of educational practice.* Upper Saddle River, NJ: Merrill.

Eisner, E. (2002). *The arts and the creation of mind.* New Haven: Yale University Press.

Elie, P. (2012). *Reinventing Bach.* USA: D & M Publishers Inc.

Encyclopedia of Art Education (n.d.). Bernard Berenson: Biography of Renaissance art historian. *Greatest Art Critics Series.* Retrieved from http://www.visual-arts-cork.com/critics/bernard-berenson.html.

English, F.W. (2008). *The art of educational leadership.* Los Angeles: Sage.

Field, D.M. (2002). *Leonardo Da Vinci.* Kent: Grange Book.

Foster, W. (1986). *The reconstruction of leadership.* Waurn Ponds, Geelong: Deakin University Press.

Fox, M. (2012). *Hildegard of Bingen: A saint for our times.* Vancouver: Namaste Publishing.

Gablik, S. (1993). Toward an ecological self. In R. Hertz (Ed.), *Theories of contemporary art* (2nd ed.) (pp. 301–307). Englewood Cliffs, NJ: Prentice-Hall.

Gaines, J.R. (2006). *Evening in the palace of reason.* New York: Harper Perennial.

Galluzzi, P. (1987). The career of a technologist. In P. Galluzzi & J. Guillaume (Eds.), *Leonard Da Vinci: Engineer and architect* (pp. 41–109). Montreal: The Montreal Museum of Fine Arts.

Gardner, H. (1995). *Leading minds: An anatomy of leadership.* New York: HarperCollins.

Gordon, I.E. (2004). *Theories of visual perception* (3rd ed.). Hove, East Sussex: Psychology Press.

Greig, G. (2013). *Breakfast with Lucian: A portrait of the artist.* London: Jonathon Cape.

Gupta, A. (2012, Fall). Simplifying Gardner's labyrinth: The role of interpersonal relationships in Pablo Picasso's artistic development. *Journal of Aesthetic Education, 46*(3), 22–35.

Hughes, R. (1979). Only in America. *The New York Review of Books.* Retrieved from http://www.nybooks.com/articles/archives/1979/dec/20/only-in-ame.

Husserl, E. (1900/1970). *Logical investigations. Vol. 1* (J.N. Findlay, Trans.). New York: Humanities Press.

Husserl, E. (1927/1971). "Phenomenology", Edmund Husserl's article for the Encyclopaedia Brittanica 1927 (R.E. Palmer, Trans.). *The British Society for Phenomenology*, 2(2), 77–90.

Ingarden, R. (1989). Phenomenological aesthetics: An attempt at defining its range. In H. Adams and L. Searle (Eds.), *Critical theory since 1965* (pp. 184–197). Tallahassee: University Press of Florida.

Kapilow, R. (2011). *What makes it great? Short masterpieces, great composers.* New Jersey: John Wiley & Sons, Inc.

King, R. (2012). *Leonardo and the last supper.* New York: Bloomsbury.

Larrington, C. (1995). *Women and writing in medieval Europe: A sourcebook.* London: Routledge.

Lawrence-Lightfoot, S. & Davis, J. Hoffman (1997). *The art and science of portraiture.* San Francisco: Jossey Bass Publishers.

Logan, F. Donald (2002). *A history of the church in the middle ages.* London: Routledge.

Maddocks, F. (2013). *Hildegard of Bingen: The woman of her age.* London: Faber & Faber.

McVicker, M.F. (2011). *Women composers of classical music: 369 biographies from 1550 into the 20th century.* Jefferson, NC and London: McFarland & Company Inc. Publishers.

Merleau-Ponty, M. (1962). *The phenomenology of perception* (C. Smith, Trans.). London: Routledge & Kegan Paul.

Milley, P. (2006). Aesthetic experience as resistance to the "iron cage" of dominative administrative rationality. In E. Samier & R. Bates (Eds.), *Aesthetic dimensions of educational administration and leadership* (pp. 79–96). London: Routledge.

Nestor-Baker, N.S. & Hoy, W.K. (2001). Tacit knowledge of school superintendents: Its nature, meaning, and content. *Educational Administration Quarterly*, 37(1), 86–129.

Palus, C.J. (2002). *The leader's edge: Six creative competencies for navigating complex challenges.* San Francisco: Jossey-Bass.

Pears, D. (1970). *Ludwig Wittgenstein.* New York: The Viking Press.

Pedretti, C. (1987). Introduction. In P. Galluzzi & J. Guillaume (Eds.), *Leonardo Da Vinci: Engineer and architect* (pp. 1–21). Montreal: The Montreal Museum of Fine Arts.

Perkins, D.N. (1994). *The intelligent eye: Learning to think by looking at art.* Los Angeles: The J. Paul Getty Trust.

Polanyi, M. (1967). *The tacit dimension.* New York: Double Day and Company.

Prosch, H. (1986). *Michael Polanyi: A critical exposition.* Albany: State University of New York Press.

Ropo, A. & Parviainen, J. (2001). Leadership and bodily knowledge in expert organizations: Epistemological rethinking. *Scandinavian Journal of Management*, 17, 1–18.

Rosenthal, S.A. & Pittinsky, T.L. (2006). Narcissistic leadership. *The Leadership Quarterly*, 17, 617–633.

Said, E. (2006). *On late style: Music and literature against the grain.* New York: Vintage Books.

Samuels, E. (1979). *Bernard Berenson: The making of a connoisseur.* Cambridge, MA: The Belknap Press.

Schroeder, H. (2007). Place experience, gestalt, and the human-nature relationship. *Journal of Environmental Psychology*, 27, 293–309.

Shamir, B., Dayan-Horesh, H., & Adler, D. (2005). Leading by biography: Towards a life-story approach to the study of leadership. *Leadership*, 1(1), 13–29.

Sinclair, A. (2005). Body possibilities in leadership. *Leadership*, 1(4), 387–406.

Truitt, A. (1982). *Daybook: The journal of an artist.* New York: Penguin.

van Manen, M. (1984). Doing phenomenological research and writing: An introduction. Monograph No. 7. Department of Secondary Education, Faculty of Education, University of Alberta.

van Manen, M. (1990). *Researching lived experience: Human science for an action sensitive pedagogy.* University of Western Ontario: Althouse Press.

van Manen, M. (2006). Writing qualitatively, or the demands of writing. *Qualitative Health Research, 16*(5), 713–722.

van Manen, M. (2007). Phenomenology of practice. *Phenomenology & Practice, 1*(1), 11–30.

Vasari, G. (1568/1996). *Lives of the painters, sculptors and architects. Vol. 1* (G. Du C. de Vere, Trans.). New York: Alfred A. Knopf.

2

A TYPOLOGY OF CONNOISSEURSHIP

The most glorious exploits do not always furnish us with the clearest discoveries of virtue or vice in men; sometimes a matter of less moment, an expression or a jest, informs us better of their characters and inclinations, than the most famous sieges, the greatest armaments, or the bloodiest battles whatsoever.

(Plutarch in Clough, n.d., p. 801)

WHAT THIS CHAPTER IS ABOUT

A typology is a classification of types. In this chapter a typology of connoisseurs is developed which separates them into three kinds. The first type are *connoisseurs of leaders*, but who were not necessarily leaders themselves, such as L. Mestrius Plutarch, Niccolò Machiavelli, Giorgio Vasari and Edward Said. Then the chapter illustrates leaders who were *connoisseurs of leadership performance*, such as Saint Mary MacKillop of Australia and Frida Kahlo the great Mexican painter. Finally the chapter focuses on leaders who were both connoisseurs of their own performance and of other leaders. We call these leaders *leader connoisseurs*. In this category are placed Paul Keating, Winston Churchill and Nelson Mandela.

Specifically this chapter addresses the following points:

* Leadership competence is first about self and may lead to an ability to engage in fine-grain judgments about leaders but may not enable a person to become a leader. This is referred to as "Connoisseurs of Leaders."

- Leaders recognized as above the norm or "great" usually develop distinctive dimensions of presenting themselves in public and have learned to sculpt themselves in ways that present effective "faces" to different publics. They are connoisseurs of their own performance or "Connoisseurs of Leadership Performance."
- "Leader connoisseurs" are those who have the competence to make fine-grain judgments about other leaders and also of themselves.
- There are different domains or fields of work in which leaders work and engage in acts of leadership or engage in judgments about those who are leaders in that field. Each of these fields has its own logic and practice which is coherent to those within it but not necessarily coherent or logical to those outside it.

Introduction

The notion that it is the little mannerisms that must be read to understand leaders is quoted in this chapter's beginning from Plutarch (AD 46–120), perhaps the most famous of the ancient connoisseurs of leaders. Plutarch's (n.d.) insistence that the small quirks of leaders were keys to their character was echoed in modern times with the U.S. Senate leadership of Lyndon B. Johnson who later became the 36th president of the country. Johnson told his young Senatorial assistants:

> Read eyes. No matter what a man [sic] is saying to you, it's not as important as what you can read in his eyes. The most important thing a man has to tell you is what he's not telling you. The most important thing he has to say is what he's trying not to say.
>
> (Johnson in Caro, 2002, p. 136)

Robert Caro (2002), Johnson's biographer, said of this capacity, "He read with a novelist's sensitivity, with an insight that was unerring, with an ability, shocking in the depth of its penetration and perception, to look into a man's heart and know his innermost worries and desires" (p. 136).

Johnson learned to be patient as he gained experience and knowledgeable perception on the 10 dimensions of connoisseurship identified in the previous chapter. When he first came to the U.S. Senate few senior Senators took time to speak to him. He just sat in the back row and he studied the men there, "not their demeanor but what lay underneath" (p. 153). And Caro (2002) wrote of these times:

> These studies took a lot of time. The session would go on for hours, and hour after hour Lyndon Johnson would sit slouched down in his chair,

head on hand, all but unmoving. All his previous life had been marked by burning impatience, by a restlessness terrible in its urgency, by an unwillingness to wait, by a feeling that he couldn't wait. But in the Senate, he had seen at once, waiting—patience—was necessary. So there would be patience.

(p. 153)

Background and Context of the Three Types of Leader Connoissseurs

The study of leader connoisseurs upon which this book is based delved into two avenues of explaining the phenomenon of connoisseurship. The first was the critical importance of leader identity or of self. This is the rock upon which a leader interacts with potential significant others. George Herbert Mead (1934) called this the "I" and "can be thought of as the essential nugget of a person that he [sic] comes to know through his own immediate subjective consciousness of self" (Ransome, 2010, p. 171). This aspect of personhood is the "inner" aspect. The "outer" self is the "me" and it is the social side and acquired as a result of social interaction with others. In the words of Mead (1934), "The process out of which the self arises is a social process which implies interaction of individuals in the group, implies the pre-existence of the group" (p. 171).

The second avenue of work in this book is that of context and transfer. Leaders do not work in a culture- and context-free social space. Rather they work within bounded social space as Pierre Bourdieu (1989), the prescient French sociologist, explained. Fields in social space have a logic of their own. Leaders within those social spaces must understand and traffic in that logic to be effective. And while some aspects of leadership performance may be transferable from one context and time to another, there is much that remains peculiar to any specific social field and time. This means that generalizations regarding the performance of any leader in any field must always be rendered with due caution and because what is ultimately transferable can almost never be made with absolute congruence or certainty. Nonetheless there remains enough to make the effort worthwhile if nothing else except to tease out the variables and nuances upon which good decisions are made.

From the data of the interviews conducted for this book and other biographical and archival information accessed, it appears to the co-authors that leadership connoisseurship consists of three types of connoisseurs. These are shown in Figure 2.1. The first dimension shown is a person who is a *connoisseur of leaders*. This is an individual who understands, appreciates and has a keen eye for differences and character assignations of leaders, but is not a leader himself/herself. This is not unusual. There are superb art, music and film critics who can recognize superior performance or a superior product but cannot themselves draw, compose and/or write. Nonetheless they have developed a keen eye for grasping essential differences and have the experience and expertise to engage in fine-grain judgments. In Renaissance times, Niccolò Machiavelli would be hard to surpass.

The second type of person is a *connoisseur of leadership performance*. This is a leader who is a master of himself/herself, someone who understands the dynamics and dimensions of followership and who can project himself/herself into a social space in which followers are attracted and/or recruited. The leaders shown in Figure 2.1 are those whom a large portion of the world would most likely agree with at least some of their accomplishments. However, as Michael Kirby (1994) reminds us, "Leadership is only as good as the direction in which we will be taken" (p. 12). Any judgment about leadership therefore has to include analysis of the leadership agenda being proffered by that leader. Kirby (1994) continues his commentary:

> There have been gifted leaders of the most horrible wickedness. A list of the top business leaders who came to mind of a survey of young Australians a few years back, now looks like a catalogue of discredited fallen heroes. Half of the list are bankrupt, in prison or charged before the courts. This is the kind of leadership Australia and its business enterprises can do without. It is proof that gifts of leadership, alone, are not enough.
>
> (p. 13)

So a connoisseur of leadership performance is a person who is a master of the one-on-one dimensions of interaction and who knows how to influence others with great skill and insight.

Finally, there is a meld of both, a leader who is a connoisseur of leadership performance and a connoisseur of other leaders, this is the *leader connoisseur*. This would be a leader who can size up other leaders quickly, appearing to be able to take the measure of other leaders nimbly and with penetration and insight. In more modern times we think here of Winston Churchill, a great leader and an uncanny appraiser of other leaders which we shall explore. A very different type of leader connoisseur was the well-known American radical Saul Alinsky who devised a strategy of how the powerless became the powerful. Alinsky (1989) created a grassroots approach whereby followers were empowered to take action themselves. Others who qualify are Nelson Mandela (1994) and the Australian Prime Minister Paul Keating (1992, 2004). These *leader connoisseurs* have developed what Miha Pogacnik (2014), himself a classical concert violinist, ascribes to superb concert musicians who have developed *gerust*, that is

> the form which you have to keep if you are professional musicians. It's the rules. You know you cannot just throw it out of the window, but then you have to get through it and it must become a "mysterium". It has to become an archetypal search for the most essential human issue which is identity and spiritual perception of the world, you know world view.
>
> (p. 3)

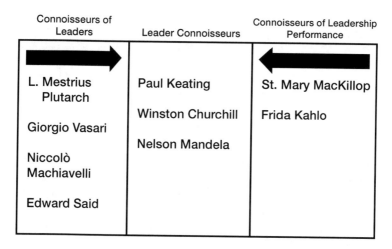

Connoisseurs of Leaders	Leader Connoisseurs	Connoisseurs of Leadership Performance
L. Mestrius Plutarch Giorgio Vasari Niccolò Machiavelli Edward Said	Paul Keating Winston Churchill Nelson Mandela	St. Mary MacKillop Frida Kahlo

FIGURE 2.1 A typology of connoisseurship: some historical exemplars

We now illustrate these three dimensions from a study of biography and history. Perhaps the most famous and quoted connoisseur of leaders was L. Mestrius Plutarchus or simply Plutarch.

Connoisseurs of Leaders

Plutarch: Portrait Painter of Ancient Personages Which Inspired Human Events Hundreds of Years Later

L. Mestrius Plutarchus (Plutarch—AD 45/50–120/127) wrote a book sometime between AD 105 and AD 115 (Grant, 1970, p. 310) in which he compared imminent Greek soldiers and statesmen to their Roman counterparts. Twenty-three pairs have survived into modern times. These pairings comprise what is known as either *Parallel Lives* or *Dual Lives*.

Whittemore (1988) says of Plutarch, "Apparently he did not conquer a single country, or tame a single wild horse. Apparently he was neither a great leader of men nor a great leader of thinkers" (p. 31). However, another scholar of Plutarch observed:

> Perhaps most striking of all, Plutarch is a thinker—a writer who interrogates the phenomena of his world in unprecedented ways. He interrogates books, symbols of cult, myths, and even natural phenomena and asks what they mean. What this indicates, first of all, is that the scope of his understanding of meaning itself is quite different from anything previously documented in Greek literature.
>
> (Lamberton, 2001, p. xiv)

So we have with Plutarch an enormously curious individual, one who is restless and relentless in his pursuit of understanding of leaders, action and context. Plutarch's work represents an intersection between his grasp of anecdote, insightful details and his vision for what comprised a great leader. His "discerning eye" was not so much on great battles, strategy or grand political spectacle, but as he himself explains in his writing about the life of Alexander who was the greatest conqueror of the ancient world, "It must be borne in mind that my design is not to write histories, but lives" (Plutarch in Clough, n.d., p. 801).

The purpose of Plutarch's portraits, he confesses, is that at first he wrote about his famous persons to inform others, but "I find myself proceeding and attaching myself to it for my own; the virtues of these great men serving me as a sort of looking-glass, in which I may see how to adjust and adorn my own life" (Plutarch in Clough, n.d., p. 293). Here Plutarch emphasizes the importance of models in learning about leadership. Models are holistic and they bring together a variety of disciplines and meld art and science together.

The other axis of Plutarch's portraits are the criteria by which he painted his subjects. Plutarch possessed a distinct vision of virtue and the life of the ethical leader. He brought to his work a keen eye towards the leaders of the times. He probed their motivation and compared them to one another, usually a Greek to a Roman. He was not a biographer in the usual sense of the word we understand today. In modern times biographers are not supposed to come to their subjects with any biases and few predilections. Plutarch had no such restrictions. He was an "ethical biographer" in this regard, and his ethics comprised his focus for public criticism which is the hallmark of a connoisseur (Eisner, 2002). These "ethics" were his ontology, that is, a manifestation of what he considered to be real and to be worthy of pursuit.

Plutarch looked for *paradeigmata*, which means patterns, models or paradigms in writing his *Lives* (Lamberton, 2001, p. 73) and he was not the least bit hesitant in including in his portraits leaders who came to bad ends as well as good ones. In this respect he said, "It likewise seems to me that we will be better spectators and imitators of the better lives if we are not uninformed about the bad and legitimately condemned ones" (Lamberton, 2001, p. 73).

The good life was one that embodied the Greek concept of *eudaimonia*, that is "the fully realized life" and the state of "being well-off" (Lamberton, 2001, p. 42). In more modern terms it is a leader who has attained "peace of mind" as the "result of certain dispositions, certain qualities of character" (Lamberton, 2001, p. 43). When a leader met a bad end it was because there were flaws in his disposition or character. This was the importance of the little anecdotes and stories Plutarch used in his *Lives*. Such inclusions were much more likely to hint at a leader's disposition or his character. And Plutarch did not neglect the role of famous women, though none appear as major players to be compared in his *Lives*, with the exception of Cleopatra in his portrait of Antony. He wrote essays on the *Sayings of Spartan Women* and the *Bravery of Women* (Lamberton, 2001,

p. 201). He also wrote essays on such things as *Advice on Marriage*; *Advice about Health*; *Moral Virtue*; *The Control of Anger*; *Shame*; *The Love of Wealth*; *Brotherly Love*; and *Talkativeness* (in Lamberton, 2001).

However, it is in his comparisons of leaders that his "discerning eye" is most explicitly revealed. As an example of his ability to grasp the fine details of leadership we review his comparison of the renowned Greek orator and speaker of the Athenian assembly, Demosthenes (384–322 BC) and the equally famous Roman orator, proconsul and philosopher Cicero (106–43 BC).

First Plutarch deals with their respective temperaments. By that is meant their emotional response to situations and their sensitivity to events and other responses. He delves into the speeches of both and says of Demosthenes that his oratory "was without all embellishment and jesting, wholly composed for real effect and seriousness; not smelling of the lamp . . . but of the temperance, thoughtfulness, austerity, and grave earnestness of his temper" (Plutarch in Clough, n.d., p. 1070). By comparison Cicero's oratory was riddled with "the love of mockery" which often ran him into "scurrility; and in his love of laughing away serious argument in judicial cases by jests and facetious remarks, with a view to the advantage of his clients, he paid too little regard to what was decent" (Plutarch in Clough, n.d., p. 1070).

Plutarch further added that Cicero "was by natural temper very much disposed to mirth and pleasantry, and always appeared with a smiling and serene countenance" (Plutarch in Clough, n.d., p. 1070) whereas "Demosthenes had constant care and thoughtfulness in his look, and a serious anxiety, which he seldom, if ever laid aside" (Plutarch in Clough, n.d., p. 1070). While Cicero often engaged in boastfulness, Demosthenes never took himself all that seriously though he was a very serious man. Plutarch summarizes and moralizes this difference when he observed, "It is necessary, indeed, for a political leader to be an able speaker; but it is an ignoble thing for any man to admire and relish the glory of his own eloquence" (Plutarch in Clough, n.d., p. 1071).

The comparison of leaders like those written by Plutarch have influenced future leaders through time. Machiavelli, another student of Roman history, took many lessons from Plutarch's narratives. Plutarch's influence also fell on Shakespeare who used the *Lives* in three of his plays and Beethoven himself was an ardent fan (Grant, 1970, p. 406). Many other world leaders also were influenced by Plutarch among them several U.S. presidents including Thomas Jefferson (Mapp, Jr., 1987, p. 60), Theodore Roosevelt (Morris, 2001, p. 285) and the 33rd U.S. president Harry Truman who even read Plutarch in the White House. We now examine the work of another *connoisseur of leaders*, Niccolò Machiavelli.

Machiavelli: The Connoisseur of Politics of His Time for All Time

Niccolò Machiavelli (1469–1527) is usually identified with only one book, *The Prince*, but in his own times he was more noted for his expertise on military preparations and strategy, his work in the Chancellery of Florence as Second Chancellor of the Signoria as a skilled and trusted negotiator, and finally as a dramatist of satiric comedies. Even as a young man he "would make up for his youth and inexperience with a formidable intellect and an impeccable education, and with tremendous amounts of energy and ambition" (King, 2007, p. 3).

Actually, *The Prince* was a knock-off of his larger work in *The Discourses* (Machiavelli, 1535/1950). What made *The Prince* revolutionary was not its form, because that was rather well established in his time. Max Lerner (1950) called it the "mirror-of-princes literature" (p. xxxi) where the rules for governing are set forth in a kind of litany of contexts based on the scholastic medieval tradition, idealism and theology. What made *The Prince* so radical was Machiavelli's rejection of this well-worn approach in favor of stark realism. Machiavelli (1535/1950) described the world of politics of his times without adornment or a resort to theological and moral arguments. His world was not the one we might wish it to be, but the world as it was.

In *The Prince* (1535/1950) Machiavelli indicated that there were three kinds of brains:

> the one understands things unassisted, the other understands things when shown by others, the third understands neither alone nor with the explanations of others. The first kind is most excellent, the second also excellent, but the third useless.
>
> (p. 86)

The Prince was banned by the Catholic church and Machiavelli was portrayed as evil incarnate, being cast as the totally evil Iago in Shakespeare's immortal play *Othello*. "Nevertheless, with us he is one of the famous idea men behind the modern state. He has even been called the founder of political science, though a better word might be *art*" (Whittemore, 1988, p. 59).

Machiavelli is so contemporary in our own times that he continues to make the opinion/editorial pages of newspapers around the world. For example his principles were reiterated when Vladimir Putin sent Russian troops into the Ukraine in 2014 (see Joffe, 2014, p. A17).

In *The Discourses*, Machiavelli (1535/1950) is able to develop his insights into more sustained argument for the points he makes. It is here that his "discerning eye" is revealed. For example, he writes on the nature of "man":

> It was a saying of ancient writers, that men afflict themselves in evil, and become weary of the good, and that both these dispositions produce the same effects: for when men are no longer obliged to fight from necessity, they fight from ambition, which passion is so powerful in the hearts of men that it never leaves them . . . The reason of this is that nature has created men so that they desire everything, but are unable to attain it; desire

being thus always greater than the faculty of acquiring, discontent with what they have and dissatisfaction with themselves result from it.

(p. 208)

Machiavelli (1535/1950) provided a useful insight as to why the past always looks better than the present to leaders. He explained that everything about the past is not known, often deeds in the past are exaggerated and contrary views erased. This gives the past a kind of roseate glow compared to the present where leaders know the characters and motives of those involved with events. The past "no longer inspires either apprehension or envy. But it is very different with the affairs of the present, in which we ourselves are either actors or spectators, and of which we have a complete knowledge, nothing being concealed from us" (p. 272).

The section in Machiavelli's work concerning how princes should, at all cost, eschew flattery still powerfully resonates today. Noting that the courts of the day were full of flatterers, Machiavelli (1535/1950) advised that the best antidote was to let "men [sic] understand that they will not offend you by speaking the truth; but when everyone can tell you the truth, you lose their respect" (p. 87). Machiavelli advised a prince to take the third way. This way involved selecting a small coterie of wise counselors and giving them the opportunity to express their opinions freely, but only when they were asked and on nothing else. But once the leader asked his counselors, he must listen intently and completely to them. Machiavelli himself had extreme difficulty in engaging in flattery even when his job required it and he was advised to engage in it (King, 2007). He concluded his observations by saying that a leader who is not wise cannot be wisely advised. The reason is that he picks inferior advisors to begin with.

Machiavelli's (1935/1950) observations and his advice to those engaged in political leadership remain vibrant and relevant today. Machiavelli was a connoisseur of leaders and contexts of his time and for all time.

Vasari: Connoisseur of Renaissance Artists

Giorgio Vasari (1511–1574) is best known for his book, *Lives of Painters, Sculptors and Architects* (1568/1996a, 1568/1996b), first published in 1550 and then again in an enlarged form in 1568. It has been described by art historians as having a "formidable influence on the discipline of art history" (Ruffini, 2011, p. 1) and esteemed as the "bible of Italian Renaissance" (Ekserdijian, 1996, p. xv).

Like Plutarch and Machiavelli, Vasari is considered a connoisseur of leaders for his ability to illuminate the lives of remarkable others (i.e. great artists) for their strengths and limitations, and how they fared against their contemporaries and the standards of the age. Vasari himself possessed superb technical competence because "[h]e was a painter and architect of distinction if not genius, which explains why he writes with such technical authority" (Ekserdijian, 1996, p. xv).

Throughout his life, Vasari traveled extensively and gained access to many collections including private ones. He was able to provide greater illumination on some artists rather than others because of his particular interests and because some of these artists were alive at the time of his writing. Not only did he have first-hand experience of some of these living artists, but he was also able to rely upon eyewitness statements and comments from others who knew or had known them so that a more complete picture of their lives and work was compiled. This was in contrast to the early artists of the 1300s who constituted the first part of Volume 1 of his book where there was much less information available on them (Ekserdijian, 1996). According to Ruffini (2011), Vasari devoted considerable time to gathering data about artists and he established very good networks in various cities, relying on his contacts for valuable information.

Ekserdijian (1996) claims that Vasari as a Florentine had greater knowledge of and interest in Florentine art than other schools and this is evident in the chapters devoted to them. Artists from his hometown of Arezzo (very close to Florence) featured heavily in comparison to artists from places like Naples (Ruffini, 2011, p. 94). Moreover, artists who were considered "lesser" received much less attention. As an example, Vasari devoted much of his second volume to Michelangelo (i.e. over 127 pages) whom he revered above all artists and considered an "absolute master." He also rated two of Michelangelo's contemporaries—Leonardo da Vinci and Raphael—very highly and devoted sizeable sections of the book to them. Yet, for "lesser" artists such as Galasso Ferrarese, just over one page was written.

Over the last two decades, scholars of art have criticized Vasari's judgment about certain artists and their works. A good example is his comparison of Raphael and Michelangelo whereby Raphael was always seen as falling short and being of a lower order, particularly when it came to human anatomy (De Vecchi, 2002, p. 130). While Vasari acknowledged Raphael's "rich inventiveness" and "variety and extent of his imitations," Raphael was not viewed as being able to achieve the "perfection" of a Michelangelo or even a Leonardo (De Vecchi, 2002, p. 346). Vasari (1568/1996a, p. 741) also referred to the significant influence that Michelangelo and Leonardo had on Raphael and how he imitated aspects of their style. Noteworthy is De Vecchi's (2002) comment that even today Vasari's ideas about Raphael (both positive and negative) continue to influence the way his work is viewed and appreciated.

Despite its flaws and idiosyncracies, Vasari's book "is our fullest guide to how people looked at art in the renaissance" (Ekserdijian, 1996, p. xlv). His magnum opus continues to exert authority in the field of Renaissance art. Ekserdijian (1996) sums up Vasari's legacy when he says that he "inspires us with a burning desire to go and see—or see again—the works of art themselves" (p. xlix). This in itself is testimony to his connoisseurship and invaluable contribution to Italian art.

Edward Said: Music Critic and Connoisseur of the 20th Century

Edward Said has been described as an important public intellectual of the 20th Century. Palestinian born, he is best known for his book *Orientalism* (1978), in which he argues against the West's limited and patronizing depictions of the Middle East, Asia and North Africa. Apart from being an "indefatigable spirit, a roving intellectual warrior against colonisations of imaginations, minds and bodies" (Saith, 2003, p. 4), Said was a contemporary connoisseur of literature, culture, music and politics. It is his work as a connoisseur leader of music that is of most interest to us in this chapter. Edward Said was the music critic for *The Nation* magazine for many years and he wrote the following books on music: *Musical Elaborations* (1991), *On Late Style: Music and Literature against the Grain* (2006), *Music at the Limits: Three Decades of Essays and Articles on Music* (2008). Daniel Barenboim and Said together wrote *Parallels and Paradoxes: Explorations in Music and Society* (2004).

As discussed earlier in this chapter, to be a connoisseur of leaders, a person does not need to demonstrate exceptional performance skills; rather, his or her great gift is that of discernment, an ability to recognize, appreciate, differentiate and evaluate. Said (1999) was acutely aware of his own limitations as a pianist and the quote below is quite telling as it reveals some of the elements he deems essential for being a truly gifted executant as opposed to a good amateur:

> When it came to music, my interest in a professional career diminished as I found myself intellectually unsatisfied by the physical requirement of daily practice and very occasional performance. And, it must be said, I realized that my gifts, such as they were, could never be adequate to the kind of professional trajectory I imagined for myself . . . I felt that there was a shadow line of raw ability I could not cross separating the good amateur from the truly gifted executant, someone like Tiegerman or Glenn Gould, whose Boston recitals I attended between 1959 and 1962 with rapt admiration, for whom the ability to transpose or read at sight, a perfect memory, and the total coordination of hand and ear were effortless, whereas for me all that was truly difficult, requiring much effort and in the end only a precarious, uncertain achievement.
>
> (Said, 1999, p. 291)

We would argue that Said would have no doubt drawn upon his knowledge as an accomplished pianist to become the connoisseur and critic he was recognized as being. According to his autobiography, he developed a strong love of music from his mother during his formative years and music was a constant companion all of his life (Said, 1999). He honed his skills as a connoisseur through the long hours he devoted to reading about music, by the lively discussions he had with musical friends and colleagues, by attending live performances, and by listening to different recordings of symphonies, concertos and musical works by different artists (M. Said, 2008, p. xii).

Said's great gifts as a music connoisseur have been noted by others such as Barenboim (2008, 2005), Saith (2003) and Yu (2006). For example, Yu (2006) said that Said was "adept at speaking about classical music or American jazz, trained to appreciate the subtleties contained in the finest compositions" (p. 19), while Saith (2003) gave homage to Said when he referred to him as "a connoisseur, an aficionado, a critic, an interpreter of Middle Eastern traditions of dance and music" (p. 3). His co-author, friend and musical collaborator, Daniel Barenboim, wrote the following about his colleague, which reveals much about Said's discerning eye:

> [Said] understood perfectly that musical genius or musical talent requires tremendous attention to detail. The genius attends to detail as though it were the most important thing and, in so doing, does not lose sight of the big picture; in fact, this attention to detail enables him to manifest his vision of the big picture. In music, as in thought, the big picture must be the result of the precise coordination of small details. When Said attended a concert of performance, he focused his attention on these details, some of which have gone unnoticed by many professionals. As a critic, he distinguished himself in many ways from his colleagues, of whom it can be said that some lack the knowledge to write about their subject matter intelligently and others lack the ability to listen without preconceptions . . . Said . . . listened with open ears and a depth of musical knowledge that allowed him to hear, and attempt to understand, the intention of the performer and his [sic] approach to music.
>
> (Barenboim, foreword in Said, 2008, p. viii)

In another piece by Barenboim (2005), he continued to praise his friend and colleague for his incredible gifts of discernment. He said:

> [Said] knew how to distinguish clearly between power and force, which constituted one of the main ideas of his struggle. He knew quite well that in music, force is not power, something that many of the world's political leaders do not perceive. The difference between power and force is equivalent to the difference between volume and intensity in music.
>
> (p. 165)

A reader would gain a strong sense of Said's musical connoisseurship in the collection of essays that constitute his book, *Music at the Limits*. In this book, he critiques artists and composers and compares and contrasts different works and performers. As an illustration, Said (2008) dedicated several chapters to the brilliant and original Canadian pianist, Glenn Gould, whom he singles out for his virtuosity. Said described Gould as

> an exception to almost all of the other musical performers in this century. He was a brilliantly proficient pianist (in a world of brilliantly proficient pianists) whose unique sound, brash style, rhythmic inventiveness, and above all, quality of attention seemed to reach out well beyond the act of performing itself. In the eighty records he made, Gould's piano tone is immediately recognizable . . . Gould's playing enables the listener to experience Bach's contrapuntal excesses . . . as no other pianist has.
>
> (pp. 3–6)

Said's (1991, 2006, 2008) essays on music and musicians are both compelling and insightful. Barenboim (2005) captures this well when he laments that Said was not only "a great thinker, a fighter for the rights of his people, and an incomparable intellectual [b]ut for me, he was always, really, a musician, in the deepest sense of the term" (p. 166). Perhaps it was this strong, even spiritual, connection to music that enabled him to focus his attention on subtleties and nuances that his contemporaries may have overlooked or not understood.

Connoisseurs of Leadership Performance

We pose here two portraits of exceptional connoisseurs of leadership performance, both of whom were women and who could not have been more different in their outlook on life and in the work that made one the first saint of the Catholic church in Australia and the second, a *mestizaje* from a Mexican mother and a German-Hungarian father of Jewish descent, into the most famous female painter in art history. Both of these remarkable women are considered connoisseurs of leadership performance for the far-reaching influence they had and continue to have on others in their respective fields. During the time they lived and worked, it can be argued that the way in which they influenced followers differed markedly due to the different types of leaders they were and the different contexts in which they operated. As a visual artist, Kahlo worked mainly on her own to create art that was inspired by Mexican and Indigenous insights as well as her own personal experiences. It was after her death that her influence has come to be most deeply appreciated not only by the art community but also by feminists who hold her up as an important symbol of female struggle and emancipation. MacKillop, on the other hand, worked with and through others in her quest to establish a religious order and schools to support disadvantaged people in the community. She was a relational leader in that she interacted on a daily basis with her sisters and others in her immediate orbit to achieve her vision and goals for the Order. Like Kahlo, her influence continues to this day and she is recognized as an outstanding leader. The next part of this chapter introduces both of these connoisseurs.

Saint Mary MacKillop: Connoisseur of Leadership Performance

Mary MacKillop (1842–1909) was an Australian nun and is the first Australian to be sainted by the Catholic church. She is considered a connoisseur of leadership performance for the leadership she exercised within her Order and within the various rural communities across the country which she served. With Father Julian Woods, she co-founded the Sisters of St Joseph of the Sacred Heart and became its first member and Superior. The Order established free schools for the poor and provided welfare and other support for the disadvantaged (such as orphanages, homes for the elderly and incurably ill) (Thorpe, 1974). During Mary's life, the Order spread from Penola in South Australia where it first started to other parts of South Australia through to Queensland, New South Wales and Victoria (Guile, 2011). Schools were also set up in New Zealand.

Mary was known for her great courage and determination in the face of adversity and for her commitment to follow the strong values and vision upon which the Order was founded. With Father Woods she wrote "Rule of the Order" which was the Order's charter (Modystack, 1995). A rule or guiding principle was that the sisters were to commit themselves to care for and educate the poor and to live a life of poverty themselves. This rule meant that sisters could not have any income and would need to get money from the public via charity and begging. Two other rules were that nuns in the Order would be led by a fellow nun; and they would take orders only from the Pope (Guile, 2011). Not surprisingly, Mary clashed bitterly with several bishops because of their unwillingness to accept her independence from their diocese. Of Mary, Fabian and Loh (1983, p. 57) state, "that a woman should aspire to extra-diocesan powers and fight for them so tenaciously was almost unbelievable." Yet Mary was unafraid to adhere to her values and to confront structures she thought were wrong.

Mary endured attacks by the clergy for decades. Much came to a head in 1871 when the Bishop of Adelaide, South Australia, excommunicated her and her sisters (i.e. those who agreed to follow her) for "disobedience and rebellion" (Bishop Shiel in Dunne, 1994, p. 23). This meant that Mary and her sisters were homeless. This lasted several months before the decision was reversed. A visit to the Pope and further correspondence with Rome meant victory for Mary as the Pope recognized the Order as being independent of diocesan control (Guile, 2011). However, some bishops continued to reject Rome's decisions and engaged in further battle with Mary. In a letter written by Mary, she shows her willingness to negotiate when she said, "If the Bishop but works with us! It is almost a growing conviction with me that we must do this, but that it can be done without destroying our unity" (MacKillop in Dunne, 1994, p. 48).

According to Burford, "Mary MacKillop did not oppose the Bishops . . . The truth is a few Bishops had their own peculiar difficulties with the type of Institute that she was setting up" (Burford in Dunne, 1994, p. 58). James Quinn who was

Bishop of Brisbane would not accept that Mary was in charge of the sisters working in Brisbane. He said, it is "impossible for me to accept the government of a woman or to have a community of nuns governed by a lady [i.e. Mary] from Adelaide. I won't allow any woman to make a disturbance in my diocese" (Quinn in Guile, 2011, p. 16). Mary realized the difficulty of this situation and the importance of staying true to the rule of the Order that maintained its independence. For this reason, she made the decision of withdrawing the sisters from Brisbane and returning them to Adelaide. She faced a similar situation when working with Quinn's brother, Bishop of Bathurst, New South Wales, who insisted that she follow his command. She again refused and removed the sisters from New South Wales. This led to an investigation orchestrated by another bishop based on claims of malicious gossip, lies and hatred towards Mary and her sisters (Modystack, 1995, p. 197). Among the allegations was that Mary had an alcohol problem. The truth was that she drank only a small amount of alcohol on her doctor's order to relieve a medical condition (Guile, 2011). The investigation cleared Mary's name and no scandal or untoward behavior by the sisters was found.

Burford, a historian and sister of St Joseph herself, describes Mary's leadership style in the following way:

Mary had an amazing ability to see things from the other person's point of view and she'd rather negotiate with people if and when a serious principle was at stake. She knew human weakness, in herself and others, and she admitted this and supported and assured others—a true peacemaker—so there was no idea of governing or ruling people. This reassuring style enabled the sisters to face difficulties and hardships and privations, and especially [regarding] the decisions which had to be made in far-flung places, to make them on their own.

(Burford in Dunne, 1994, p. 43)

The sisters of St Joseph depended on charity and received little money from the dioceses. Support for their work came from all sectors of the community and from people representing different religious views. In January 1883, the *Victorian Journal*, a monthly review, stated:

The consensus of opinion in Adelaide amongst protestants as well as Catholics is that the Sisters of St Joseph are doing really good work . . . The proof that they are esteemed by all classes is the liberal support they get from Protestants, as well as from their own creed.

(in Dunne, 1994, p. 61)

As well as battling Bishops, Mary was to face a number of battles with Father Woods who was the Director of the Institute of St Joseph and who worked closely with Mary during the first years of setting up the Order. His behavior could be tactless, difficult and self-righteous (Fabian & Loh, 1983, p. 64). Mary found it difficult to remain silent when she observed injustice, dishonesty, stupidity or unkindness in others. According to Modystack (1995, p. 44), Mary was known to speak up in a firm yet kind way. An illustration of this was that, as Mary grew in maturity and confidence, she did not hold back from letting Father Woods know that he acted tactlessly or unkindly. The following extract comes from a letter she wrote to him:

> If you would only consider the feelings of others a little more, and not act quite so hastily in some things, I am sure that much good you really wish to do, would thus be so easily done. Make allowance for those who do not see as you do—I mean make it in time, not when, through some want of thought or haste on your part, someone has been grieved or perhaps provoked to irritation . . . Sometimes, without meaning it, you slight others, and cause them much bitterness and pain.
>
> (MacKillop in Modystack, 1995, p. 45)

We see that Mary MacKillop was a connoisseur of leadership performance. She showed genuine openness to others and prized good relationships with all. In her work and life she met people representing all classes and ranks yet she was not impressed by titles (Gardiner, 1994, p. 484). Gardiner (1994, pp. 5–6) claims that Mary "looked beyond what she could see and hear and smell, and attended to what her faith told her of the dignity of every human person. This attitude called for a rare nobility of mind." She had a great love of humanity and respected people even when they were at their worst. Her life seemed littered with one battle after the other with those who sought to undermine her moral authority yet she acted justly and respectfully to everyone (Gardiner, 1994). She had a discerning eye when it came to understanding people: their motivations, their strengths and their weaknesses, just as she was aware of her own weaknesses.

It was her strong faith that enabled her to work to achieve her vision to serve the poor, the homeless and the disenfranchised in Australian society during the 1800s and early 1900s. She was guided by an aesthetic vision that came from a higher moral purpose to serve God and to do that in a practical way by serving the least advantaged of his people. It could be said that her discerning eye was framed within her commitment to the rules that governed the Order and always in the service of the least advantaged.

As a leader, she showed strength of character, conviction, self-belief, and resilience. She had a very strong identity and exercised belief in the rightness of what she was doing. She was said to exude charm and warmth and many people admired her, not only members of the public who provided financial support over decades, but also the growing group of sisters who followed her. Not only did she establish the Order from nothing in 1867, but it numbered

120 sisters in 1871 (McCreanor, 2011, p. 341) at the time of her and her sisters' excommunication. When she passed away in 1909, there were 750 sisters working across 117 schools (Guile, 2011). That she was able to inspire so many sisters to follow her into a life of harsh poverty, little material comforts, and one of supreme service to others, is a testament to her ability to lead in an exceptional way.

Frida Kahlo: Connoisseur of Mexican Culture, Life and Loving

Frida Kahlo (1907–1954) is arguably the most famous female painter in the world. She was a connoisseur of life and love, eventually becoming a world cult figure celebrated in books and film. She lived for a brief 47 years, a life filled with pain, first from polio as a child which left her with a permanent limp, and then enduring injuries from a terrible accident when she was riding in an electric street car that collided with a bus. From this collision:

> Kahlo suffered multiple injuries: her spinal column was broken in three places; her collarbone and two ribs were broken; her right leg and eleven factures and the right foot was crushed; her left shoulder was out of joint and her pelvis was broken in three places. Most horrifying of all, as the medical records document in chillingly laconic terms, she suffered a 'penetrating abdominal wound caused by iron handrail entering left hip, exiting through the vagina and tearing left lip'.
>
> (Ankori, 2013, p. 51)

Frida's life was completely shattered and she was not expected to live. Instead she spent a long and painful recovery, that while it enabled her to eventually walk again and to paint, it ended her ability to have children and to have anything comparable to a "normal life."

One of Frida's biographers, Hayden Herrera (1983), summarized the impact of this accident on her life:

> Painting was part of Frida Kahlo's battle for life. It was also very much a part of her self-creation: in her art, as in her life, a theatrical self-presentation was a means to control her world. As she recovered, relapsed, recovered again, she reinvented herself. She created a person who could be mobile and make mischief in her imagination rather than with her legs. "Frida is the only painter who gave birth to herself" said an intimate friend of Frida's.
>
> (p. 75)

In her quest to live life and to cover her physical deformities and flaws, Frida Kahlo created unforgettable dresses and traditional Mexican jewelry. By wearing

Tehuana blouses and skirts, she was able to transform her public persona into what was called "La Mexicana." "This clothing tradition involved using costumes from the Isthmus of Tehuantepec, known for its matriarchal society of strong and beautiful women" (Ankori, 2013, p. 168).

Frida Kahlo was twice married to the Mexican muralist Diego Rivera who, while also gifted, was a faithless husband and filled her with regrets, sorrow and additional emotional pain. Hamill (1999) observed that "Diego was a grand mythomaniac; Frida was one of the century's most gifted narcissists. They fed each other, and fed *off* each other, in a union that had its own rules, its own hidden dynamics" (p. 135).

Despite all of the handicaps Frida Kahlo created paintings that are etched in the memory of the artistic world and exhibited in major museums and sell today for millions of dollars. Her husband Diego Rivera first saw her early work, even before it became famous, and wrote this about it:

> The canvases revealed an unusual energy of expression, precise delineation of character, and true severity. They showed none of the tricks in the name of originality that usually mark the work of ambitious beginners. They had a fundamental plastic honesty, and an artistic personality of their own. They communicated a vital sensuality, completed by a merciless yet sensitive power of observation.
>
> (Rivera in Hamill, 1999, pp. 134–135)

Another of Frida Kahlo's biographers, Gannit Ankori (2013), provided a glimpse behind Frida's artistic accomplishments, indicating she was way ahead of her times:

> Her knowledge in the sciences, humanities and arts was deep and up to date. An analysis of the books in her library and information gleaned from her voluminous correspondence reveal her erudition in art, literature, medicine, botany, psychology, philosophy, archaeology, history and linguistics. She was also personally acquainted with many of the artists, poets, musicians and intellectuals of her day.
>
> (p. 171)

Despite her fame today, in her own time Frida Kahlo was exceptionally self-critical, writing in a letter to Diego Rivera, "The conclusion I've drawn is that all I've done is fail" (Kahlo in Ankori, 2013, p. 7). The most any of her paintings ever sold for in her life was $400. Today they are worth millions and, as Ankori (2013) notes, "A Google search of her name yields more than three million hits in a tenth of a second" (p. 192). Today she has totally eclipsed her former famous husband as time has revealed her true genius. Frida is said to have remarked to her caregiver days before her death, "Love is the only reason for living" (Ankori, 2013, p. 123).

Leader Connoisseurs

Paul Keating: Australian Leader Connoisseur

Paul Keating was the 24th Prime Minister of Australia and Leader of the Labor Party. He held office from 1991 to 1996. Prior to taking up the prime ministership, he was Treasurer of Australia working closely with Bob Hawke in the Hawke Government from 1983. From 1983 to 1991, Hawke and Keating were viewed as a formidable force in politics and their productive partnership yielded a spate of successful economic reforms (Watson, 2003). However, their partnership came to an end when Keating successfully challenged Hawke for the prime ministership in late 1991. Paul Keating won the 1993 election but lost the next election to John Howard in 1996. During his time as prime minister, Paul Keating continued Labor's progressive reform agenda and "big picture" achievements included his proposal for reform to make Australia a republic; Mabo legislation that recognized land rights for Indigenous people; and external policy development towards the Asian region (Keating, n.d.).

In the discussion that follows, we discuss how Keating presented himself as a *leader connoisseur*, that is, he was both a *connoisseur of leadership performance* because he was a master leader himself and a *connoisseur of leaders* because he had the ability to "size up" other leaders and provide fine-grain judgments about their policies and performance.

In discussing leadership, Keating (2004) said:

> leadership is about interpreting the future to the present; having the ability to see over the horizon; letting those wider coordinates inform one's thinking. Giving one the ability to move forward more profoundly, and by moving forward I mean not having one foot in the safe house of incrementalism.
>
> (p. 1)

For Keating, incrementalism implies taking little risk and is unlikely to lead to any significant advances. What he prefers is "quantum leaps and leaders [who] are the instruments by which [quantum] . . . changes occur" (Keating, 2004, p. 2). Keating referred to the need for leaders to have "a big picture" or a framework and, once this is known, then it's a matter of providing the detail or to "get the coordinates of your circumstances right" (Keating, 2004, p. 1). Yet Keating was often criticized for his big picture ideas because of their corresponding lack of human detail and for their focus on the general rather than the local (Watson, 2003, p. 92).

Keating (2004) claimed that the success of bringing Australia from a protectionist economy to an openly competitive one during the Labor Party reign (i.e. between 1983 and 1996) was due to strong leadership and radical change. He said that the changes

> occurred because a handful of politicians—individuals—recognised that the old paradigm had outlived its usefulness, had come to its end. A new paradigm had to be put into place. And it was—an outcome of leadership, and only leadership.
>
> (p. 3)

Don Watson (2003), his former speech-writer, who wrote a substantive biography on Keating, said Keating was

> a political leader who more than any other in the last quarter of a century was determined to be master of his environment rather than an opportunist waiting for the times to suit him . . . He practised politics precisely for the purpose of mastering events because politics was the only means by which he could turn this thing of his imagination into something real. Politics was power, it was the hunt, the game, a way to the unrivalled pleasure of destroying his enemies—but it was, as well, always an act of creation.
>
> (p. xi)

Keating was a connoisseur of leadership performance as he combined imagination with agency in his quest to achieve his vision for Australia. One illustration is that he inspired the nation with his Redfern speech (Keating, 1992) where he acknowledged the legacy of dispossession of Indigenous people and argued for the importance of Aboriginal reconciliation. Watson (2003, pp. 288–290) claims that a key principle of the speech was the need for imagination because without imagination, there could be no hope, resolution or confidence in redressing Indigenous people's plight. The speech was well received by all Australians, including Aboriginal leaders (Watson, 2003, p. 291). The Redfern speech was one of a number of speeches that Keating gave that mapped out his big picture views for the nation.

Another biographer, John Edwards (1996), alluded to Keating's big picture outlook when he described him as someone who

> thought by flashes, intuition, by discarding everything that was not big and essential. Compared to Whitlam [Australia's Prime Minister from 1972 to 1975], Keating was more interested in the whole than the analysis of the parts, more interested in being able to grab something intuitively through practical experience . . . he found that his strength was to grasp the main point and to hold on to it.
>
> (p. 100)

A key strength of Keating's was his ability to understand political leadership and to read people and situations and respond accordingly. He learned from observing and talking with other Labor leaders and this helped him to develop his discerning eye. Edwards (1996) said that Keating was able to interpret other people's

> hidden motives from outward but unintended signals, of the need in politics to judge what people said in the light of their customary degree of optimism or pessimism, with appropriate weights for their characteristic clarity or confusion, intelligence or stupidity, to make allowances for the usual way in which egotism or insecurity would affect a person's views, the myriad of ways in which partialities of various kinds—love, political partisanship, ambition, pride, self-hatred—might create small or large errors of assessment.
>
> (p. 183)

Not only did Keating develop discerning skills in reading situations but, on occasion, he also disregarded sensible advice because as leader he saw things or felt things differently from others (Edwards, 1996, p. 101). Keating said that leadership is "not about being popular. It's about being right and about being strong . . . It's about doing what you think the nation requires, making profound judgements about profound issues" (Keating in Watson, 2003, p. 21). Not surprisingly, some of those decisions were unpopular and he was criticized for them by his opponents and the media.

Whereas Keating was described by the media as aloof and arrogant, he saw himself as the "Placido Domingo of Australian politics" (Watson, 2003, p. 23). Watson explained this by saying that Keating viewed himself as giving quality performances and those performances would usually outstrip those of his opponents. He could do this by his quick wit, keen intelligence and ability to persuade others to see his view. As Watson (2003) claimed, Keating "could sell an idea better than anybody else in the government" (p. 24).

In addition to being a connoisseur of leadership performance, Keating can be described as a connoisseur of the arts and connoisseur of leaders. He has been called a very "different" type of prime minister due to his aesthetic sensibilities and esoteric knowledge of classical music (particularly Mahler), antique furniture and architecture. According to Edwards (1996, p. 48), Keating is considered a world class expert on French decoration from 1790 to 1814 and his views are sought by dealers and curators in the United States and England.

Keating is a person who is "charmed by beauty" and, during his political career, it was music and the decorative arts that "filled the bottle up" and replenished him (Edwards, 1996, p. 49). As a great lover of classical music, Keating said in a radio interview for a New York radio program that he "restructured the Australian economy on the backs of . . . composers [i.e. Mahler, Bruckner, Chopin and Korngold]" (Keating in Smith, 2009, p. 1). According to Smith (2009), Keating is probably considered the world's most knowledgeable former prime minister on Gustav Mahler's music.

Of interest to us is that he began his journey into connoisseurship of both the arts and leadership as a teenager. At this time, he subscribed to a magazine called *Connoisseur* which featured stories on antiques and classical music (Watson, 2003). At the same time, he embarked on his lifelong love of reading biographies, autobiographies and history. Through the reading of leaders' biographies, he came to appreciate greatness in leaders such as Roosevelt, whom he saw as humane, and Churchill whom he viewed as inspiring because of his courage and desire to pursue what he saw as right (Edwards, 1996). Keating claimed that Churchill was "one of the reasons I am in public life" (Keating in Edwards, 1996, p. 51). Keating realized early on that it was in politics "where one would have a great influence on events, where the canvas was broader and all that I ever read convinced me this was true" (Keating in Edwards, 1996, p. 50). Hence, it was a life of politics he pursued and he served as a politician for 27 years.

Keating had a discerning eye about other politicians and what they stood for. He was in awe of Gough Whitlam when he first joined politics and was able to state how he himself differed from Whitlam on a number of key issues. Of Whitlam he said he

> was a process man: reform, the constitution, the federal structure . . . he was also into social, foreign and other areas of policy, whereas my interests were . . . to try and see what made the structure of the country, what held the structure together, what made it tick, and how it could tick better.
>
> (Keating in Edwards, 1996, p. 100)

Having a discerning eye is necessary in politics particularly when important decisions need to be made. Edwards (1996, pp. 458–460) gives an example of a key decision Keating was faced with after being newly elected prime minister in 1993. The decision was to choose a Treasurer of the Government with whom he could work closely. The choice was between two persons: the safe choice who was intelligent, critical, experienced with the role but a skeptic when it came to change OR the risky choice who had a lot of ideas and a track record of successfully implementing policy yet was described as manipulative and attracted to "gimmicks" (Edwards, 1996, p. 460). After much deliberation, Keating chose the latter. Commentators have claimed that Keating's style of leadership was that of a risk-taker ('t Hart & Walter, 2014; Watson, 2003).

Keating's strengths as a leader were many. He was, first and foremost, an "ideas" person who had the courage to take the country in a direction that he saw was best. He was also an outstanding negotiator due to the authority or "weight" which he brought to negotiations (Watson, 2003, p. 434). He surrounded himself with very able public servants and colleagues who provided excellent advice. Moreover, his charismatic style enlivened his arguments and provided a type of genuineness at the same time (Watson, 2003, p. 434). For these reasons and those discussed above, we consider him to be a *leader connoisseur*.

Winston Churchill: British Leader Connoisseur

The renowned philosopher Isaiah Berlin once remarked that Winston Churchill was "the largest human being of our times" (Manchester, 1988, p. xvii). Historian Max Hastings (2010) similarly agreed, noting that "Churchill was the greatest Englishman and one of the greatest human beings of the twentieth century, indeed of all time" (p. 3). When he passed away at age 90, John Keegan (2002) observed, "The British people recognized in his death the passing of not only one of the greatest of their fellow countrymen who had ever lived but also of a supremely heroic moment in their own life as a nation" (p. 183).

Winston Leonard Spencer Churchill (1874–1965) sets a high standard as the leader connoisseur for this book. He had a passion for life and power, held eight cabinet posts in government before becoming prime minister at age 65 during Britain's most tenuous moment as a weak nation facing Hitler's Nazi legions which had just overrun France in 1940. Churchill's cabinet secretary said of him at that moment, "Everything depended upon him and him alone. Only he had the power to make the nation believe that it could win" (Hastings, 2010, p. 5). More than anything else it was Churchill's words, his defiant and articulate speeches in Parliament that gave the British people courage and connected them to their glorious past. "Morally Churchill set the agenda of the Second World War. Its realization determined, after 1945, the future of the world" (Keegan, 2002, p. 145).

Few realized, however, that Churchill the oratorical giant, the supreme public speaker who galvanized the backbone of a nation during a time of peril, had a speech impediment. He lisped and he worked very hard to conceal that lisp with stringent rehearsals of his speeches. For a 40-minute speech he would spend six to eight hours of preparation (Manchester, 1988, p. 32). Every word was dictated and written out including crib notes about where to pause and what gestures should be used at the appropriate turn of the phrase. To bystanders and those unfamiliar with his words, they appeared to be extemporaneous. Nothing could be further from the truth.

Just as Plutarch has indicated in his writings of famous statesmen and generals, it was the small things that reveal a person's character and provided insight into their personalities. Churchill was no exception. He worked his personal staff, his phalanx of secretaries extremely hard. He was an "atrocious" taskmaster and "his attitude toward his employees is difficult to understand or, at times, even to excuse" (Manchester, 1988, p. 34). When dictating his speeches, often in the wee hours of the morning, it was common for him to weep, "his voice becomes thick with emotion, tears run down his cheeks (and his secretary's)" (Manchester, 1988, pp. 32–33). Once, when a male servant stood up to him and talked back, Churchill exclaimed, "You were very rude to me you know." The servant replied, "Yes, but you were rude too," to which Churchill responded, "Yes, but I am a great man" (Manchester, 1988, p. 36). In all of this Manchester (1988) summarizes:

> What is striking is that those who work for him, toiling long hours, underpaid, and subject to savage, undeserved reprimands, agree with him. They feel the sting of his whip. Yet he continues to command their respect, even their love. Those who are shocked by Churchill's treatment of his employees all have this in common: they never worked for him.
>
> (p. 36)

Churchill's beginnings were not auspicious. Though born into a substantial family palace estate and the grandson of a duke, Churchill did not enjoy the affection of his father. His mother loved him but had little time for him. His school record was mediocre. He was labeled a disciplinary problem and dumped into some of the lowest level classes possible. He flunked many exams and his poor record denied him any chance of attending Oxford or Cambridge. He never completed college. He did attend Sandhurst, Britain's equivalent of West Point. Using his mother's contacts he got himself into military active duty, first in India and later in South Africa. It was in the military service he plunged into arduous reading of the classics and wrote articles for newspapers. Coming back to England he was elected to Parliament and was a cabinet minister at age 33. In 1911 he was First Lord of the Admiralty and as Britain entered the Great War the British navy was prepared with a new type of battleship called the Dreadnought (Massie, 2003).

Despite British naval superiority, the Great War, which had begun in August 1914 when Germany invaded Belgium, ground to a bloody and futile stalemate on the Western Front (Massie, 2003, p. 430). Quite early in the war Churchill began to ponder an attack through the Dardanelles as a way of relieving Turkish pressure on Russia and of using the Royal Navy as a wedge to do so (Gilbert, 1991, p. 290).

It is within this context that the plans for a naval attack through the Dardanelles which would lead to a direct attack on the Gallipoli peninsula and then an attack on Istanbul (then Constantinople) would take Turkey out of the war. This was the soft underbelly that might relieve the stalemate on the Western Front and become decisive and end the war. The idea of sending old battleships through the Dardanelle straits to take out the forts there and land troops at Gallipoli was thus hatched. But it came to disaster. The Turks mined the straits, old battleships were sunk with nearly all hands drowned; troops put ashore at Gallipoli were slaughtered as they tried to break out from Turkish defenses. As Massie (2003) notes, "The front was stalemated. The Allies could not seize the ridges; the Turks could not hurl their enemies back into the sea; and the killing ground of the Western Front was reproduced at Gallipoli" (p. 480). The result was entirely blamed on Churchill and he took the political hit that saw him dismissed from the Admiralty (Massie, 2003, p. 491). Gallipoli became Churchill's cross to bear for over 20 years. Later his wife Clementine wrote of this time, "When he left the Admiralty, he thought he was finished . . . I thought he would never get over the Dardanelles: I thought he would die of grief" (Massie, 2003, p. 491).

Churchill's long comeback in politics was marred by his crossing the aisle in Parliament, the equivalent of a Democrat becoming a Republican and later to re-cross the aisle again. In 1922 he was unable to secure a seat in Parliament, the first time in 22 years (Gilbert, 1991, p. 456). He took to writing his memoirs and began painting to deal with his depression which he called his "Black dog" (Gilbert, 1991, p. 230). Painting totally absorbed him. It forced him to focus. He wrote about his experience as follows:

> When I left the Admiralty at the end of May, 1915, I still remained a member of the Cabinet and the War Council. In this position I knew everything and could do nothing. The change from the intense executive activities of each day's work at the Admiralty to the narrowly measured duties of counsellor left me gasping . . . I had great anxiety and no means of relieving it . . . I had long hours of utterly unwonted leisure in which to contemplate the frightful unfolding of the War . . . and then it was that the Muse of Painting came to my rescue.
>
> (Churchill, 1921/1922, p. 53)

Even in his days out of politics, Churchill labored to paint, read and write. He was eventually to win the Nobel Prize in Literature in 1953 for his histories. But it was the emergent rise of Hitler's Germany that would eventually win the respect of the British public and bring him to the role of prime minister in Britain's "finest hour."

Churchill was prescient, a true visionary, and as Lukacs (2002) writes long before anyone in Britain recognized the threat Hitler posed to the peace of Europe, Churchill was writing in 1934 that Hitler

> has succeeded in restoring Germany to the most powerful position in Europe, and not only has he restored the position of his country, but he has even, to a very large extent, reversed the results of the Great War . . . When Hitler began, Germany lay prostrate at the feet of the Allies. He may yet see the day when what is left of Europe will be prostrate at the feet of Germany.
>
> (pp. 6–7)

Churchill began to try and warn his people and his nation about the dangers Hitler's rise was posing. But this earned him isolation and charges he was exaggerating the threat and that he was a warmonger. He cautioned against appeasement and never wavered in his assessment of the intentions of Hitler. He had the Führer pegged right from the outset. He also correctly assessed the threat of Communism following the war in his famous Iron Curtain forebodings and speech in the United States (Gilbert, 1991, p. 866). However, even Churchill's famous vision failed him with his resistance to granting Dominion status to India. He was not a perfect human. Lukacs (2002) recounts a story told by a young woman whom Churchill had expressed some interest in before his marriage to Clementine when she said, "The first time you meet Winston you see all his faults, and the rest of your life you spend in discovering his virtues" (p. 145).

Nelson Mandela: Leader Connoisseur and Father of His Country

Millions of people on the planet know the basic outline of the life of Nelson Mandela (1918–2013), the black freedom fighter who was imprisoned for some three decades of his life and who emerged to win the first free election in the history of South Africa as well as the Nobel Peace Prize in December of 1993.

Nelson Mandela was first a connoisseur of self-image when he appeared in court in traditional tribal dress of the Xhosa people. It was through a display of his African heritage that he demonstrated his understanding of the need for a public image (Mandela, 1994). He demonstrated it again when, as president, he endorsed the formerly all-white South African rugby team the Springboks and urged black South Africans to root for them in the world championships. In turn the nearly all-white rugby team learned the Xhosa song *Tshotsholoza* which was "popular with soccer fans and which Mandela and his fellow prisoners on Robben Island used to sing when working in the lime quarry" (Meredith, 2010, p. 526). The rejoicing among the entire country when the Springboks won the world championship brought the nation together. It is memorialized in the film *Invictus* released in 2009 starring Matt Damon as South African team captain Francois Pienaar and Morgan Freeman as Mandela.

But perhaps Mandela's greatest feat was accomplished as prisoner 466/64 in a small seven foot square cell on Robben Island off Capetown, South Africa. There, in a seven foot square cement room,

> there was no bed. Mandela was provided with a sisal mat on which to sleep, three flimsy blankets, a toilet bucket and a plastic bottle of water. In the winter months, his cell was so cold he slept fully dressed in prison garb.
> (Meredith, 2010, p. 279)

Mandela endured days in solitary confinement and other forms of humiliation and deprivation but he never buckled. John Battersby (2009), a South African journalist and editor who interviewed Mandela many times, conducted a near final chat with him a year after he was no longer president and when he was 82. Battersby (2009) said that Mandela's goal of bringing South Africa towards coming together was based on the African concept of *ubuntu* which was defined by Archbishop Desmond Tutu as:

> A person with Ubuntu is open and available to others, affirming of others, does not feel threatened that others are able and good, for he or she has a proper self-assurance that comes from knowing that he or she belongs in a greater whole and is diminished when others are humiliated or diminished, when others are tortured or oppressed.

> (Tutu in Battersby, 2009, p. 6)

Mandela (as cited in Battersby, 2009) indicated that his time in prison was one which "had taught him to respect even the most ordinary people, and that he was always surprised how wrong one could be in judging people before speaking to them and finding out their unique story" (p. 7).

Nelson Mandela represents the leader connoisseur, one who understands his or her role in leading. His sense of what white South Africa had to hear from its first black leader was impeccable. "No matter what personal hardships he had to endure, he never lost sight of the goal of non-racial democracy in South Africa, believed that white fear of it could eventually be overcome" (Meredith, 2010, p. 573). Mandela demonstrated a "generosity of spirit . . . after his prison ordeal [and it] had a profound impact on his white adversaries, earning him measures of trust and confidence which made a political settlement attainable" (Meredith, 2010, p. 573).

And while Mandela's sense of political timing was correct on many occasions, there were lapses at times in judging very close friends and specifically with his ex-wife Winnie, whom he appointed as Minister for Arts, Culture, Science and Technology and eventually had to fire her, only to reappoint her and fire her again. Her involvement in shady dealings and get-rich-quick schemes embarrassed the new government and when she took to publicly criticizing it Mandela acted quickly. He was also hot-tempered at times, even with close allies and friends including Archbishop Desmond Tutu (Meredith, 2010, p. 544).

On the domestic side of South Africa "Major strides were made in the provision of housing, sanitation, piped water and electricity. But however much Mandela tried to focus attention on the poorer sections of society, the immediate beneficiary of the new South Africa was the black middle class" (Meredith, 2010, p. 569). But Mandela's legacy for the new South Africa was much more than these advancements. It was the personal Mandela, his "radiant smile, his self-deprecating humour, his benign presence, indeed the touch of magic he brought to everyday life" (Meredith, 2010, p. 599). He was simply larger than life. Mandela mused over his own life when he observed, "I was not a messiah, but an ordinary man who had become a leader because of extraordinary circumstances" (Meredith, 2010, p. 599).

Summary

This chapter has presented three types of portraits of connoisseurs: (1) connoisseurs of leaders; (2) connoisseurs of leadership performance; and (3) leader connoisseurs. An attempt has been made to show that these types represent men and women from many nations and international cultural identities of the world. A connoisseur of leaders may not necessarily be a leader himself/herself. Likewise, a connoisseur of leadership performance may not extend to being a connoisseur of other leaders. These two dimensions represent the internal and external worlds of connoisseurship which can come together into one integrated whole resulting in the *leader connoisseur*.

IMPLICATIONS FOR POLICY AND PRACTICE

Connoisseurship is a Social Creation Which is Dynamic and Fluid

The manifestations of connoisseurship involve self and the construction of self in a dynamic and fluid field of social interaction. From the perspective of George Herbert Mead (1934) the self consists of two parts, the "I" and the "me." Mead envisions the "me" part of self as socially constructed as does Erving Goffman (1959) who believed the self was merely a projection of a community upon the person. For Goffman, the self is a fleeting image of interaction between a community of believers or followers and the social interaction with a leader. It is thus an internal vision which is fragile and continually under interrogation and revision.

The database for this book was aimed at gaining a more nuanced understanding of how leaders develop their own *discerning eye*, the knowledge base of explicit and tacit knowledge to gain extraordinary insight and competence as a leader. Such knowledge is developmental and evolutionary with experience acting as a kind of scaffolding to make sense of the social interactions involved with leading. From Goffman's (1959) description in the analogy of self as a form of dramatic performance, *leading* is a kind of acting while *leadership* is the play. *Leadership* involves roles and audience expectations.

Notions of the practice of *leading* schools based on ideas that leadership emanates from a stable base are illusory. A bureaucratic role may have some sort of social permanency *as a role,* but the person in it is anything but permanent. Just as an actor may "stuff up" his or her lines in a play and be rejected or replaced, so can leaders occupying organizational roles be similarly disposed of.

Many contemporary versions and visions of educational leadership based on behavioral skill lists and "competencies" used in leadership preparation at the university or college level pay scant attention to the requirement of leadership identity and how it shapes and is in turn shaped by interactions with followers and significant others. Such an understanding undermines the fluid base upon which effective *leading* is actually embedded. This approach to leadership practice is not only misleading but strips the process of *leading* of its actual notion of performance, substituting instead the idea that the only way of judging effectiveness is student learning results. From this overly simplistic view, *leading* as a practice remains in a black box, present only as the equivalent of a Rorschach inkblot.

Key Chapter Ideas

• Differentiation of Connoisseurs

There are at least three types of connoisseurs in leadership. Both connoisseurship and leadership rest on differentiation of self and self-identity as the lynchpin of *the discerning eye.* The self is comprised of a personal and private structure called by Mead (1934) the "I" of identity, and subsequently the "me" which is constructed in social interaction with others. These constitute the inner and outer selves of a leader and of a connoisseur of leaders. This type of connoisseur may not be a leader but has developed a fine-grained eye towards those who occupy leadership positions which we call *connoisseurs of leader.* Then there is a *connoisseur of leadership performance* which refers to leaders who are connoisseurs of themselves and the craft of leadership in their respective roles. Finally there are *leader connoisseurs* who are both connoisseurs of leaders and connoisseurs of leadership performance.

• Field of Practice/Logic

According to Bourdieu and Wacquant (1992) a *field* is a dynamic and fluid juncture or intersection within a specific social space. The logic of practice within this social space is governed by the rules which are observed there. All players, even those who are disadvantaged in that space, usually uphold those rules. Persons or agencies located in this social space view for power and legitimacy and the players are arranged hierarchically according to the power to influence other persons or agencies situated there.

- **Contextual Transfer of Connoisseurship in Social Spaces**

Connoisseurs work in designated social spaces and are subject to the rules of logic and practice which are regnant within them (Bourdieu, 1993). As a practice, connoisseurship is the result of social construction within a dynamic and interactive social space. In some cases connoisseurs can transfer their competence and knowledge to other fields and retain their hierarchical position of influence and in other cases they cannot (see Gardner, 1995). Much depends on public perception of their sphere of expertise and the issue at hand in which they are expressing an opinion.

References

Alinsky, S.D. (1989). *Rules for radicals: A practical primer for realistic radicals.* New York: Vintage Books.

Ankori, G. (2013). *Frida Kahlo.* London: Reaktion Books Ltd.

Barenboim, D. (2005). Maestro. In H.M. Bhaba & W.J.T Mitchell (Eds.), *Edward Said: Continuing the conversation* (pp. 163–167). Chicago: University of Chicago Press.

Barenboim, D. (2008). Foreword. In E. Said, *Music at the limits: Three decades of essays and articles on music* (pp. vii–x). London: Bloomsbury.

Barenboim, D. & Said, E. (2004). *Parallels and paradoxes: Explorations in music and society.* Edited by A. Guzelimian. London: Bloomsbury.

Battersby, J.D. (2009). *Nelson Mandela: A life in photographs.* New York: Sterling.

Bourdieu, P. (1989). *Distinction: A social critique of the judgment of taste* (R. Nice, Trans.). Oxford: Taylor & Francis.

Bourdieu, P. (1993). *The field of cultural production.* New York: Columbia University Press.

Bourdieu, P. & Wacquant, L.J.D. (1992). *An invitation to reflexive sociology.* Chicago: University of Chicago Press.

Caro, R.A. (2002). *The years of Lyndon Johnson: Master of the senate.* New York: Alfred A. Knopf.

Churchill, W. (1921/1922). Painting as a pastime. *Strand* magazine. As cited in D. Coombs and M. Churchill (2003). *Sir Winston Churchill: His life and his paintings* (pp. 51–70). Philadelphia: Running Press Book Publications.

Clough, A.H. (Ed.). (n.d.). *Plutarch's lives* (J. Dryden, Trans.). New York: Modern Library.

De Vecchi, P. (2002). *Raphael.* New York and London: Abbeville Press Publishers.

Dunne, C. (1994). *Mary MacKillop: No plaster saint.* Sydney: Australian Broadcasting Commission.

Edwards, J. (1996). *Keating: The inside story.* Ringwood: Penguin Books.

Eisner, E. (2002). *The arts and the creation of mind.* New Haven, CT: Yale University Press.

Ekserdijian, D. (1996). Introduction. In G. Vasari (1568/1996a). *Lives of the painters, sculptors and architects. Vol. 1* (pp. xv–xlix) (G. Du C. de Vere, Trans.). New York: Alfred A. Knopf.

Fabian, S. & Loh, M. (1983). *The changemakers: Ten significant Australian women.* Milton: The Jacaranda Press.

Gardiner, P. (1994). *An extraordinary Australian: Mary Mackillop.* Alexandria: E.J. Dwyer (Australia) Pty Ltd.

Gardner, H. (1995). *Leading minds: The anatomy of leadership.* New York: Basic Books, Inc.

Gilbert, M. (1991). *Churchill: A life*. New York: Henry Holt and Company.

Goffman, E. (1959). *The presentation of self in everyday life*. New York: Doubleday Anchor.

Grant, M. (1970). *The ancient historians*. New York: Barnes and Noble Books.

Guile, M. (2011). *Stories from Australia's history: Mary MacKillop's path to sainthood*. South Yarra: Macmillan Education Australia Pty Ltd.

Hamill, P. (1999). *Diego Rivera*. New York: Harry M. Abrams, Inc. Publishers.

Hastings, M. (2010). *Winston's War: Churchill 1940–1945*. New York: Alfred A. Knopf.

Herrera, H. (1983). *Frida: A biography of Frida Kahlo*. New York: HarperCollins.

Joffe, J. (2014, March 6). Dear Vladimir: Congratulations. You read my book. *The Wall Street Journal*. A17. Retrieved from www.wsj.com/articles/SB10001424052702 30382420457942313357451 3024.

Keating, P. (n.d.). Biography. Retrieved from http://www.keating.org.au/page/biography/html.

Keating, P. (1992). Redfern speech: Year of the World's Indigenous People. Delivered in Redfern Park on December 10, 1992. Retrieved from http://www.keating.org.au/shop/item/redfern-speech-year-for-the-w. . .

Keating, P. (2004). Human resource management: The role of leadership—11 May 2004. Address given to the Australian Human Resources Institute, Melbourne, May 11, 2004. Retrieved from http://www.keating.org.au/shop/item/human-resource-management-the-role-of-leadership-11-May-2004.

Keegan, J. (2002). *Winston Churchill*. New York: Viking.

King, R. (2007). *Machiavelli, philosopher of power*. New York: HarperCollins.

Kirby, M. (1994). Inaugural Williamson Community Leadership Lecture. Parliament House, Melbourne, Australia. Unpublished Manuscript.

Lamberton, R. (2001). *Plutarch*. New Haven, CT: Yale University Press.

Lerner, M. (1950). Introduction. In N. Machiavelli, *The prince and the discourses* (pp. xxv–xlvi). New York: Modern Library.

Lukacs, J. (2002). *Churchill: Visionary, statesman, historian*. New Haven, CT: Yale University Press.

Machiavelli, N. (1535/1950). *The prince and the discourses*. New York: The Modern Library.

Manchester, W. (1988). *The last lion: Winston Spencer Churchill. Alone 1932–1940*. Boston: Little Brown and Company.

Mandela, N. (1994). *Long walk to freedom: The autobiography of Nelson Mandela*. London: Little, Brown.

Mapp, A.J. Jr. (1987). *Thomas Jefferson: A strange case of mistaken identity*. New York: Madison Books.

Massie, R.K. (2003). *Castles of steel*. New York: Random House.

McCreanor, S. (Ed.). (2011). *Mary McKillop and a nest of crosses: Correspondence with Fr Julian Tenison Woods 1869–1872*. North Sydney: Sisters of St Joseph of the Sacred Heart.

Mead, G.H. (1934). *Mind, self and society from the standpoint of a social behaviorist*. Edited by C.W. Morris. Chicago: University of Chicago Press.

Meredith, M. (2010). *Mandela: A biography*. New York: Public Affairs.

Modystack, W. (1995). *Blessed Mary Mackillop: A woman before her time*. Sydney: Lansdowne.

Morris, E. (2001). *Theodore Rex*. New York: Random House.

Plutarch, L.M. (n.d.). *Plutarch's lives* (Dryden, Trans.). Edited by A.H. Clough. New York: Modern Library.

Pogacnik, M. (2014). Sternstunde: Interview with Miha Pogacnik, classical concert violinist and leadership consultant on what business can learn from classical masterpieces. *Age of Artists*. Retrieved from www.ageofartists.org.

Ransome, P. (2010). *Social theory for beginners*. Bristol, UK: The Policy Press.

Ruffini, M. (2011). *Art without an author: Vasari's lives and Michelangelo's death*. New York: Fordham University Press.

Said, E. (1978). *Orientalism*. New York: Vintage Books.

Said, E. (1991). *Musical elaborations*. New York: Columbia University Press.

Said, E. (1999). *Out of place: A memoir*. New York: Vintage Books.

Said, E. (2006). *On late style: Music and literature against the grain*. New York: Vintage Books.

Said, E. (2008). *Music at the limits: Three decades of essays and articles on music*. London: Bloomsbury.

Said, M. (2008). Preface. In E. Said, *Music at the limits: Three decades of essays and articles on music* (xi–xiii). London: Bloomsbury.

Saith, A. (2003). Word and reed as weapon and shield: A laudation for Edward Said. Delivered on the occasion of the award of the degree of Doctor Honoris Causa to Edward Said at the Lustrum Ceremony on the 50th Anniversay of the Institute of Social Studies, The Hague, The Netherlands, May 21. Retrieved from www.iss.nl/fileadmin/ASSETS/iss/Documents/Academic_publications/said_lecture.pdf.

Smith, M. (2009). Keating promoted culture as something to celebrate. Retrieved from http://www.smh.com.au/federal-politics/keating-promoted-culture-a.

't Hart, P. & Walter, J. (2014). Distributed leadership and policy success: Understanding political dyads. Paper prepared for delivery at the 2014 Annual Meeting of the Australian Political Studies Association, University of Sydney, September 28–October 1, 2014.

Thorpe, O. (1974). Mackillop, Mary Helen (1984–1909). *Australian Dictionary of Biography*, 5, 1. Retrieved from http://adb.anu.edu.au/biography/mackillop-mary-helen-4112.

Watson, D. (2003). *Recollections of a bleeding heart: A portrait of Paul Keating*. Milsons Point: Vintage.

Whittemore, R. (1988). *Pure lives: The early biographers*. Baltimore, MD: The Johns Hopkins University Press.

Vasari, G. (1568/1996a). *Lives of the painters, sculptors and architects. Vol. 1*. (G. Du C. de Vere, Trans.). New York: Alfred A. Knopf.

Vasari, G. (1568/1996b). *Lives of the painters, sculptors and architects. Vol. 2*. (G. Du C. de Vere, Trans.). New York: Alfred A. Knopf.

Yu, H. (2006). Reflections on Edward Said's legacy: Orientalism, cosmopolitanism and the enlightenment. *Journal of the Canadian Historical Association*, 17(2), 16–31.

3

EDUCATIONAL LEADERS
AS CONNOISSEURS

And anybody who communicates, whether a musician, or writer, or a painter, is obviously trying to have a certain amount of power not only over the material, but over the craft itself. Ruskin says, for example, that when you look at a great work by Michelangelo, you're impressed not only with the nobility of the work but also with the idea of power in the work—that is to say, that Michelangelo was able to compel stone and create with his hands a human figure of a sort that never lets you forget it wasn't done by any ordinary effort. So, there's that kind of power, as well: the power to impress and the power to sustain attention.

(Said in Barenboim & Said, 2004, pp. 71–72)

WHAT THIS CHAPTER IS ABOUT

This chapter focuses exclusively on educational leaders who were connoisseurs in their time and place in the world. Since it was impossible to interview them inasmuch as most of them are no longer alive, our sources were biographical and archival. Both of these sources have been used in the past by other researchers to construct portraits of deceased leaders and to examine the decisions they made in their times (see Barber, 1985; Carlyle, 1935; Gardner, 1995; Keegan, 1987).

We would remind our readers that while it is natural for them to compare themselves to these leaders, they are cautioned not to become discouraged. Connoisseurship is not only distinctive but developmental. It comes from very hard work over a sustained period of time. While theoretically all leaders have the potential to become connoisseurs, very few attain that status. Perhaps as more information is gleaned from the work in this book and from additional research that this study may inspire, more educational leaders may attain that connoisseurship status.

Specifically this chapter addresses the following points:

- Educational leaders who were also connoisseurs developed views and voices opposed to the tenets and pedagogy of traditional education in many different countries.
- Educational leaders who became connoisseurs functioned as the equivalent of Weber's (1920/1993) "switchmen," individuals who blazed new tracks and onto which many other educators then followed.
- Educational leaders who became connoisseurs often voiced opposition to a broad range of conventional beliefs beyond pedagogy. Their questioning attitude took many forms of opposition, of which conventional schooling was only one area.
- The influence of many of the educational leaders as connoisseurs is still being felt around the globe.

Introduction

The international educational leaders described in this chapter advanced ideas that changed the way subsequent educators thought about pedagogy and other educational issues. Max Weber (1920/1993) termed such innovative ideas the equivalent of a railroad "switchman." Once formed and explicated, these new ideas created a new vision in which other interests than those used before could be pursued on a new track. We view the educators in this chapter as an example of the Weberian "switchman" and see this term as applying to both men and women. For some of our readers we want to remind them that over time the radicality of these innovators has become somewhat humdrum and it is easy to forget how revolutionary their ideas were at the time they thought and wrote about them.

One of the requirements that seems obvious for someone to become a "switchman" is that they had to have a grasp of the intellectual/cognitive field before they could position their new ideas against it. This knowledge is the foundation of connoisseurship and, as we have argued before, much of it is "tacit" or understood but not necessarily overtly expressed. Tacit knowledge exists because a person has deep knowledge of a particular area or field.

We now highlight internationally known educational leaders who were connoisseurs. In terms of our typology of connoisseurs discussed in the previous chapter, we consider our five educational leaders in this chapter to be "connoisseurs of leadership performance" for their outstanding performance as leaders themselves. All of them developed "the discerning eye," whether it be in philosophy as in the case of John Dewey, or a practitioner-scholar as in the case of Tsunesaburō Makiguchi of Japan, Paulo Freire of Brazil or Maria Montessori of Italy. We also include the contribution of Jacob Riis, for his public advocacy and education work that led to tenement reform for poor citizens living in New York in the first part of the 20th Century.

Because their work ranged outside of their immediate cultural and political contexts, these educational leaders transcended the political boundaries of their countries to create ideas and perspectives that have universal appeal applicable beyond their own nationalities, culture and context.

Paulo Freire of Brazil (1921–1997)

Paulo Freire was an educator, philosopher, academic, political activist and public intellectual and is considered to be "one of the most heralded educators of the twentieth century" (Mayo, 2004, p. 1). He is well known for his socially transformative vision of adult education (Hall in Schugurensky & Bailey, 2014, p. 11) and revolutionary pedagogical theory of literacy based on his early work with adults (Giroux, 1987). Freire is recognized as one of the founders of critical pedagogy since he brought ideas together from politics, education, imperialism and liberation (Schugurensky & Bailey, 2014). Freire's extraordinary influence has been felt not only in the developing world but also many parts of Europe, the United States and Australia (Mayo, 2004). Widely esteemed by his colleagues and the profession, he was made honorary professor of 28 universities around the world (*Encyclopedia of Biography*, 2004). Freire passed away in 1997, yet his ideas and prolific writings (25 books translated into 35 languages) (*Encyclopedia of Biography*, 2004) live on. The number of books, papers and articles re-examining and extending his idea continues to grow (Mayo, 2004).

Although born into a middle-class family in northeast Brazil in 1921, Freire was exposed to poverty and family economic hardships because of the depression. This early exposure to poverty no doubt sensitized him to social inequality and social injustice. Growing up he was greatly influenced by Christian liberation theology and, later, he and his wife were members of the progressive Catholic action movement (Schugurensky & Bailey, 2014). Freire was employed as a secondary teacher of Portugese before studying and practicing law. However, the law did not sustain him and he returned to education where he spent 10 years working as a director of the Department of Education and Culture of the Social Service of Industry (SESI) in Pernambuco, Brazil. In this position, he was responsible for creating programs to better the living standards of workers and one of his initiatives was the establishment of workers' clubs where workers could discuss common problems and come up with answers. It was this experience that formed the foundation of his doctoral dissertation (Schugurensky & Bailey, 2014).

Later, as director of the University of Recife's Cultural Extension Service, he brought literacy programs to thousands of peasants in northeast Brazil. At that time Brazil was an extremely poor country and illiteracy was high. Without literacy, the peasants were not able to vote. His alternative and very successful system of teaching literacy to adults attracted the attention of the president of Brazil and he later implemented his program nationally. However, a couple of years later, in 1964, the military overthrew the left-wing Goulart government with the consequence that Freire's adult literacy program, viewed as politically subversive, ceased. Freire was imprisoned and then exiled (Schugurensky & Bailey, 2014). Many years and decades later, he was employed by revolutionary governments around the world to help them establish literacy programs (Mayo, 2004). During his 16-year exile from Brazil, he traveled extensively and engaged in a variety of projects in many different parts of the world (Bhattacharya, 2011).

It was not until 1980 that Freire moved back to Brazil where he remained until his death. In Brazil, he became active in political affairs and was a founding member of the Workers' Party of Brazil. For a couple of years he held the position of Secretary of Education in São Paulo whereby he aimed to improve access to schooling, democratize school administrations, improve the quality of education for children and working youths and adults, and develop critically responsible citizens (Schugurensky & Bailey, 2014, p. 36). These goals were very ambitious given the widespread poverty, limited resources, traditional methods used in schools, poor infrastructure and high staff turnover. According to Schugurensky and Bailey (2014), he brought many of his early ideas about education to his role as director. These included:

> the notion of education as a tool for social and cultural emancipation, the role of students and teachers as subjects of their own learning process, the importance of "reading the word" through "reading the world", the democratization of student–teacher relations, the recognition of education as a political-pedagogical project.
>
> (p. 39)

Freire reflected on his time as Secretary of Education and claimed that he did not abuse his authority nor had power corrupted him. He said the following to a group of educators:

> If I die, for instance, this year, I would not have written the four books I wanted to write, but I proved myself in a job that I needed to perform before dying. Much more necessary than writing those four books was to know how I would behave holding power, and I would like to tell you that I behave well, with a relative coherence.
>
> (Freire, 1990, in Schugurensky, 1998, p. 21)

A key part of his leadership practice was to set up teams of five to six advisors who would work autonomously and substitute for him. In describing how he worked with his team in this context, Gadotti (1994), a colleague who worked with him for over 20 years, said:

> Paulo Freire would ardently defend his opinions, though he knew how to work in a team, contradicting the spontaneism of which he was so often accused. He had authority but exercised it democratically and confronted difficult situations with considerable patience.
>
> (p. 99)

Freire maintained that the important changes he instigated during his time in office were structural changes that enabled schools to have greater autonomy and the creation of school councils and student unions (Gadotti, 1994, p. 100). While there were many achievements, Schugurensky and Bailey (2014) claim that the administration led by Freire was not completely successful as Freire and his team endeavored to bring about too many initiatives at one time. Other factors that impacted upon the success of the reforms included resistance by teachers and fellow bureaucrats and limited resources to support the changes.

Freire has been described as a Marxist humanist for his love of the poor, oppressed and marginalized and for his vision of a "material reorganization of society . . . [and] a dismantling of colonial structures and ideologies" (McLaren & De Lissovoy, 2002, p. 1). His aesthetic vision is a moral one concerned with the fight for social justice. In his work and life, he showed a commitment to social justice through his involvement in political activities, the social movements he established and was part of, and his own humanity as a person and an educator.

An important theme in Freire's work is the place of love and humility in teaching (Mayo, 2004, p. 93). For Freire, teachers should be open, humble and willing to learn from their students and others. Not surprisingly, Freire himself was described as a person of great humility. A colleague and friend, the lay Dominican Friar, Frei Betto, who worked with Freire, and who used his method to educate others, said the following of him:

> he allowed himself to be educated by the workers, before presuming to be their educator . . . He was a simple person, an unpretentious intellectual, who never wished to show off his erudition, who did not favour one person over another in a relationship.
>
> (Betto, 1999, in Mayo, 2004, p. 3)

Freire was seen by his colleagues as a gifted teacher who loved his students and provided constructive and supportive feedback (Munoz in Schugurensky & Bailey, 2014, p. 42). Giroux (2010, in Schugurensky & Bailey, 2014) said:

Paulo stands out as exceptionally generous, eager to help younger intellec-
tuals publish their work, to write letters of support, and to live as much as
possible of himself in the service of others.

(p. 42)

A concept that Freire identifies as critical for revolutionary educators is
coherence (Freire, 1998) and by coherence he refers to a type of consistency
between what is said and what is done as well as consistency between theory and
practice. Gadotti (1994) claims that Freire was coherent yet not totally supportive
of coherence since this would make a person incapable of change or unprepared
to question his or her own prejudices. Thus, Freire demonstrated cultural
awareness and reflectivity as he was able to both trust and distrust his own
perceptions by engaging in self-criticism and reflection (Schugurensky & Bailey,
2014, p. 42). In Freire's later works, he referred to the quest in life as gaining
coherence and by this he meant developing a fuller awareness of his
"unfinishedness" (Freire in Mayo, 2004, p. 94). As a critical intellectual, he
continued to rethink and refine his ideas and their applicability to practice
throughout his life. He showed considerable self-awareness and understanding.
In one of the last books he wrote, he said:

I am a totality and not a dichotomy. I do not have a side of me that is
schematic, meticulous, nationalist, and another side that is disarticulated or
imprecise, which simply likes the world. I know with my entire body, with
feelings, with passion, and also with reason.

(Freire, 1998, p. 30)

An important insight Gadotti provides on Freire is his humanness:

Paulo Freire also suffers frustrations like all of us. He can leave a seminar
angrily, if he thinks he hasn't reached his objectives. He goes through
moments of anguish because the world is not the way he dreamed it should
be. He also often finds it difficult to believe that other people cannot accept
him. He becomes angry although he is an even-tempered man. He's proud,
despite being democratic. He's passionate, but he doesn't separate his
passion from his ideas.

(Gadotti, 1994, p. 137)

There is no doubt that Freire had developed a knowledgeable perception over
decades of experience and focused discipline in his various capacities as an activist,
educator and humanist. He shared his knowledgeable perception and discerning
insights with others while at the same time always respected others' views. The
quote from Gadotti (1994) illustrates this well:

Paulo Freire always pays attention; he is always analysing his practice and the concrete action around him. As a teacher, he always analyses at length what a student says. And when he doesn't agree, he doesn't answer aggressively but strongly defends his points of view . . . This shows his respect for his interlocutor. But this respect doesn't make him lose his attention. Autonomy doesn't mean abandonment . . . He always intervenes, he nevers stays out of the discussion, and he constantly gives his opinion.

(p. 86)

As a leader, Freire was a visionary who used his imagination to envisage possibilities. Central to his pedagogy is the power and place of imagination to enable a seeing of what is possible and therefore imagination is a precondition to change (McLaren & De Lissovoy, 2002). Referring to Freire's work in this area, McLaren and De Lissovoy (2002) explain:

more than a cognitive or emotional potential, the human imagination . . . is capable of a radical and productive envisioning that exceeds the limits of the given . . . the educator-student and student-educator work together to mobilize the imagination in the service of creating a vision of a new society.

(p. 2)

This notion of imagination is tied up with Freire's strong belief in the role of education to bring about social justice. Freire was the consummate connoisseur. His life and work breathe of his aesthetic vision where theory and practice, and imagination and agency, were brought together. As Darder (2003) claims, Freire refused to accept fatalism. "At every turn, he emphatically rejected the idea that nothing could be done about the educational consequences of economic inequalities and social injustice" (p. 500).

Freire had a strong sense of identity and purpose. A good illustration was how he coped whilst in exile. Freire (1998) discusses this time as painful to himself and his family. Yet during those 16 years where he continued his work in unfamiliar contexts, he revised and renewed his purpose and vision. Whether he was working with illiterate peasants in remote villages, government officials, fellow academics, or teachers and students, he was acutely aware of the power differentials within and across societies and redressing power imbalances was the impetus for his life project of social justice.

Maria Montessori of Italy (1870–1952)

Maria Montessori was an influential educator, medical doctor and feminist. She is recognized internationally for pioneering a system of educating children which was referred to as "the Montessori Method." *The Montessori Method* was also the title of her first book, published in 1912 in Italy and then translated into 20 languages. The book reached second place on the U.S. non-fiction list for 1912 (Montessori Australia, n.d.). Montessori's method has been described as "a comprehensive educational theory; it embodied a general philosophy of education, a psychology of learning, and a method of instruction" (Gutek, 2003, p. 178).

Montessori started her professional life as a medical doctor. She was the first woman to enroll and then graduate in medical school with a medical degree in her native Italy. This was no small feat given the conservative values regarding the role of women that were pervasive in Italy at the turn of the 19th Century. Yet she excelled at university and won several scholarships for her outstanding work (Standing, 1998). After Montessori graduated from university, she was chosen to represent Italy at a feminist congress where she argued for the rights of working women. At a similar conference a couple of years later, she championed the cause of ending the exploitative practice of employing child labor in the mines in Sicily (Standing, 1998). Defending the "underdog" was to be a cause she continued throughout her life. Standing (1998), a colleague who knew her for 30 years and who wrote her biography, puts it thus, "she felt the duty of going forth as an apostle on behalf of all the children in the world, born and as yet born, to preach for their rights and their liberation" (p. 61).

After graduating, Maria worked at the University of Rome psychiatric clinic with developmentally challenged children (May, n.d.). She embraced the writings of two French physicians, Jean-Marc Itard and Édouard Séguin, and adopted their important ideas regarding the need to respect and understand all children. She went on to develop a range of stimulus materials to help disabled and disadvantaged children develop their motor skills. Montessori later applied these ideas to children who did not have any specific learning problems (Montessori Australia, n.d.). These were children from the slums and also children from privileged backgrounds. It was found that when children had the opportunity to choose their own activities within a structured environment, they were not only happy and motivated but also learned (*Montessori International*, 2002). The key principles of Montessori's method are spontaneous activities and independent learning (*Montessori International*, 2002).

Montessori set up a number of children's houses, referred to as *Casa dei bambini*, throughout Italy where she implemented her method of teaching. Soon these schools or houses spread to other countries. She spent a number of decades of her life traveling the world, to places such as the United States, the United Kingdom, Spain, The Netherlands and India, where she visited newly founded schools and provided training programs to educators. She received three nominations for the Nobel Peace Prize in recognition of her life's commitment to education (Montessori Australia, n.d.). Today, it is estimated that there are more than 8,000 Montessori schools across six continents making her method of education the "single largest pedagogy" in the world (May, n.d., p. 1).

Her ideas on children's education were revolutionary for the time. Her training meant that she used a scientific approach when coming to understand children. She worked closely with them, observing them, and these observations enabled her to create her method and develop materials to enhance their learning. In the early 1900s, the dominant perspective was that children were in need of adult control and strong intervention (*Montessori International*, 2002). Like John Dewey in the United States, Montessori questioned the prevailing traditional pedagogy of the day. Yet her work was different from Dewey's. Dewey and his colleagues' progressive educational approach focused on children's social interaction and problem-solving skills while Montessori's work with children was seen as emphasizing the cognitive aspects of child development, more so than creating opportunities for them to develop their social and cooperative skills (May, n.d.).

Montessori was a very strong-willed and principled person who was not afraid to chart her own course. Gutek (2003) gives the example of the time when Montessori accepted an invitation from the Fascist Government in Italy to set up Montessori schools and a training institute. When some years later the regime wanted to use her as an ambassador to support Fascism, Montessori refused. Her desire was to preserve her independence and to maintain more of an international role (Gutek, 2003). Moreover, she realized that an education focused on developing free and strong personalities could not thrive in a totalitarian environment (Standing, 1998). Not surprising, Mussolini closed down her schools and Montessori left Italy in exile (Gutek, 2003).

Gutek (2003) described Montessori not only as an independent and forceful person, but also as

> a somewhat doctrinaire leader who wanted her disciples to implement her method exactly as she designed it, without change or innovation. For her the scientific method meant the precise implementation and use of materials as she intended them to be used.

(p. 186)

Kramer's (1989) biography of Montessori provides further comment and critical insights into her character and work. While praising her for her innovation and intuition that helped in the exploration and creation of new methods for educating children, Kramer points out that over time, Montessori remained isolated from other important movements that were taking place in both education and psychology. The effect was that "the movement had become a fortress. It protected those within from external dangers but left them with a rather impoverished set of experiences, seldom seeing new faces, hearing other voices than their own" (Kramer, 1989, p. 378). It was this isolation that prevented her from cross-pollination of ideas and growing intellectually (Kramer, 1989). Her other biographer, Standing, referred to Montessori's strong sense of self and belief in her abilities and direction. He said, "the spirit of the pioneer was strong in her; and she felt—as the genius generally does—a confidence in her own powers." The following quote sums up Standing's (1998) view of Montessori's character, vision and leadership abilities:

> Her profound insight into the soul of the child; her long and varied experience; her scientific outlook combined with maternal tenderness and sympathy; the lucidity of her discourses and their originality; her strong yet charming personality, at once humble yet dignified; the passionate sincerity of her devotion to her mission—all of these combined to make her the perfect advocate of her cause, which was the cause of the child.
>
> (pp. 65–66)

In many ways, what Standing says in the aforementioned quote resonates with all of our dimensions of connoisseurship: Montessori had an aesthetic vision that was closely tied to her moral purpose and moral commitment to children; she was incredibly gifted (not merely competent); she showed a very strong desire to succeed and succeeded through working hard over many decades; she was disciplined and engaged in rigorous observation and study; she became experienced and through that developed expertise; she had a good understanding of practice and its links to theory; and she had a strong identity. Her life was one where she transcended her cultural conditioning and, by so doing, traveled her own path and created her own destiny. Not only did she challenge traditional barriers facing women through education, but she also challenged the barriers that exist between teachers and pupils (Kramer, 1989).

Tsunesaburō Makiguchi of Japan (1871–1944)

Tsunesaburō Makiguchi was an elementary school teacher and principal in Japan who developed for his time a revolutionary pedagogy which was based on "respect for and faith in children's agency in the creation of value—mirrored by a sense of respect for the agency of those engaged in guiding" children's development (Goulah & Gebert, 2014, p. 17).

Abandoning the formalism of instruction then regnant in Japanese schools, Makiguchi took his students intellectually into the real world. He worked to connect them to their immediate environs and the geography in which they and their families lived and toiled. He began by asking his students to write a story on the Soseigawa River which ran through the city. Later he shifted to mountains. The idea was to start with the familiar and work in new material which his students then incorporated into their expanding view and work. This approach, today called *constructivism*, was radical because learning then was linked to rote memorization and geography consisted of memorizing the names of rivers, mountains, cities and political subdivisions.

In his early 20s Makiguchi began writing a book, *The Geography of Human Life*, which was a 1,000-page tribute to his ideas about life and learning. This work was "archaeological in nature, in that it tried to dig into and understand the dialectic relation between humans and both their physical and social environment" (Ibrahim, 2014, p. 107). Makiguchi, whose early childhood was one of some stress, having been abandoned by his seaman father when he was only five years old, could have taken a deterministic view of human nature being shaped by impersonal forces beyond his control. Instead Makiguchi adopted the perspective that humans brought meaning to their environment and were active architects of it. Because of this connection, humans had to take special care to be in harmony with nature. In addition, in his path-breaking book, Makiguchi argued for peace and global citizenship at a time when Japanese militarism was a cascading force in Japanese society. This conflict was to be the essential flashpoint which ultimately landed him in prison as a "thought criminal" where he died in 1944 at the age of 73, an opponent of the war and of the alleged divinity of the Japanese emperor.

During his educational career as a school leader between 1913 and 1932, Makiguchi continued to write, publishing his second book *Research in Community Studies*. Refusing to bend to the pressures for favored treatment of some wealthy students, Makiguchi ran afoul of parental complaints and was summarily transferred to another school. He was ultimately principal of five schools in Tokyo. He developed a mature pedagogy, one which centered on the joy of learning. He rebelled against the relentless pressure of testing students in an environment of intense competition and the destructive effects on their lives, remarking that in his struggle against this kind of "education," "I cannot be distracted by the question of reputation, the random praise or censure of others" (Makiguchi in Ibrahim, 2014, p. 109).

Gebert (2009) compared Makiguchi's philosophy with that of John Dewey and noted the similarities that "Like Dewey Makiguchi rejected the idea that education is preparation for future living. Rather, education is living, and living is education. Thus, the benefits afforded by authentic (value-creating) education must be experienced now, in the process of education" (p. 163).

Even in solitary confinement in prison near the end of his life, Makiguchi insisted to his police interrogators his view that "The emperor is a common mortal . . . Nor is the emperor without error" (Ito, 2014, pp. 24–25). This criticism was a threat to the militaristic foundation of the Japanese state which took its power from the alleged divinity of the emperor. Ito (2014) also notes that Makiguchi's religious beliefs in Nichiren Buddhism were inseparable from his educational theories and he perished without compromising either.

Today, Makiguchi's philosophy of education is carried on with SOKA education, a perspective on learning and teaching that embodies his ideas and values regarding the joy of learning and the happiness of children. It stands in stark contrast to the dicta of the neo-liberal forces trying to destroy the foundation of creating in schools places of learning and joy with more tests, standards and so-called "accountability" that has erased school as a place of learning that never gives up on any student (Bethel, 1973).

John Dewey (1859–1952) of the United States

Jay Martin (2002), John Dewey's biographer wrote of him:

> Dewey was the last American philosopher to claim attention from the public and to hold it over a long period of time. Perhaps culture can do without philosophers, but it cannot do without philosophy. How do we judge a society? Perhaps the standard is what we find in its schools.
>
> (p. 498)

John Dewey remains American education's most pre-eminent philosopher and spokesperson. He lived during "the American Century," that period of time when the United States came to dominate the world, economically, militarily and culturally. His output was prodigious. He published his first article in 1882 and Martin (2002) indicates that in his 67 years through 1949 he wrote "about a thousand essays, books, reviews and works in other forms and he had not yet written his last work" (p. 478).

While Dewey is most acclaimed for the ideas behind "Progressive Education" he realized that many of his views had been miscast and misinterpreted. He was associated with the "child centered school" but he lamented that that had never been his objective. He asked a friend in 1950, "Why do writers and teachers insist on saddling me with the 'child-centered' school? Anyone who has read me knows that it is the socially centered school that I have sought" (Dewey in Martin, 2002, p. 498).

In contemporary times in the early 21st Century, John Dewey is connected to pragmatism as a philosophy, another linkage he denied. He is viewed more than half a century after his death as a kind of dry and stuffy intellectual more discussed than read except by the rare graduate student who takes time to more fully investigate his thoughts. What is not well known is that Dewey was an emotional man who often made impulsive decisions and that personal reflection advanced by logic and sound scholarship often followed his emotional displays.

Lynd (1966) indicated that John Dewey was what he termed an *instrumentalist* and that Dewey's perspective was based on the following principles:

- *There are no eternal truths* and trying to find immutable truth is a fool's errand. Dewey rejected the Greek mind versus body dualism and insisted that only experience itself as a human being interacted with the environment produced worthwhile knowledge.

- *The only test for truth lies in determining its consequences for human living* and the most appropriate means to determine this is through scientific activity.
- *The search for knowledge must be continuous but will not lead to some idea of ultimate reality.*
- *There is no mind or soul outside of the material aspects of man's existence.*
- *There are no fixed moral laws; however, democracy is a moral value* (Lynd, 1966).

In his early life as an academic, Dewey was involved in intensive investigations into psychology and philosophy that led to the creation of the Lab School at the University of Chicago. It was during these early years that he developed his interest in all matters pertaining to pedagogy. After the death of two of his children, the latest his son Gordon dying of typhoid fever in Europe, Dewey transferred to the Teachers College Columbia University in New York where he remade his academic career and shifted his academic work to focus more directly on matters of public democracy and politics. He had a passion for the underserved and ill-served people in the world. He became a world traveler and visited many countries between 1919 and 1934. He worked to establish citizen groups to advocate for wider participation in democracy. The focus of his writing and his tone reflected this change. As Martin (2002) remarks, "much of his writing was polemical and controversial. He was attacked and he counterattacked" (p. 243).

Dewey believed that "the collective experience of a democratic society should be seen as a resource for solving future problems" (Bowen & Hobson, 1974, p. 169). His focus shifted to the role of teachers and the fact that teachers had to have a stronger voice in school affairs and decisions. He helped organize the American Association of University Professors (AAUP), a still active organization in the United States. He was an active participant in the creation of the National Association for the Advancement of Colored People (the NAACP), the American Civil Liberties Union (the ACLU), and the New York City Teachers Union and later the American Federation of Teachers. Dewey not only wrote about democracy, he practiced it.

Dewey's most popular book was *The School and Society* released in 1899 and based on a series of lectures Dewey gave at the University of Chicago. This book went through extensive editions and was revised by Dewey in 1915. In this book, Dewey (1899/1990) sketched out a picture of "the old education" which unfortunately is still the dominant picture of many schools today:

> its passivity of attitude, its mechanical massing of children, its uniformity of curriculum and method. It may be summed up by stating that the center of gravity is outside the child. It is in the teacher, the textbook, anywhere and everywhere you please except in the immediate instincts and activities of the child himself. On that basis there is not much to be said about the life of the child. A good deal might be said about studying of the child, but the school is not the place where the child lives.
>
> (p. 34)

Dewey (1899/1990) also spoke of waste in education, not from the usual materialistic dimensions about time or class size, but from the perspective of the individual student. On this matter he wrote:

> From the standpoint of the child, the great waste in the school comes from his [sic] inability to utilize the experiences he gets outside the school in any complete and free way within the school itself; while, on the other hand, he is unable to apply in daily life what he is learning at school. That is the isolation of the school—its isolation from life.
>
> (p. 75)

Despite the talk of Dewey's influence in his day in the schools, his actual ideas were hard to translate and often mistranslated. He shouldered the blame for many of the ills he wanted to change in the schools. He was accused of being a subversive and the FBI opened a file on him to track his thoughts and work. His alleged teachings were criticized directly by Dwight Eisenhower, president of the United States, and a high ranking U.S. Naval Admiral, Hyman Rickover, also falsely accused him of implementing ideas that weakened the rigor of the schools. But these are but testimony to the breadth of his writing and the exceptional range of his influence. He remains the pre-eminent philosopher of education in the United States.

Jacob Riis (1849–1914) of the United States

Jacob Augustus Riis rose from a poor Danish immigrant background to be praised by Theodore Roosevelt as "the best American I ever knew" (Yochelson & Czitrom, 2007, p. 3). Though not an educator working in the schools, Jacob Riis took advantage of his public role as an advocate for tenement reform and adequate social services for the urban poor to be an educator of the general public on the extreme effects and the grinding degradation of poverty on the lives of the citizens of New York City.

Jacob Riis came to America in 1870 with little money but he was a skilled carpenter and he spoke some English. He moved around the country for a while doing odd jobs but finally back in New York City he landed a role as a newspaper reporter and bought a small newspaper. He became a crusading journalist and learned about the advantages of using photographs in publishing. He became a reporter on the police beat and was exposed to the criminal underbelly of the city's poor. He wrote feature articles for Danish newspapers on New York personalities, crime and the foibles of those in high society. In this way Riis learned the ins and outs of life in the slums. In his writing, Yochelson and Czitrom (2007) noted that

> Riis evolved a distinctive and highly clinical approach, one that fused empathic descriptions of human misery and resilience, statistical data culled

from policy and other government sources, and a fierce scepticism directed at popular myth and the more sensational mysteries of the city.

(pp. 12–13).

The squalid conditions of the city's poorest immigrants living in the tenement houses became Riis' special project and crusade. "By 1880 over 600,000 New Yorkers lived in 24,000 tenements . . . and thousands of buildings were in terrible sanitary condition, with seriously defective plumbing, and often no ventilation or sewer condition, with seriously defective plumbing and often with no ventilation connections" (Yochelson & Czitrom, 2007, p. 20). These terrible health conditions accounted for the annual deaths of 3,000 children below the age of five and thousands of cases of contagious diseases. By using the power of the photograph and especially the use of flash powder to provide light at night, Riis took pictures of the most notorious slums, housing quarters in dark and damp basements where over 30,000 people slept at night. He put together a slide show in which he projected images on large screens. These images became an integral feature of his lectures, which raised awareness about the ravages and dangers faced by people living in the slums. He personally narrated these public exposés. Finally in 1890 he published the photographs and personal stories in a best-selling book, *How the Other Half Lives: Studies Among the Tenements of New York.*

Riis' work in documentary photography and muckraking journalism won him fame and led to laws, policies and changes in the living conditions of hundreds of New York City's poor. Later he mused in a letter to his son, "I had no special genius, no special ability. I had endurance, and I reached at last the heart of men; [sic] that is all I can claim" (Riis in Yochelson & Czitrom, 2007, p. 119).

Summary

This chapter has focused briefly on describing educational connoisseurs from different countries and times. These connoisseurs were compared to Max Weber's railroad "switchman," a provocative metaphor he used to describe how new ideas create innovative pathways for material interests to be pursued. Such ideas are inevitably linked to the human beings who formulated and wrote about them.

Based on historical and archival data, a perusal of the portraits included in this chapter provide evidence that nearly all of the educator connoisseurs included were linked to Eisner's 10 dimensions of connoisseurship (see Chapter 1), that is, they demonstrated such characteristics as knowledgeable perception, the ability to reflect, interpret and assimilate a wealth of experiences as well as having competence and the ability to frame problems and issues. All of the educators possessed a personal passion for improving themselves and the field of education. They understood how practice is formed and should be changed in different contexts. Nearly all possessed aesthetic vision. They were provocative and inspirational. Their lives included time for serious introspection. Nearly all were not interested in improving traditional educational practice, that is, they were not interested in making schools as they existed more "effective." For them, "effective" meant doing things differently. In creating their ideas they became examples of Weber's "switchmen" and created new tracks for subsequent educators to follow.

IMPLICATIONS FOR POLICY AND PRACTICE

Questioning Conventional Ideas of Pedagogy and Education is Part of a Gestalt of Skepticism About Orthodox Social and Cultural Beliefs in General

The brief portraits of educational leaders as connoisseurs presented in this chapter clearly demonstrate from sources of life writing about them that they were skeptical and critical not only of educational conventions, but of many other attitudes and practices also deemed conventional of their times. These ranged from beliefs regarding religion to other metaphysical notions within their cultures such as Dewey's rejection of Greek (and hence Christian) dualism. Many questioned and wrote against the orthodox political/social/economic dominant hegemonies of their times with some being placed under surveillance by agents of their governments as subversives and at least one dying in prison as a "thought criminal."

The discussion presented in this chapter would suggest that opposition to dominant forms of education and schooling are part and parcel of opposition to other forms of orthodoxy embedded in a society's cultural beliefs and practices. The implication for educational practice is that candidates for leadership positions should be exposed to many forms of cultural hegemony and oppositional perspectives so that they are able to form a coherent position of their own educational principles and practices.

Key Chapter Ideas

- ### Switchman

This term comes from Max Weber (1920/1993) and refers to individuals who blazed new tracks onto which others followed and set a new direction for a particular field.

• Dissatisfaction is a Key Motivator to Re-Conceptualize Pedagogy and Education

All of the educator connoisseurs included in this chapter became dissatisfied with traditional forms of education that dominated their times. The sources of this dissatisfaction were varied, but nearly all observed that the methods and assumptions of rote memory and pursuit of the idea that children were empty vessels to be filled up were antithetical to helping children learn to think independently and to become thoughtful, participatory citizens in their countries. Traditional forms of pedagogy stamped out the joy of discovery and learning which is essential to human growth, development and happiness.

References

Barber, J. (1985). *The presidential character.* Englewood Cliffs, NJ: Prentice-Hall, Inc.

Barenboim, D. & Said, E. (2004). *Parallels and paradoxes: Explorations in music and society.* Edited by A. Guzelimian. London: Bloomsbury.

Bethel, D.M. (1973). *Makiguchi the value creator: Revolutionary Japanese educator and founder of Soka Gakkai.* Tokyo: Weatherhill.

Bhattacharya, A. (2011). *Paulo Freire: Rousseau of the twentieth century.* Dordrecht: Springer.

Bowen, J. & Hobson, P.R. (1974). *Theories of education: Studies of significant innovation in western educational thought.* Sydney: John Wiley and Sons Australasia Pty. Ltd.

Carlyle, T. (1935). *On heroes, hero-worship, and the heroic in history.* London: Oxford University Press.

Darder, A. (2003). Teaching as an act of love: Reflections on Paulo Freire and his contributions to our lives and our work. In A. Darder, M. Baltodano & R.D. Torres (Eds.), *The critical pedagogy reader* (pp. 497–510). New York: RoutledgeFalmer.

Dewey, J. (1899/1990). *The school and society.* Chicago: University of Chicago Press.

Encyclopedia of Biography (2004). Paulo Freire. Enclopedia.com. Retrieved from http://www.encyclopedia.com/utility/printdocument.aspxx?id=IG2.

Freire, P. (1998). *Pedagogy of the heart.* New York: Continuum.

Gadotti, M. (1994). *Reading Paulo Freire: His life and work.* Albany: State University of New York Press.

Gardner, H. (1995). *Leading minds: An anatomy of leadership.* New York: Basic Books, Inc.

Gebert, A. (2009). The role of community studies in the Makiguchian pedagogy. *Educational Studies, 45*(2), 146–164.

Giroux, H. (1987). Introduction. In P. Freire & D. Macedo (1987), *Literacy: Reading the word and the world* (pp. 1–27). London: Routledge Kegan Paul.

Goulah, J. & Gebert, A. (Eds.). (2014). *Tsunesaburo Makiguchi (1871–1944).* London: Routledge.

Gutek, G.L. (2003). Maria Montessori: Contributions to educational psychology. In B.J. Zimmerman & D.H. Schunk (Eds.), *Educational psychology: A century of contributions* (pp. 171–186). Mahwah, NJ: Lawrence Erlbaum Associates.

Ibrahim, A. (2014). Media review. In J. Goulah & A. Gebert (Eds.), *Tsunesaburo Makiguchi (1871–1944)* (pp. 104–111). London: Routledge.

Ito, T. (2014). Reading resistance: The record of Tsunesaburo Makiguchi's interrogation by wartime Japan's "thought police." In J. Goulah & A. Gebert (Eds.), *Tsunesaburo Makiguchi (1871–1944)* (pp. 23–35). London: Routledge.

Keegan, J. (1987). *The mask of command*. New York: Viking.

Kramer, R. (1989). *Maria Montessori: A biography*. London: Hamish Hamilton.

Lynd, A. (1966). Who wants progressive education? The influence of John Dewey on the public schools. In R.D. Archambault (Ed.), *Dewey on education* (pp. 191–208). New York: Random House.

Martin, J. (2002). *The education of John Dewey: A biography*. New York: Columbia University Press.

May, S. (n.d.). Maria Montessori. Talbot School of Theology, Catholic Educators. Retrieved from http://www.talbot.edu/ce20/educators/catholic/maria_montessori/.

Mayo, P. (2004). *Liberating praxis: Paulo Freire's legacy for radical education and politics*. Westport, CT: Praeger.

McLaren, P. & De Lissovoy, N. (2002). Paulo Freire (1921–1997). *Encyclopedia of Education*. Retrieved from http://www.encyclopedia.com/topic/Paulo_Freire.aspx.

Montessori Australia (n.d.). A biography of Dr Maria Montessori. Retrieved from http://montessori.org.au/montessori/biography.htm.

Montessori International (2002). The life history of Dr Maria Montessori. Retrieved from http://seekeronline.info/journals/y2005/jul05.html.

Schugurensky, D. (1998). The legacy of Paulo Freire: A critical review of his contributions. *Convergence, Tribute to Paulo Freire, xxxi*(1 & 2), 17–29.

Schugurensky, D. & Bailey, R. (2014). *Paulo Freire*. London: Bloomsbury Publishing.

Standing, E.M. (1998). *Maria Montessori: Her life and work*. New York: Plume.

Weber, M. (1920/1993). *The sociology of religion*. Boston: Beacon Press.

Yochelson, B. & Czitrom, D. (2007). *Rediscovering Jacob Riis*. Chicago: University of Chicago Press.

4

HOW ARTISTS AND LEADERS THINK AND WORK[1]

Connoisseurs notice in the field of their expertise what others may miss seeing.
(Eisner, 2002, p. 187)

WHAT THIS CHAPTER IS ABOUT

This chapter reports the research of artists and leaders upon which this book is defined and framed. The research process began with artists because of our conviction that continuing the traditional line of inquiry from the social sciences and main line research on school leadership was not apt to yield much in the way of new insights. In short, what was desired was to bring "new eyes" to old landscapes. In this pursuit we found this assumption well founded.

This line of inquiry of the research reported in this chapter was also developmental, that is it began with a study of creativity and morphed into one involving connoisseurship. In retrospect it was a "natural" kind of progression, but at the time a thoughtfully considered crossroad in the conduct of the research. Specifically this chapter addresses the following points:

- Based on the work of Elliot Eisner (2002) there are at least seven ways that the arts can enhance education and quite possibly educational leadership.
- The four key cognitive functions of the arts are reviewed.
- The three phased study of artists and educational leaders is described and illustrative comments indicated which are connected to Eisner's epistemic frames.

- How and when artists developed their *discerning eyes* is discussed.
- Educational leaders' comments connected to Eisner's epistemic frames are indicated and illustrated.
- Initial findings regarding the development of the *discerning eye* for educational leaders are described.
- Similarities and differences between artists and leaders are described.
- The "transactive account" is indicated as thoughtful practice.

Introduction

Elliot Eisner (2002) advanced seven propositions of how the arts could enhance education and by extrapolation educational leadership. The examples are:

1. There can be more than one answer to a question and more than one solution to a problem; the variability of outcome is OK.
2. The way something is formed matters. Form and content interpenetrate and cannot be cleanly separated.
3. The importance of imagination is given license in the arts. True innovation and change will not always be tidy, linear or concrete.
4. The capacity of an art form to touch us depends on the relationships that are composed by artists. Relationships "cannot be reduced to rule or recipe or formula or algorithm. Judgment depends on feel, and feel depends on a kind of somatic knowledge that enables one to determine if the form at hand has . . . 'rightness of fit'" (p. 201).
5. Intrinsic satisfactions matter. Such satisfactions improve longevity and resiliency and offer more powerful rewards than extrinsic ones. Intrinsic satisfactions relate to the notion that one's work should bring joy and be joyful.
6. Literal language and quantification are not the only means through which human understanding may be secured or represented. Non-quantifiable, non-literal and non-linear representations are central to a complete range of human communication.
7. One's work should be "flexibly purposive" and in which the ends of the work are held as open-ended (p. 206).

Schama (2006) provided support for Eisner's claims in his book *The Power of Art*:

> The power of art is the power of unsettling surprise. Even when it seems imitative, art doesn't so much duplicate the familiarity of the seen world as replace it with a reality all of its own. Its mission, beyond the delivery of beauty is the disruption of the banal.
>
> (p. 7)

Both Eisner (2002) and Schama (2006) suggest that art provides a new and active way of seeing that enables a person to fully appreciate what is happening in the world or, as Oscar Wilde (1913/2007) once said, "the mission of true art—to make us pause and look at a thing a second time" (p. 41). According to Perkins (1994), works of art require us to look at them both "persistently and intelligently" (p. 21) since it is unlikely there will be one meaning but multiple interpretations since "art functions as a symbol system" (Perkins, 1994, p. 21). "One cannot make . . . judgements about what [one] . . . cannot see or experience" (Eisner, 1979, p. x) and it is this idea that lies at the heart of connoisseurship which can be understood as "the art of appreciating what is educationally significant" (Eisner, 1979, p. x) or "the rightness of fit" (Eisner, 2002, p. 2).

Taylor (2012) distinguishes between the amateur and the professional (and here we could substitute connoisseur):

> And the difference may not be a difference of originality or insight but a difference of mastery. The professional, by dint of sheer extra hours of practice, can do things with the medium that the amateur can't, and so they are able to express things more strikingly, more subtly, more beautifully and more truthfully than the amateur.
>
> (pp. 25–26)

The Four Cognitive Functions of the Arts

According to Eisner (2002), the arts perform a number of key cognitive functions. One of these is representation which is "aimed at transforming the contents of consciousness within the constraints and affordances of a material" (p. 6). In other words, artists undergo a process whereby they move from an idea or an image to the end product (i.e. a finished painting, a choreographed piece of dance). Oscar Wilde (1913/2007, para. 64) describes this process as "the fulfilment of a prophecy: for every work of art is the conversion of an idea into an image." And this is where the "contents of consciousness are made public" (Eisner, 2002, p. 8). There are four key non-linear and inter-related processes that constitute representation through which artists traverse:

1. Inscription—which starts with an idea or image that is made concrete.
2. Editing—a "process of working on inscriptions so they achieve the quality, the precision, and the power their creator desires" (p. 6).
3. Communication is "the transformation of consciousness into a public form" (p. 6).
4. Discovery refers to "ends in process which in turn generate surprise" (p. 7). Eisner maintains that surprise is not only of the satisfying aspects of working in the arts but also it enables learning to occur that can be applied later on.

An important decision artists make, then, is choosing the medium with which they think they will be best able to represent the idea (Eisner, 2002). The medium both constrains and liberates the art-making process.

The Research of Artists and Leaders

The empirical study that constituted the work and reported in this chapter was part of a three phased line of inquiry which occurred in Australia and America between 2012 and 2015 and is shown in Table 4.1.

TABLE 4.1 Delineation of critical phases in connoisseurship

Study phase	Major focus	Key questions*
I	How do artists retain their creativity and resiliency when facing major barriers in their work?	1. What are the major types of limitations that artists confront in their work? 2. How does the medium in which an artist works frame it and/or limit it? 3. What inspires artists to keep working?
II	How and under what conditions do artists develop "the discerning eye" and become connoisseurs of their and others' work?	1. How do artists describe the ways they differentiate their work and the development of the skills which are used to complete it? 2. Are interpersonal relationships important as factors of influence in the identity and subsequent work of an artist?
III	How do educational leaders develop a "discerning eye" in their practice? Does this development parallel or imitate the same process with artists?	1. Can educational leaders recall significant junctures (critical incidents) where their ability to problem solve was markedly enhanced? 2. How has a leader's identity as an effective problem solver been developed over time?

Note: * See Appendix for a list of interview questions.

A qualitative methodology drawing upon semi-structured interviews was used in all of the phases of this research. Phases 1 and 2 solely involved artists while Phase 3 involved leaders. Questions asked during each phase of the study can be found in the Appendix. The next part of the discussion reports on findings from Phase 1.

Phase 1: Findings From the Artists

The participants for Phases 1 and 2 consisted of 10 former or current artists representing a variety of artistic fields. Nine of the 10 artists were Australian and

TABLE 4.2 Illustrative comments from artists to Eisner's epistemic frames

Participant	Artistic focus	Current work environment	Illustrative comment	Connection to Eisner's epistemic frames
Scott	Actor, director	Higher education	"An aesthetic response is the most truthful response. The body has an innate sense of the truth. The basis of all sub-text. Performance is a lie to expose a greater truth"	4, 6
Carol	Visual artist	Self-employed consultant	"The use of art enables people to gain a different language and start talking in a different way. It is moving beyond your own language. It is a new way of perceiving"	3, 6
Maree	Choreographer, former ballet dancer, film maker	Public sector	"What lasts over time are the emotional connections. You remember how it [the dance] made you feel"	4, 5, 6
James	Trained as an opera singer; cabaret performer and songwriter	Higher education	"In the performing arts, you always have that uncertainty—rehearsal covers for some anxiety—I'm methodological with the rehearsal—never tell where the audience is going to go—in cabaret the audience can actually talk to you"	1, 3, 6, 7
Ken	Composer, sonic experimenter	Higher education	"I always think about how the medium limits and the issue of aesthetic, authenticity. Within music or any of the arts you've got to tread the balance between familiarity and newness. The medium shapes the message"	1, 2
Caitlin	Sculptor	Self-employed	"Ambiguity is part of the process—a challenge, sometimes you play with the clay; that's when you come up with the answer when you are not thinking about what you are doing. Then you often come up with the solution"	1, 7

continued

TABLE 4.2 Continued

Participant	Artistic focus	Current work environment	Illustrative comment	Connection to Eisner's epistemic frames
Sarah	Choreographer, former ballet/ folk dancer	Higher education	"At the university you are working with intelligent people, but they are intelligent in a particular way. And so often as an artist you could be intimidated. Here there are times I feel like a genius. I have a different way of thinking about things that could solve a problem. The scientific way gets stuck. There are other ways here"	1, 6, 7
Jim	Music/song-writer, former visual artist, writer of short stories	Higher education	"The medium is part of the creative process; essentially the medium is the mode; I like the technology. I like the computer. It's fun to do"	3, 5, 7
Greg	Writer	Self-employed	"One has to have an open attitude towards ambiguity. You define it positively. It can suddenly become a tool or medium you use for the benefit of an audience"	1, 5
Alberto	Painter/ ceramicist/ print-maker	Higher education/ Jesuit priest	"Art allows me to perceive reality as a whole and not just as a problem. I can celebrate what I already have. Art allows me to be practical and not strategic"	1, 4, 5

known to one of the researchers as either family members, friends, colleagues, or friends of friends. Our tenth interviewee, however, differed in three main ways from our other artist participants in that he was a South American artist working in an American university, not known to either of us at the time when we approached him, and a Jesuit priest.

The artists interviewed had been or were currently involved in a range of artistic pursuits including dance and choreography, cabaret performing, acting and directing, visual art, painting, print-making, sculpting, writing, and musical composition. Of the 10 artists, six worked within a higher education environment where they exercised varying degrees of leadership in their respective units, one worked within the public sector, and three were self-employed. Of these three, one was a consultant, and the remaining two artists had previously left their public sector positions to pursue full-time work as artists. Table 4.2 presents information pertaining to the 10 artists (the names used are pseudonyms), identifies the focus of their artistic role, their current work environment, and provides an illustrative comment tied to one of Eisner's seven epistemic frames regarding the value of the arts.

Eisner's Epistemic Frames

Comments from all of the 10 artists reflected one or more of Eisner's epistemic frames about the value of the arts. For example, a number of the artists alluded to the value of the arts in enabling them to see there are many paths that can be traveled and there is never one answer to a problem (Eisner's Epistemic Frame 1). An open attitude (Greg), "a new way of perceiving" (Carol) and a tolerance for ambiguity (Caitlin) are part of the process. Taylor (2012) concurs when he says that "creativity is about making choices, but not about making a choice from a set of well-defined alternatives using analytic reasoning. Rather it is about making a choice based in intuitive understanding" (p. 85).

Eisner's Epistemic Frame 4 that highlights the aesthetic dimension of feeling was captured well by Maree and Scott. Maree referred to the emotional connections inherent in dance and the power of dance to enable you to remember how you feel when you were dancing or when you are watching another person dance. Regarding the theater, Scott referred to the aesthetic response (rather than an intellectual one) as being "the most truthful." As an artist, he saw his role as providing audiences with pleasure and passion. Alberto referred to art as a deep human experience; a living force.

The artists in the sample used a variety of mediums to create the performance and/or the product/s. Apart from Greg the writer whose medium lay in words, the other artists transcended "literal language and quantification" (Eisner, 2002, Epistemic Frame 6) to communicate understanding in their work. The mediums the artists chose were those with which they were most comfortable and in which they had some background training. As an example, James said he had "always thought in music" so song was the medium he used to express himself. As a composer, Ken referred to working primarily in popular music genres but had experience working in choral and classical music as well as "sonic experimentations." Alberto referred to a variety of mediums he called upon and these included ceramics, painting and print-making. He said that while drawing enabled him to be "spontaneous," print-making was totally "calculated" and involved a lengthy process that began with hundreds of drawings and then selecting only five to seven to take further.

The artists in the sample were more than aware of the constraints as well as the possibilities the medium in which they choose to work raises for them. They recognized that the selection of the medium was critical in what they were aiming to produce. One of the artists (Jim) referred to the aid of computer technology in helping him write songs and enabling creativity. The artists had no difficulties in identifying particular types of constraints. A quote from Scott (director) captured the sentiments raised by all of the participants when he said, "any genre limits the expression of anything." Other comments were: "I always think about how the medium limits" and he went on to say, "the medium shapes the message" (Ken). "Tools limit" was a comment made by the writer (Greg) who went on to say that writing is possibly the most abstract art form there is.

Carol, the visual artist, referred to art as being a form of inquiry that means being in a state of vulnerability. One of the choreographers (Sarah) referred to the medium of traditional ballet which draws upon strict and upright technique and this can be inhibiting in contrast to folk dance music that is more earthy and collaborative. She also made mention of music as dictating the nature and type of dance undertaken.

For the sculptor, Caitlin, clay was her primary medium and she gave the example of relying on armatures when building figures. She explained that armatures, while providing structure and support, also inhibit because the artist is required to adhere to the armature/design.

In this study artists spoke about ambiguity not as being stressful or problematic but as being part and parcel of the process of creating. For example, James said, "in the arts you are always uncertain when you perform." Yet the artists were not fazed by ambiguity and their comments indicated they approached their work in an open-ended way which resonates with Eisner's (2002, p. 206) Epistemic Frame 7. As Caitlin said, ambiguity is part of the process and it is a challenge. The director said "the task is to do your best" and "there is no right or wrong way" (Scott). The choreographer referred to handling ambiguity by having "trust in the artists you are working with. You let people take more risks" (Sarah). Scott, the director, said it was critical to "turn limitations into assets." The artists welcomed ambiguity and recognized that it provided opportunities for creative space to be afforded. This is not surprising as Eisner (2002) states that a function of the arts is the development of "a disposition to tolerate ambiguity, to explore what is uncertain, to exercise judgement free from prescriptive rules and procedures" (p. 10).

The next part of the discussion refers to the four cognitive functions of representation that lie at the heart of creating art. Each of these is considered in relation to the artists:

The Four Cognitive Functions of Representation

1. Inscription

According to the artists, the inspiration for creating often came from an idea or image they had in their minds for some time. One of the artists put it well when he said that an idea for a project depends on where the impetus is coming from and whether the artist her/himself is initiating it or a brief is coming from someone else (Greg). Regarding the former, some of the artists referred to significant life events as providing ideas/material to pursue in their art. A good example was Alberto who referred to the loss of a friend to cancer and how he created an exhibition of work to celebrate her life and suffering. While a number of the artists referred to ideas that they initiated and felt compelled to pursue, others referred to commissions (e.g. Ken, Scott, Sue, Caitlin, Alberto) or particular opportunities that presented themselves (James). In these cases, often the medium selected was proposed by the person who was paying the artist for the work. This was the case for Ken who is often asked to produce music from a variety of genres and Sarah who has been commissioned to create specific choreographic works.

The process of inscription or making the idea concrete (Eisner, 2002) became apparent when the artists took the first steps of engagement with the medium. For example, Sarah the choreographer referred to the necessity to have ideas and questions in her mind for the project so that she is prepared for the first rehearsal with dancers (Sarah).

2. Editing

According to Eisner (2002), editing is not only a function in which writers engage; all artists are involved in the process of editing their work to ensure the final product is of quality. Ken, Maree and Caitlin said that it is not always easy to recognize when the work is finished but at some point a decision has to be made to this effect. As Henri (2007) said, "no work of art is really ever finished. They [the artists] only stop at good places" (p. 177).

The artists who tended to work on their own (i.e. Greg, James, Caitlin, Jim, Alberto) referred to relying on themselves to make judgments during the editing and refining phase. Greg said it involved bringing a certain type of objectivity or discipline to the art to know where to go with it. He went on to say that it is about knowing whether to restructure or "kill it dead" (Greg). Eisner (2002) would refer to this as attending to the details of the work.

For those artists who worked closely with others, such as the choreographers, the film maker, director and musical composer, they commented on feedback from others as a key part of the process. This is connected to Eisner's (2002, p. 6) comment that editing is not only about working on details but also involves attending to relationships with others. For example, Scott, the director, referred to himself as a builder who works with actors, a space and an audience. He referred to the importance of collaboration where everyone has a role to play and is encouraged to express themselves. Similarly, Sarah, the choreographer, referred to working collaboratively with dancers, building a comfortable and collaborative environment where risks can be taken and trust can be built.

A number of the artists said that when things were not working the way they had hoped, they took a "pause" (Greg), returned to it later (Caitlin) or as Sarah said, you "come back to it." By doing so, the time away allowed a different "seeing." Taylor (2012, p. 16) refers to this time away from the creative process as "time off."

According to Eisner (2002), a key part of editing is drawing upon one's imagination since it "enables us to try things out . . . without the consequences we might encounter if we had to act upon them empirically" (p. 5). The process of trial and error was identified by Jim. Moreover, James referred to the importance of rehearsal to help minimize uncertainty.

3. Communication

According to Eisner (2002), communication is moving the work into a public form so that it can be understood by others. Those others might be other artists if it is a type of collaborative project (as in choreography, play direction, and so on) so that communication and editing are similar processes. Alternatively, communication can be construed as communicating with an audience via a performance or receiving feedback from others regarding one's composition or creation. As Greg said, there would be little point in creating if there was not someone with whom you were communicating. Many of the artists referred to the importance of communicating and seeking feedback from others regarding their work. For example, James as a sole performer referred to gaining feedback from each audience for whom he presents. He said, "the audience tells you if they understand and gives you feedback." Another example was provided by Alberto who said he invites external persons, such as other artists, teachers and students, to give him feedback on his work and to tell him what they see.

4. Discovery

According to Eisner (2002) discovery is described as something that happens in the creation of art that is not necessarily envisioned when the work is started. It is at the discovery phase that surprises emerge and these surprises are viewed as providing opportunities for going in new and different directions. The artists we interviewed alluded to discoveries they made by accident. These discoveries emerged when they dealt with unexpected obstacles or were confronted with constraints and had to solve new types of problems. Sarah referred to working in the studio with dancers as "an exciting period of discovery. Like a scientific experiment." She said that making things work and solving problems was part of the discovery process. Ken also referred to the creative process in the sound studio: "it's about knowledge and wanting to discover something new under the stone."

Surprises can also come in the form of things working when there is no explanation or reason for them working, as was indicated by the director, Scott. Jim said that surprise occurred for him when the music sounds a lot better than anticipated and when the initial idea is matched to the product that is produced. Greg the writer referred to surprise and serendipity as twins. The surprise occurs when you look back on what you created and you are satisfied with it, while the most striking thoughts are those that are produced through serendipity.

All of the artists talked about the joy they experienced in creating art. Ken said "once you get engaged in a song it is a joyous time." Alberto referred to the "joy of creating" while Sarah talked about "getting a great rush" when working with dancers and the fun environment that studios can be. Scott said that "creativity should be joyful." Maree referred to the joy she feels when she steps on stage and performs. Jim referred to fun associated with recording music. The wonderful satisfaction of being immersed in art fits with Eisner's fifth Epistemic Frame that refers to the joy of one's work. The sculptor in our study referred to being lost in sculpting where hours would pass and she would not be aware of time. This notion of getting lost in the work has been referred to as "flow" (Csikszentmihalyi, 1990). The next part of the chapter discusses findings from Phase 2 interviews.

Phase 2: Findings and Discussion About the "Discerning Eye"

Phase 2 sought to explore artists' understandings of how they developed a "discerning eye." Eight broad themes discussed below point to the ways in which this was achieved.

1. The Discerning Eye is Developmental, Evolutionary and Dependent on Others

The interview data indicated that the development of "the discerning eye" was developmental, evolutionary and dependent on interactions with significant others such as family, friends or strangers. A number of the participants talked about "maturity," "experience" and how the passage of time enabled them to become more discerning in their work. James said, "as I matured . . . I have been able to bring an agenda to my cabaret work that helps me identify more specific performance criteria." Sarah, the choreographer, referred to a number of key activities that have enabled her to have a more discerning eye about her work. She said:

> As well as analyzing your own experience you have this other growing knowledge from your own judgment of others' works. You learn about how they have approached experiments, you learn from what you think succeeds. Probably learn from what you see fails and why. And I suppose in a general sense one of the big learnings for me was about the strength of the idea or concept at the beginning of a work. You can look at work and assess that the starting point was not interesting enough, wasn't new enough. The way that these things are set up is often what sets them out to fail.

Caitlin, the sculptor, referred to her growth as an artist as being due to her work being shown in exhibitions and having received affirming feedback from members of the public. She reflected that in her early work, she focused on honing her skills and producing beautiful figures but as she has grown in confidence and maturity she has been able to gravitate to projects that have moved beyond demonstrations of skill towards more meaningful content.

Greg pinpointed a differentiating moment when he moved away from journalism which he described as "a perfunctory profession" to a more erudite type of writing that requires him to think more deeply about what he is doing and the central ideas he wishes to explore.

2. The Discerning Eye Can Begin in Early Childhood and the Early Environment

Early childhood and the kind of environment in which a child grows up as either nurturing or not, is critical for the kind of unstated parameters and expectations which, subtly or not, propel or enable development to take on certain life trajectories over others. All of the artists referred to either early exposure to their artistic field or a nurturing environment or significant others during their formative years that helped shape their development. For instance, Sarah said she started dance at the age of five and her life since then has been involved in the arts. In contrast with the other artists, Greg lamented that his early family life did not provide a nurturing environment and he received little if any encouragement from his parents. He said, "had it been there the effects would have been radical and I believe I may have made the transition a lot earlier." What became important was the personal awareness of his own ability to write and the "realization that I was actually good enough to do that."

3. The Discerning Eye Emerges From Hard Work and is Influenced by Factors of Serendipity

Few of the respondents had attained deliberate plans or specific outcomes. While their development and/or accomplishments were a product of hard work, factors of serendipity were taken advantage of, and opportunities were exploited as they became apparent. Berenson (1948) similarly noted that:

> The real artist, if at the moment of creation he [sic] thinks at all, thinks of little but his craft, the action and arrangement chiefly, and of all the skill and mastery he has acquired previously—I mean how to draw, how to paint, what proportions, what types to give his figures. These are now his style, that is to say his habitual way of visualizing and executing, his habitual handiwork.

(p. 113)

Berenson's (1948) observation was illustrated in Phase 1 where all of the artists acknowledged that it took long hours of dedication and practice to develop their art-based skills. In Phase 2 a couple of the participants referred to opportunities they had been afforded to produce particular types of work and these opportunities led them in a direction in which they may not have traveled without this invitation. Two illustrations provided by Caitlin were being given a commission to create the bust of a significant historical religious figure and creating a piece of art that would conform to the parameters of a contemporary art competition. Other artists (i.e. Sarah, Scott, Maree, Ken, Alberto) made mention of invitations to create works for particular audiences and these invitations provided them with opportunities for creative growth.

4. The Discerning Eye is the Result of Personal Efforts to Attain Competency

For the artists in this study, the discerning eye was the result of personal efforts to attain competency in a specific endeavor and the overt and covert shifts in direction because of interactions with significant others: family, sponsors, friends, even strangers who made comments about their work which were then considered and even adopted as the larger web in which the respondents worked.

The development of the discerning eye relied a great deal on the personal efforts and competencies of the artists themselves and what they deemed was good work. All of them recognized the central place of technical competence and a good grounding in the discipline which comes with practice and hard work. For Greg, competence in writing constitutes not only good technique including grammatical structuralism but also originality. In relation to dance and dance performance, Sarah said, "the longer you practice, the less self-conscious you become." The idea of competence was connected to the development of confidence. There would be very few biographies or autobiographies of artists that would not speak of the toil and sheer hard work involved in gaining competence and developing a discerning eye. A good example is Lucian Freud, the British figurative artist who painted every day of his life and was driven to constantly improve his work (Grieg, 2013).

All of the artists referred to significant interpersonal relationships that included family and friends as well as fellow artists who were viewed as key sources in providing valuable feedback and at times reassurance. A couple of the artists alluded to "mentors" who gave them not only psycho-social support (through encouragement, support, friendship, guidance) but also useful technical and business advice as well as offering a different perspective. A good example of mentoring was given by Caitlin who referred to an experienced colleague and fellow bronze artist who continues to give her feedback regarding all aspects of her work. For the artists in the study, relationships with others (including mentors) were seen as central to their development and identity as artists and provided them with ongoing nourishment. As an illustration, Sarah underscored the necessity for effective interpersonal relationships with dancers and this is unsurprising given dancers are the "tools used for creating dance."

A relevant concept here is that of Bourdieu's (1977) *habitus* which embodies aspirations, expectations, the learning of social rules and class life patterns, bodily deportment and dispositions, and thinking outside of those patterns. The "discerning eye" is both contained and not contained in the habitus. The respondent's work has to stay somewhat within the habitus to communicate understood meanings as a matter of communication. On the other hand it also has to transcend the habitus in order to provide a work that will provoke reflection, even if only a remembrance of something that is "beautiful." The "discerning eye" has to understand how far to push the limits of symbolic communication whether in an art piece or a literary effort.

5. The Discerning Eye is an Outcome of the Respondent's Increasing Differentiation in His or Her Work

The development of "the discerning eye" is a "natural" outcome to the respondent's increasing differentiation in his/her work environment which can be major or subtle; it also represents an increasing ability to evaluate their own work and contribution. This notion of increasing differentiation is connected to Eisner's (2002) point about editing and reworking. All of the participants referred to the importance of working and reworking. Yet, for the artists, there was a constant search for meaning and purpose that involves technique and the development of technique but it is also beyond technique.

All of the artists reflected that their artistic pursuits were personally meaningful to them. Not only that, the themes they pursued in their work were often a reflection of what was happening in their personal relationships or other parts of their life. Caitlin said, "whatever is happening [in my personal life] moves me to create something relevant." The nature, type and choice of creation was described as a reflection of this emotional state. The great poet Walt Whitman captured this idea nicely when he said, "in my poems, all revolves around, concentrates in, radiates from myself. I have but one central figure, the general human personality typified in myself" (in Kapilow, 2011, p. 89). Similarly, Oscar Wilde (1913/2007, para. 90) noted that "between my art and the world there is now a wide gulf, but between my art and myself there is none."

Only one of the artists had a contrary view. Jim said that unlike other artists, he tries to detach himself from the work. So while the themes he pursues are very much of interest to him they are not necessarily reflective of his life. He gave the example of writing songs about notable characters in history and literature who appeal to him in some way.

6. Feedback, Via Public Recognition, Helps to Develop Artists' Discerning Eye

Public recognition of one's work was considered a valuable form of feedback since art is created for a purpose and the audience plays its role. As Gardner (1973) wrote, "neither creator or performer can continue to function without an audience . . . who will behold the artwork, seek to comprehend it, and in all likelihood have some sort of affective reaction to it" (p. 28). The artists in our study were acutely aware of the necessity for public recognition and the types of response they are able to generate from the public/audience for whom they presented their work. Greg summed it up well when he said, "there has to be a symmetry of resonance between the artist and the audience . . . What you are trying to do is to open a circuit in somebody else's brain with your own idea . . . It's all about communication."

James, the cabaret performer, went as far as saying that "the public access is the most important part of the development of my creative work." While Sarah concurred, she indicated that there are other considerations. In relation to choreography, she raised the following questions: Are you happy with what you produced? Did you achieve everything you set out to achieve? Was it a good experience for the artists? Was it a good experience for the others involved in the production (e.g. stage hands, lighting technicians, and others)?

7. Benchmarking is a Process That Helps to Develop the Discerning Eye

According to Kapilow (2011), "the difference between good and great is both enormous and infinitesimal. It is hundreds of small, inspired choices made by a composer—note by note, rhythm by rhythm, measure by measure" (pp. 187–188). While Kapilow was referring to good and great in the context of classical music, the same could be said about any work of art. Benchmarking is a process that enables artists to ask how good is their work compared with others. Where do they fit into the scheme of things? Where is the medium going and where is art at? And how do artists categorize themselves compared to others (see Bloom, 1997)? The notion of benchmarking was one that emerged from the artists' comments where they referred to great artists (both living and deceased) they admired and who influenced their work. Moreover, being aware of their contemporaries' work and comparing this work to their own was described as an important process in helping them to make judgments about their work. For example, James said, "As I look at other cabaret performers, it [has] helped me to define where my own work fitted." He went on to say that he recently observed another cabaret performer who was working within a feminist mode and observing her helped him to articulate and label the particular mode that best describes his work.

Jim talked a great deal about how he was influenced by the sound recordings of well-known bands and how in his compositions, he has sought to create similar sounds by using the same types of computer technology utilized by these bands. He said, "the better grasp of the technology in music, the better it enables you to express yourself or come up with a vision or a sound that you want." On a lighter note, Jim said that sometimes listening to the music of his peers is a confidence booster as "It's so terrible and I'll endeavour not to do anything so bad!!"

8. The Discerning Eye is Aware of the Tension That Exists Between Tradition and Innovation

The issue relating to the tension between tradition and innovation lies at the heart of art creation: on the one hand preserving the traditions of the past and on the other charting new frontiers and new works (Ehrich & English, 2013b). The artists acknowledged how the history of their discipline had shaped them and provided them with a grounding and accompanying core skills and knowledge in their respective fields. They were also aware that the creative process can be about taking a risk to assert one's position or statement. Greg reinforced this point when he said that for artists, "it is about being prepared to take a risk," yet he went on to say that various pressures can sometimes make one disinclined to embrace fully this type of idea.

Phase 3: Conversations and Findings From Educational Leaders

As discussed earlier in this chapter, our empirical investigations commenced with artists to enable us to gain insights into the nature and evolution of the discerning eye as a key concept for understanding leadership. The purpose of Phase 3 interviews was to build upon our findings from Phases 1 and 2 and relate those new learnings to the field of leadership. Thus the questions we asked leaders were informed by evolving understandings about artists and connoisseurship. This next section of the chapter begins by providing some background discussion on each of the 10 leaders before providing illustrative comments that fit with Eisner's epistemic frames.

All of the leaders were known to us in our capacity as university lecturers and professional colleagues. Three of the six Australian leaders were currently employed as school principals (Robert, Bernard and Peter), while two had held at one time the position of school principal (Matthew and Sandra). For instance, Sandra was working as a supervisor of school principals for a religious school district in Queensland, Australia, while Matthew was employed as a leader/manager of education programs in an arts-based organization. Unlike the other leaders in this sample who had experience in the principalship, Miriam was working as a self-employed community arts educator/leader. She had several years' experience leading/choreographing a dance project for women of various disabilities and abilities. Her involvement in our sample was significant because she was both an artist and a leader.

Of the four American leaders, two were school principals (Tanya, Donovan), one was a school superintendent (Templeton), and the fourth leader (Julia) was previously a school principal and administrator in the Department of Education, but now working as an educational consultant.

Eisner's Epistemic Frames and Their Applicability to Leaders

Our interviews with artists provided many illustrations of Eisner's epistemic frames and showed artists' openness to learning and creating. From interviews with leaders, we were able to find illustrations that also matched Eisner's seven key frames and these have been included in Table 4.3. Although the leaders were operating from a different context and used different language to explore their work and outlook, there were points of commonality.

All of the leaders talked about the "intrinsic satisfactions" (Epistemic Frame 5, Eisner, 2002, p. 202) that came with their work. This involved the satisfaction of seeing children achieve and enjoy school (e.g. Robert, Peter, Bernard, Donovan, Tanya, Templeton) and participate in arts-based education programs (Matthew, Miriam). Bernard, for example, commented on the satisfaction of seeing a school that is "humming" along where students are laughing and where there is trust and good relationships among staff. For Miriam the creative work which she facilitated was "deeply pleasurable and nourishing." Sandra described her work and the work of the leaders whom she serves in her capacity as a senior education officer as "complex, exciting and evolving." Tanya referred to the importance of leaders and teachers having passion for their work. She commented that she regularly checks to see if teachers in her school have that "thrill" and, if not, she works closely with them to see what is missing and thus tries to help improve the situation. Noteworthy is that the leaders in our sample chose their profession because of their love of children and many of them (Donovan, Miriam, Templeton, Robert, Julia) expressed a strong desire to improve the life chances of particular groups of disadvantaged or minority children or adults (in Miriam's case). For example, Templeton, the African American school superintendent, said, "I always pull for the underdog . . . I want them [the students] to feel satisfied once they leave school."

As with the artists, the leaders in the sample were aware of the complexity and open-ended nature of leadership. As Eisner (2002) has stated, there is always more than one answer or solution to every question (Epistemic Frame 1) and "flexible purposing" suggests the "capacity to improvise [and] to exploit unanticipated possibilities" (Eisner, 2002, p. 206, Frame 7). A good example of both Epistemic Frames 1 and 7 was illustrated by Robert, primary school principal,

TABLE 4.3 Illustrative comments from leaders to Eisner's epistemic frames

Participant	Current work environment	Illustrative comments	Eisner's epistemic frames
Robert	Primary principal	"I became a principal to make a difference; I thought I could do better than my peers" "Mine was an anti-model"	1, 7
Bernard	Primary principal	"Being a leader is as much about the heart as it is the head"	4
Peter	High school principal	"It's an immense privilege to be a head"	5
Matthew	Previous primary school principal; now arts administrator	"We are touring primary schools with a new show. We are simply telling stories through art"	6, 1
Sandra	Senior education officer/supervisor of school principals (religious school district)	"In my role as a senior education officer you expect the unexpected. There are no two days the same. There's no real routine"	7, 1
Miriam	Self-employed community arts leader	"The focus of the dance program was to create a high quality experience (process) for participants and a performative outcome (performance) that was inclusive of diversity"	3, 4, 5, 6, 7, 1, 2
Tanya	Elementary school principal	"When people say they love working here [at the school] that matters to me"	5, 7
Donovan	Newly appointed school principal	"Hard work and curiosity can carry you a long way because while having a high IQ is good, curiosity means you are going to continue to learn"	1, 3, 7
Templeton	School superintendent	"Nothing excites me more than to hear a former student talk to me about something which was born out of the vision I generated, when they say I did what I did because of you. Students have an uncanny ability to tell the truth"	4, 5
Julia	Previous principal and administrator; now educational consultant	"You can't lead others unless you can lead yourself"	4, 5

when he referred to what propelled him to become a school principal. He indicated that unlike some of his colleagues, he was determined not to become a school principal who followed the dominant rational/technical model. He also conceded that he did not have all the answers but that it was important to be mindful and realize there are multiple options to every problem. Both Tanya and Templeton referred to the complex nature of their work and the importance of being "flexible." As an illustration, Templeton said, "Things used to be black and white and now I live in the land of gray." He gave a further example where he described himself as being an onion consisting of multiple layers. He said:

> I'm complex. I can project and be a mirror. I'm a situational leader who can adapt and meet the needs at hand. Sometimes I make the decision and other times I say these are the options and let's talk about it.

One of the leaders who provided ample illustrations of Eisner's Epistemic Frame 6 (concerned with the message that human understanding is not only achieved through language but also non-discursive forms) was Miriam. Miriam referred to her 10-month dance project that involved weekly classes with women of various disabilities that culminated in an end-of-year performance based on collaborative workshops developed throughout the year. She said:

> the creative process within performing arts lends itself beautifully to practices and approaches that develop connection between people without relying on language. Shared creative experiences engaging in improvisational movement and sound bring people together in more embodied ways, bypassing much of what gets in the way of people connecting with each other.

Another example of Eisner's Epistemic Frame 6 was provided by Tanya who explained how she manipulated the physical environment of her office in order to send a clear message to staff and students that she is open, willing and available to meet and greet visitors. She indicated that the previous principal at the school had barricaded herself behind a huge desk in an office whose door was closed most of the time. One of Tanya's first undertakings as principal was to buy more furniture, including a smaller desk, a conference table and chairs where meetings could be held with teachers and parents, and installing a window.

In terms of the importance of language, Sandra underscored the need for leaders to have very good communication skills (such as listening and talking) since poor communication means misrepresented information which can then have detrimental effects. Other leaders also alluded to the need for clear communication. Tanya said, "I do have a sense of how to word something. The ability to say what needs to be said, to change the wording to create a different effect" was identified as paramount particularly when dealing with people over sensitive matters.

All of the leaders alluded to the importance of not only "seeing" but seeing things other than the way they are. This fits with Eisner's (2002) Epistemic Frame 3 regarding imagination and the ability to imagine a different present and future. A good example of this came from Peter who observed the school he inherited (some years before) as being "traditional, rigid and command and control." He said that since taking on the headship of this school, he has pushed, questioned and challenged people and asked them "why do we do this?" He said that with the support of his team he has been able to realign the school and move it from what was done before to what we want to do now.

According to Eisner, form and content cannot be separated but are inter-connected (Epistemic Frame 2). In other words, what and how cannot be separated. The comments from leaders indicated that they were aware of how important it is for leaders to be credible so there is not a big gap between what they say and how they act. All of the leaders talked about the importance of good relationships that are necessary for building trust. As Bernard said, "micromanaging is not demonstrating trust." Donovan referred to the need to build collaborative relationships with staff in the school but also with members of central office. He said, "you have to get people around you who shore up your weaknesses and build on your strengths."

Epistemic Frame 4 also resonated in the comments by leaders. This frame concerns the need for individuals to be able to demonstrate a sensitivity to rightness of fit when making judgments (Eisner, 2002). Miriam said that over time and with experience her attitude towards the difficulties she faced in her work as choreographer/leader of the dance project changed and she was able to become more flexible. She said she learned how to be "hard nosed" about some things yet more flexible with others. Learning from experience and a certain intuition played a role in determining her way of making judgments. The other leaders referred to using a variety of strategies to help them make fit or sound judgments and often these included conversations and consultations with staff so that they had a better understanding of where their staff were at on various issues.

As an illustration, Julia, a native American Indian educational consultant, talked about her abilities as a leader in being both sensitive and responsive to others. She said, "one of my great strengths is being able to connect and interact with people no matter where they come from." Yet she lamented that there have been times when she has had to turn to others for guidance and support. She said, "I was totally terrified of the first time I had to speak to the State Board of Education. I received some coaching from others and then each time I spoke it got easier."

The aforementioned discussion has shown how Eisner's (2002) frames were reflected in the comments made by leaders. The next section provides a discussion of the themes that emerged from an analysis of the summaries of interviews with the 10 leaders. While analysing the leaders' summaries, we were guided by the eight themes that emerged from Phases 1 and 2 of the study. We found that seven of these eight themes reflected the types of comments that the leaders made. The eighth theme—"the discerning eye is aware of the tension between tradition and innovation"—was not pertinent to the content of leaders' interviews and therefore not included in the discussion that follows. The focus of the questions we asked leaders concerned competence, what they perceived as outstanding practice, and where they saw themselves as fitting on a continuum of outstanding practice (see Appendix for a list of Phase 3 interview questions).

Themes Regarding the Development of the "Discerning Eye" for Leaders

1. The Discerning Eye is Developmental, Evolutionary and Dependent on Others (Such as Mentors)

Like the artists in the sample, the leaders recognized the key role of experience in shaping their work practices and providing the grounding for them to become competent. As Peter said, "principals become principals through experience." The leaders in the sample also acknowledged some critical incidents in their life trajectories that provided direction and afforded opportunities for development. For example, Peter referred to being "molded by critical events and incidents" over a period of some 15 years as a principal. He gave the example of the death of students and parents, an episode of stalking in the school, and police protection issues as among the very difficult situations he faced. He said that some of these events have helped him to understand his motivations, his values, and develop competence.

A critical incident for Sandra was her first appointment as an assistant school principal where she learned on the job and observed others making mistakes. This foray into leadership helped her formulate a collegial approach to leadership which she followed when she became a school principal. For Julia, a critical incident was the death of her mother in a road accident back in 2001. She said that her mother was the "core foundation of her being" and this event caused her to look within herself for strength. What also helped her at this time was her participation in an especially targeted program for developing leadership capacity in leaders. Julia remarked that becoming part of this program and working with a cohort of leaders was transformative as it allowed her to embark on a personal journey of growth with the support of like-minded peers.

The leaders also referred to mentors or previous colleagues/bosses who have played an important role in helping them develop their skills and abilities. For example, Sandra highlighted how important mentors had been for her when she was learning to become a school leader. She also referred to "collegial networks" that helped to sustain her for many years in the job. She had the fortune of being part of a close-knit network of eight people and those people became sounding boards for her over a period of time. That support made her feel she was not alone. Bernard indicated that he has three or four mentors who are quite different from him but who provide support and advice from time to time. Robert referred to a "noble friend" who plays the role of mentor and provides challenging conversations to stimulate critical thinking. Matthew referred to colleagues and previous bosses who had given him support and guidance when he was starting out as a school leader.

Julia recalled a number of important mentors, especially her first principal who taught her about the importance of understanding the value of fairness and consistency in discipline. She also referred to learning key skills about working in teams and empowering others from various mentors who supported her growth as a teacher and administrator. Donovan shared that he had had several helpful mentors who assisted his growth. One of these mentors taught him that "details matter. You can skate along with the big picture but sooner or later details will get you." Another mentor taught him the value of silence. He pointed to his father as a mentor and described him as "an incredibly ethical person."

2. The Discerning Eye Can Begin in Early Childhood

All of the U.S.-based leaders alluded to early life experiences as being formative in the development of their discerning eye. For example, Tanya referred to developing a passion for nurturing others due to her own experiences growing up where she noted an absence of nurturance and stability. She described the features of her home life as one where there was little money, of parents who divorced and then reconnected with new partners, some of whom were of dubious character, and where both parents suffered from mental health problems. In her work as a school leader she has worked hard to create nurturing and protective environments for both students and staff where everyone can feel valued and where their skills and abilities are appreciated.

The other three U.S. leaders, Templeton, Donovan and Julia, referred to developing core values about social justice and improving the achievement gap for all students based on their early exposure to inequality either first-hand (as in Templeton and Julia's case) or vicariously as in Donovan's case. For instance, Donovan recalled his mother's involvement in the civil rights movement and how she took Donovan with her when she visited homes of African Americans who were living in abject poverty. The experience of observing poverty left a lasting impression.

Only one of the Australian leader participants provided discussion that indicated how her early life played a key role in shaping her worldview and field of focus. Miriam reflected on her growing up years and said she felt disconnected from the rest of the world yet her inner life was very strong and imaginative. She developed a strong sense of social justice from an early age and this value flowed through her creative life. She said:

my creative work has helped me to heal some of the feelings of being "different." In particular, working inclusively brought out my capacity to work with difference as a strength and as something that is creatively exciting and challenging.

While the other leaders in the sample did not allude to the importance of their early life in shaping their worldview or practice, this does not mean that this was not the case but merely that the questions we asked them did not provide them with an opportunity to comment.

3. The Discerning Eye Emerged From Hard Work and is Influenced by Factors of Serendipity

All of the leaders alluded to the necessity for hard work in order to develop skills and competence in leadership. For example, Templeton mused that "much of what I've accomplished is not because I'm brilliant. It's my work ethic and my competence is in being able to legitimize my work and have credibility with the folks I serve." Miriam talked about the sheer hard work of running a dance project over a 10-month period for eight years. The deep commitment and dedication to their work was evident in the way all of the leaders spoke about leadership and the leadership activities in which they engaged.

The notion of serendipity was not as apparent in the interviews with leaders as it was with artists. It seemed that the decision to become a school principal was a deliberate one for the principals we interviewed. All of the principals in our sample started their careers as teachers but all made the conscious decision of moving into school leadership as a career choice. All of them commented that they were very young when they took up the role. They were keen to do so to make a qualitative difference to the lives of students in their care.

However, there was one clear example of serendipity and it was provided by Matthew who said that he had been granted the opportunity to be seconded (i.e. especially invited) to work in an arts-based education organization for a period of two years while his current position would be left open for him to return to after that time. It was this change of direction in his career that has since led to his ongoing work as a manager of an arts organization and to leave site school leadership.

4. The Discerning Eye is the Result of Personal Efforts to Attain Competency

All of the educational leaders conceded that they have a way to go to be competent in all aspects of leadership. Sandra commented that in terms of her own growth as a leader she sees she is "continually evolving" and as her role changes, she is required to develop new skill sets and move in different directions. Julia reflected on her growth as a leader by saying that "we are all gifted with certain strengths." She saw herself as being on a continuum where she continues to grow and where there is no end point to her development. Donovan said that competence is "something that takes a long time to earn and is quick to lose. You demonstrate it day after day." He, along with Bernard, Robert and Peter, said that it is possible to be competent in one area but not others. Peter went on to say that many leaders fall down because they don't reflect on how they can do better. He said that competence in leadership is if the leader's ego is not dominant. When it is dominant, we see leaders who pursue power, control and it's all about them and not the students.

According to Peter, a fundamental barrier to competence for a leader in education is an inability to reflect on one's behavior and to build relationships and trust. For Templeton, incompetence in a leadership is often evident in "unorganized chaos," where the school culture is toxic and where there is a lack of genuine collaboration between staff. A key comment made by the leaders in the sample regarding how to attain competency was the need for reflection; reflection on one's self and school situation and the ongoing need for feedback from others regarding their decisions and actions. A clear example of the importance of reflection was underscored by Julia. She referred to the need to return to her own set of core values and her identity particularly when faced with difficult decisions.

A point raised by Templeton and Julia only was the notion of developing competency when working in different cultural environments. Because of their cultural identity, Templeton as an African American man and Julia as a Native American Indian woman, they referred to the importance of working well within the mainstream culture without compromising their cultural identity or core values. Here Templeton used the term "code switching," which refers to the ability to "read" situations and decide which way to act, while Julia said she feels comfortable working in a white world, a native world, and somewhere in between. For both of these leaders, their cultural positioning has enabled them to navigate both worlds and appreciate competence from different perspectives.

5. The Discerning Eye is an Outcome of the Respondent's Increasing Differentiation in His or Her Work

All of the leaders, to various extents, gave an indication that they are engaged in differentiating their work and are aware of the subtleties that contribute to great as opposed to good leadership. For instance, a comment by Peter that he himself is not a good teacher but he knows good teaching when he sees it, implies a discerning eye. For Robert, he came to the realization that it is important to keep a balance of what is and what should be/not be in a school so that every effort can be made to work towards improvement building on this discrepancy.

Miriam said that with experience she had become better at recognizing situations and how best to respond to them. She said:

> this work is tricky because although it is professional and you are there in a "work" role, you can't separate out the personal aspect of it. The nature of community art projects is that participants' personal lives can't be left at the door, they do impact on the creative work and you cannot help but become involved to some extent . . . As a creative facilitator you are personally involved—you are vulnerable to some extent. Sometimes it can be tricky finding the right balance.

Reflecting on 16 years of his life in school administration, Templeton mused that with experience, he has been able to come to recognize the finer nuances and complexities of leading schools and this has helped him to understand himself as a leader and how to differentiate himself from others. Similarly, Tanya confessed that she has grown greatly in her emotional and interpersonal skills. Whereas once she would respond immediately to difficult interpersonal situations, she said, "now I'm a bit slower to respond . . . Now my answer to some questions is, 'I'd like to think about that'." This demonstrated the development of a type of mindfulness about her work.

6. Feedback, Via Public Recognition, Helps to Develop Artists' Discerning Eye

All of the leaders referred to feedback from others and who these others were depended on the actual context of their work. For example, for all of the principals in the sample (i.e. those in Australia and the United States), feedback via public recognition came from staff, students, parents, the wider community and colleagues. Members of the senior management team in his school were Peter's most valuable source of feedback, support and discussion. He said that the value of the team is that it challenges him to rethink his platform on issues and the diversity of ideas meant that better decisions are made.

Both Sandra and Templeton as systems leaders referred to feedback not only from the principals with whom they worked but also other partners such as Boards of Education and systems leaders. Templeton said he didn't realize how public and how political his job was until he took on the superintendency. He said that previously he had been isolated from the public aspect of his work. For Matthew, public recognition came from schools and students, work colleagues, but also the artists with whom he engaged to work on various projects.

For Miriam, feedback was received from her co-facilitator, participants, and the audience at large. Similar to the artists in Phase 1 interviews, Miriam referred to audience feedback from the annual performance given by the women participants in the dance project. For all of the performances she directed over eight years, she said that members of the audience informed her of how they appreciated the "highly original and emotive" dance experience and how it had challenged them to rethink conventional dance and the performativity of people with disabilities.

7. Benchmarking is a Process That Helps to Develop the Discerning Eye

Although working in different countries and somewhat different contexts, both Sandra and Templeton performed the role of supervising and supporting school principals. This position afforded them the opportunity to visit many schools and see first-hand a diversity of leadership approaches and principals who possessed different skill sets. Although she didn't use the term "benchmarking," Sandra was fully aware of the tremendous diversity of abilities of school principals within her district where some school principals have strengths in leading others and are very personable while others have low EQ, low empathy and are not intuitive enough to recognize the source of difficulties they face. She concluded that not all leaders have the required skill sets for the job. A key part of her role is to coach principals to think through their situations and oftentimes how to tune in to others. She noted the frustration some principals have demonstrated because they find it difficult to develop effective people skills that result in positive relationships and improved work productivity. A frustration for her was not having the resources to offer more support to those principals who are struggling.

In Templeton's work as a superintendent, he visits schools and watches school principals in their own environment. He finds this more telling than if they visited him at his office. Observing a great number of principals has enabled him to benchmark principal performance. For Miriam, benchmarking was not an option as she said she was the only person in her capital city to be running community-based dance classes for women who have diverse abilities. However, she was aware that there were others in Australia who were doing similar work to her. On reflection she said that perhaps she should have made connections with others and reached out for support. This would have enabled her to benchmark her work against others.

Comparative benchmarking was not a key practice that leaders reported in their interviews with us. Even so, it seems likely that they were aware of the trailblazers in their professional field. All of the leaders in the sample were able to describe examples of poor and good leadership. All of them recognized their own strengths as well as their limitations.

Comparing Artists and Leaders: Similarities and Differences

The data gathered in this study has underscored some important differentiations in how leaders perceive and work in educational decision-making contexts. An important distinction has been made by Weick (1993) between decision-making in organizations and *sensemaking*. In the former concept, decision-making is perceived as following economic and mathematical models which are logical and predictable. In the later circumstance, *sensemaking* involves a much more personal perspective in which:

> individuals are not seen as living in, and acting out their lives in relation to, a wider reality, so much as creating and sustaining images of a wider reality . . . They realize their reality, by reading into their situation patterns of significant meaning.
>
> (Morgan, Frost & Pondy, 1983, p. 24)

The researchers in this study see the promise of the arts in restoring to organizational decision-making the full spectrum of *sensemaking*, for as Henri (2007) notes:

> I have no sympathy with the belief that art is the restricted province of those who paint, sculpt, make music and verse. I hope we will come to an understanding that the material used is only incidental, that there is an artist in every man [*sic*]; and that to him the possibility of development and expression and the happiness of creation is as much a right and as much a duty to himself, as to any of those who work in the especially ticketed ways.
>
> (pp. 223–224)

The data derived from this project were especially insightful in the way that artists confront constraints. Educational leaders are apt to see constraints or limitations as doors closing, that is their overall objectives have to be compromised or reduced. On the other hand, artists see limitations as possibilities, opportunities and alternatives with a result that can be superior than that originally intended. The artists interviewed had a more positive perspective on constraints. They tended to enter the creative process with an implicit understanding that constraints will always be present and to expect them. Nothing will ever be perfect and few things will result in perfection. The turning of constraints and limitations into assets is their bent.

Another important difference is how artists conceived of collaboration. The artists in this study conceived of collaboration as a genuine form of sharing where distinctions in formal roles were often non-essential in a discourse about an ongoing performance or a product. This genuine form of sharing is not always found in educational contexts.

Then there is the whole aspect of joy. For artists what is rewarding is the "joy" of the activity. It is a personal side of enactment. It is what keeps artists going. The school leaders we interviewed also spoke of joy but in a slightly more nuanced way. Joy for school leaders was a positive place for students where their development and learning were publicly displayed and felt. Artists and school leaders both understand that joy is the key to passion for their work and the emotional force which sustains them as they often struggle within the constraints they encounter.

The artists interviewed also underscored the importance of stories or narratives. For as Gardner (1995, p. 9) observed, "Leaders in the arts characteristically inspire others by the ways they use their chosen media of artistic expression, be they the phrases of a sonata or the gestures of a dance." Story is the key. Art is about the telling of a story and connecting at an emotional level. It is about "the logic of things." Artistic job satisfaction is working out the puzzle and collaboration. Artists live in the world of ideas or, as Perkins (1994) noted, a world where powerful dispositions of thinking reside. Our artists were not afraid to explore ideas and they understood that they had to fight for those ideas and convince others of them. Based on our interviews they had a knack of making things work. One actor director described what he does as a form of "turd polishing," an earthy expression of the importance of overcoming obstacles no matter how unpleasant.

Several artists acknowledged that their work in the aesthetic realm is dependent on passion and emotion and how it deals with the truth of the body. But it is also a creative arena in which one is exposed and will ultimately be judged. It is making oneself vulnerable.

There were many similarities between artists and school leaders in the case of connoisseurship. Where artists depended on working with people such as actors, directors and choreographers, trust and good interpersonal relationships were crucial to their success. The same resonated with educational leaders. Where artists worked solo this was not a factor, though even here the response of the public to their works was crucial to their success and their own self-confidence.

Artists and educational leaders had little problem in reflecting on their skill development on continua that were common. The one very large difference was that educational leaders look at their outcomes as student growth and success, and with staff, while artists usually created a product or a performance which became their yardstick in determining their success.

Educational leaders acknowledged that their work was bounded by an organization because it was that organization in which their formal roles were embedded. Within the constellation of roles they practiced their craft and art. Their success depended upon being able to share their passions, respecting the many persons with whom they worked, building on the strengths of their people, and understanding the large and small interconnections which link people functioning in different positions and often quasi-independently of one another. This is the communal nature of educational leadership in a service-oriented activity dealing with a public good. This was the distinctive feature which separated artists and educational leaders.

Towards the "Transactive Account" as Thoughtful Practice

Robert Henri (2007), well-known American artist and teacher, contrasts the artist with the non-artist and then makes the cogent point that what is needed is finding the value in the work itself:

> When the artist is alive in any person, whatever his [sic] kind of work may be, he becomes an inventive, searching, daring, self-expressing creature . . . He disturbs, upsets, enlightens, and he opens ways for a better understanding. Where those who are not artists are trying to close the book, he opens it, shows there are still more pages possible. The world would stagnate without him, and the world would be beautiful with him; for he is interesting to himself and he is interesting to others. He does not have to be a painter or sculptor to be an artist. He can work in any medium. He simply has to find the gain in the work itself, not outside it.
>
> (p. 11)

Our study restores to the question of leadership perspective and preparation the notion that leaders, especially educational leaders who are involved in the development of human potential, must possess the full range of human attributes, including emotional development and recognition of the role of creative expression in themselves and in performing their jobs. Perkins (1994) saw this as critical in transforming and reforming schools to create more thoughtful future graduates. He concluded that:

> art has a distinctive role to play. The liberal borders of art help us to carry good thinking dispositions nurtured in the context of art to the wider world. Art is an extrovert. Art connects because artists make it connect, because artists strive to express not just the anatomy of bodies but the anatomy of the human condition and of the universe that impinges upon it. If most disciplines dig moats, art builds bridges.
>
> (p. 70)

It is in this inclusive perspective that the idea of connoisseurship in leadership is located. It involves the full range of human intellect and thoughtful practice which combines both science and art, one complementing the other into what Eisner (1998) calls "a transactive account [in which] the idea that truth exceeds belief is itself a belief in the possibility of an ontological objectivity" (p. 51). The reason is that we "seek more than what ultimately is referenced to our own beliefs after using criteria appropriate for holding them is to appeal to a higher authority or to seek a main line that bypasses minds' mediation of nature" (p. 51). This is the essence of connoisseurship as thoughtful practice.

Summary

We began our study with a conjecture regarding the potential of the arts to enhance not only the study of leadership, but its practice in educational contexts. That conjecture prompted us to ask a broad array of artists working in different fields questions about their practice and perspectives about their work.

The decision to reach into the arts echoed a position advocated by Eisner (2002) and by experts in the field of leadership studies. For example, Heilbrunn (1996) observed:

> To date, the study of leadership has successfully identified many important traits of leaders and made valuable contributions to our understanding of how leaders and followers in organizations interact. But to grow as a discipline, it will have to cast a wider net. Doing so, it may discover that the most important things about leadership lie far beyond the capabilities of science to analyze.
>
> (p. 11)

Our empirical foray reported here has served to create an expanded base for the consideration of leadership. The artists we interviewed legitimated Temes' (1996) definition that "leadership is the action of ideas to make change, through the agency of individuals" (p. 74) and in so doing underscored the seven tenets advanced by Eisner (2002) regarding how the arts could enhance education and by logical extension leadership in education. We believe these initial linkages of the arts could help establish a transactive account for an improved corpus of work in leadership studies and research. We believe that is a promise worth pursuing.

Implications for Policy and Practice

The Arts Offer a Promising and Restorative Perspective to Understanding and Enhancing Leadership Practice

The fully functioning human being as leader is both rational and emotional. The emotional side of leadership is comprised of intuition, moral judgments, ethical considerations, and aesthetic sensitivities. The social science view of leadership, which has been dominant in educational leadership, has marginalized the complete range of human considerations and actions. In lists of skills, dispositions and competencies most governmental agencies use to license school leaders, the artistic and aesthetic dimensions have been erased.

The work of Elliot Eisner (2002) provides some examples of how the arts can be restorative to the full range of leader decisions. The arts emphasize imagination, the consideration of multiple "right" answers, and pay attention to how things are formed because that process leads to some questions being raised and others eliminated before decisions are even considered. In short, the entire process of "framing" is one of the most provocative functions of the artistic process.

Some Educational Leaders Display Movement Towards Connoisseurship as a Kind of "Natural" Progression but Largely as a Matter of Personal Biography

The interviews of educational leaders in Australia and America revealed that they were moving towards advanced competencies in areas amounting to the development of connoisseurship in their roles, albeit some were moving faster than others. Nearly all of the leaders interviewed were reflective about themselves and their own growth. Some were more articulate about their advancement than others. Very few, if any, leaders cited their university-based preparation as containing content that provoked them to delve deeply into something like Eisner's epistemic frames. If leaders were illustrating dimensions of connoisseurship it tended to be more the result of their own upbringing and life biography than anything formal in their university preparation.

Key Chapter Ideas

Epistemic Frame

Epistemology is concerned with knowledge and the nature of what is true. An epistemic frame is a way of forming a question or an assumption that is revelatory about the nature of knowledge or truth embedded in it. It is closely related to one of the four key cognitive functions of the arts, that is how an idea or an image is transformed into an end product within the constraints of the material or medium selected to represent it.

Benchmarking

A comparison of the performance of self or others to a well-established "model" of competence as an educational leader.

Sensemaking

A term used by Karl Weick (1993) to refer to how a leader creates meaning in situations that make sense to them. It is a non-linear and non-mathematical model of reasoning.

Note

1   Portions of this chapter previously appeared in Ehrich and English (2013a).

References

Berenson, B. (1948). *Aesthetics and history*. Garden City, NY: Doubleday & Company, Inc.
Bloom, H. (1997). *The anxiety of influence: A theory of poetry*. New York: Oxford University Press.
Bourdieu, P. (1977). *Outline of a theory of practice*. Cambridge: Cambridge University Press.
Csikszentmihalyi, M. (1990). *Flow: The psychology of optimal experience*. New York: Harper Perennial.
Ehrich, L.C. & English, F.W. (2013a). Towards connoisseurship in educational leadership: Following the data in a three stage line of inquiry. In S. Eacott & R. Niesche (Eds.), *Empirical leadership research: Letting the data speak for themselves* (pp. 165–198). Niagara Falls, NY: Untested Ideas Research Center.
Ehrich, L.C. & English, F.W. (2013b). Leadership as dance: A consideration of the applicability of the "mother" of all arts as the basis for establishing connoisseurship. *International Journal of Leadership in Education, 16*(4), 454–481.
Eisner, E. (1979). *The educational imagination: On the design and evaluation of school programs*. New York and London: Macmillan Publishing Co. & Collier Macmillan Publishers.
Eisner, E. (1998). *The enlightened eye: Qualitative inquiry and the enhancement of educational practice*. Upper Saddle River, NJ: Merrill.
Eisner, E. (2002). *The arts and the creation of mind*. New Haven: Yale University Press.
Gardner, H. (1973). *The arts and human development*. New York: John Wiley and Sons.
Gardner, H. (1995). *Leading minds: An anatomy of leadership*. New York: Basic Books.
Grieg, G. (2013). *Breakfast with Lucien: A portrait of an artist*. London: Jonathon Cape.
Heilbrunn, J. (1996). Can leadership be studied? In P.S. Temes (Ed.), *Teaching leadership: Essays in theory and practice* (pp. 1–11). New York: Peter Lang.
Henri, R. (2007). *The art spirit*. New York: Basic Books.
Kapilow, R. (2011). *What makes it great? Short masterpieces, great composers*. Hoboken, NJ: John Wiley and Sons.
Morgan, G., Frost, P. & Pondy, L. (1983). Organizational symbolism. In L. Pondy, P. Frost, G. Morgan & T. Dandrige (Eds.), *Organizational symbolism* (pp. 3–35). Greenwich, CT: JAI Press.
Perkins, D. (1994). *The intelligent eye: Learning to think by looking at art*. Santa Monica, CA: The Getty Center for Education in the Arts.
Schama, S. (2006). *The power of art*. New York: HarperCollins.
Taylor, S. (2012). *Leadership craft, leadership art*. New York: Palgrave Macmillan.
Temes, P.S. (1996). Teaching leadership / teaching ethics: Martin Luther King's "letter from Birmingham jail." In P.S. Temes (Ed.), *Teaching leadership: Essays in theory and practice* (pp. 73–83). New York: Peter Lang.
Weick, K.E. (1993). The collapse of sensemaking in organizations: The Mann Gulch disaster. *Administrative Science Quarterly, 38*(4), 628–652.
Wilde, O. (1913/2007). *De Profundis*. The Project Gutenberg eBook. Retrieved from https://www.gutenberg.org/files/921/921-h/921-h.htm.

5

PORTRAITS OF ARTISTS

There is and can be no self-knowledge based on theoretical assumptions, for the object of self-knowledge is an individual—a relative exception and an irregular phenomenon.

(Jung, 1958, p. 17)

WHAT THIS CHAPTER IS ABOUT

Moving towards connoisseurship is a continuum of development. It is evolutionary and follows a number of trajectories. Using a model of the stages of the development of connoisseurship which is explained in this chapter, interviews with artists are presented as close-up portraits of this evolution. The portraits were derived after two phases of interviews and they are presented as examples of connoisseurship *in progress*.

Introduction

When the idea was first developed for this book, we decided that our investigation of leadership connoisseurship should begin by interviewing artists first rather than school leaders. The reason was that we wanted to initiate an inquiry into a new and different area of competence and activity in the hope that heretofore unnoticed and overlooked areas of leadership competence might be revealed. It is much the same with conducting an anthropological study in a different culture. One is often most observant and sensitive to differences when they are encountered initially and are fresh. The longer one works or lives in a culture the less one often sees of it.

Some Assumptions About Artistic Connoisseurship

To breathe life into the concept of a connoisseur in the arts and in leadership, four portraits of artists we interviewed are sketched out in this chapter. The next chapter considers portraits of a selection of the leaders we interviewed. Four important points are made prior to discussing the methodology of portraiture itself. They are:

1. Connoisseurship Occurs on a Continuum That Can Be Mapped

After several rounds of interviews of both artists and educational leaders, and reflective discussions regarding our findings, we posit that connoisseurship is not an absolute status, but that it occurs on a continuum of development. While on this continuum we discerned that there are distinctive stages or gradations of this continuum. These are shown in Table 5.1. These are roughly explained as follows.

TABLE 5.1 Stages of connoisseurship

Ten dimensions	Stage 1	Stage 2	Stage 3	Stage 4
1. Perception 2. Experience 3. Competence 4. Framing 5. Desire 6. Practice 7. Aesthetic vision 8. Awareness 9. Discipline 10. Identity	Awareness of potentiality	Conscious movement towards expertise and early accomplishment	Substantive accomplishment	Advanced accomplishment and public recognition

Stage 1: Awareness of Potentiality

In this stage a potential connoisseur comes to a self-realization that he/she has an abiding interest in a subject or concept or an occupation and/or skill. This interest is more than a "normal" curiosity. It becomes a compelling area of attention and interest and eventually development. This stage is marked by the awareness that the area of interest is different from others and how they may be interested in the same topic or area. It may occur at a relatively young age.

Stage 2: Conscious Movement Towards Expertise and Early Accomplishment

At this stage the young novice connoisseur begins to move towards a conscious acquisition of greater expertise, knowledge and engages in projects that begin to show promise. Early works may draw praise and interest from others.

Stage 3: Substantive Accomplishment

At this stage the connoisseur begins to attain or achieve a growing reputation and public awareness of his/her work or competence.

Stage 4: Advanced Accomplishment and Public Recognition

This final evolutionary stage is marked by acclimation and recognition for the work of the connoisseur in his/her chosen field or area. This person is almost always listed at the top of his/her field and pointed to as an acknowledged expert whose opinion is often considered definitive and final.

2. Assessment of Connoisseurship is Nominal and Ordinal

Previously in Chapter 1, 10 dimensions of connoisseurship were presented. The portraits in this chapter are benchmarked against these 10 dimensions. Measurement can occur only in four different types of scales. They are nominal, ordinal, ratio and interval. Typically achievement tests employ ratio and interval data. No such specificity is possible at this point with the concept of connoisseurship. Rather, nominal scales are like dictionary definitions. They define properties of something, an objective or a term or concept. Ordinal scales assess strength and usually relate to more or less of the capacity being discussed. An example might be with height or weight. Two or more individuals can be compared to one another on height or weight. One person might be said to be tall and when compared to the other person or persons "taller" than the other. Once measurement is discussed as with inches for height or pounds for weight, then the last two types of scales are involved.

Our discussion of these artist portraits (and leader portraits in the following chapter) involve only nominal and ordinal assessment. A person can be said to possess one of the dimensions or not and if it is possessed then one can say either it is with greater or lesser intensity or presence than others interviewed. It should be mentioned that the assessment itself is not objective in the traditional sense in which that term is usually employed in measurement. There is no objective scale we know of that something like "desire" could be determined as long as part of that assessment involves a "reading" of some inner state or quality in another human being. But this is the nature of and beauty that lies behind the idea of connoisseurship; it spans the usual binary of objectivity and subjectivity. And as previously discussed, leadership studies have been dwarfed by the lack of development of the full human being because of the impact of behaviorism as the dominant epistemic frame utilized in such studies.

3. Connoisseurship is Not Confined to Bureaucratic Roles

The true connoisseur is not necessarily the one at the top of professional hierarchies, that is, the superintendent of schools may not be a leader connoisseur, but such persons may be principals, coordinators or teachers. Connoisseurship is neither confined nor defined by formal organizational roles; rather it is a capacity of the individual occupying that role. While we think that leaders who are connoisseurs will be better leaders, there are plenty of leaders who are good leaders but not connoisseurs, and there are connoisseurs in our educational organizations who have very little formal organizational authority. In such organizations the benefits of connoisseurs are denied to the organizations in which they serve.

4. An Identified Connoisseur May Possess Only Some of the Ten Dimensions

There is no magic number by which one person may be called a "connoisseur" and another not. Rather, the dimensions of connoisseurship represent a kind of rough benchmark by which connoisseurship may be assessed. Connoisseurship therefore represents a cluster of dimensions, some of great intensity and others more moderately so. In some cases some dimensions may be small or perhaps even absent. But a person has to have at least some of the dimensions in some significant amount or he/she cannot be a connoisseur.

About the Methodology of Portraiture

Portraiture is a type of ethnographic research (Lawrence-Lightfoot & Hoffman Davis, 1997) and is a form of third person life writing (English, 2006). Sarah Lawrence-Lightfoot (1983) defines it as "a method framed by the traditions and values of the phenomenological paradigm, sharing many of the techniques, standards, and goals of ethnography" (p. 13). As such it resists simplistic categorization and draws upon the traditions of art and science.

A recent example in the art world is Simon Schama's (2006) *The Power of Art*. Earlier examples in the literature of educational leadership include Harry Wolcott's (1973) *The Man in the Principal's Office: An Ethnography*; Larry Cuban's (1976) *Urban School Chiefs Under Fire*; Sarah Lawrence-Lightfoot's (1983) *The Good High School: Portraits of Character and Culture* and Peter Ribbins and Brian Sherratt's (1997) *Radical Educational Policies and Conservative Secretaries of State*.

These examples are representative of a method which aims to "capture the richness, complexity, and dimensionality of human experience in social and cultural context, conveying the perspectives of the people who are negotiating those experiences" (Lawrence-Lightfoot & Hoffman Davis, 1997, p. 3).

Refined by Sarah Lawrence-Lightfoot of Harvard University, she described the methodology as a kind of life drawing with words which occurred at the intersection of "aesthetics and empiricism" (Lawrence-Lightfoot & Hoffman Davis, 1997, p. 6). Like Plutarch centuries before who was concerned about ethical behavior, Lawrence-Lightfoot was focused on capturing "goodness" in her subjects beginning with how they defined goodness (Lawrence-Lightfoot & Hoffman Davis, 1997, p. 9). The resultant characterization, a portrait, "creates a narrative that is at once complex, provocative, and inviting, that attempts to be holistic, revealing the dynamic interaction of values, personality, structure, and history" (Lawrence-Lightfoot & Hoffman Davis, 1997, p. 11).

The focal point for portraiture is to reveal the context in which a person lives and works. "Context becomes the framework, the reference point, the map, the ecological sphere; it is used to place people and action in time and space and as a resource for understanding what they say and do" (Lawrence-Lightfoot & Hoffman Davis, 1997, p. 41). In an echo of Plutarch (in Clough, n.d.) who believed that it was in small incidents that a person's character was revealed, Lawrence-Lightfoot and Hoffman Davis (1997) said that, "We have no idea how to decipher or decode an action, a gesture, a conversation, or an exclamation unless we see it embedded in context" (p. 41). Similarly, Plutarch said of his biographees that "sometimes a matter of less moment, an expression or a jest, informs us better of their characters and inclinations" (Plutarch in Clough, n.d., p. 801). Plutarch compared himself to a portrait painter who was more interested in the lines and facial features of his men because it was there that he found "indications of the souls of men" (Plutarch in Clough, n.d., p. 801).

As we interviewed our subjects to discern characteristics of connoisseurship, the context became the setting in which it was defined and exhibited. We did not inform our respondents that we were searching for evidence of connoisseurship in the questions we posed to them. Our approach was to talk with those respondents about their work and the purpose of their work.

In this chapter we build on the previous chapter by providing a more detailed and nuanced discussion of a selection of our artist participants. As discussed in Chapter 4, the artists and leader connoisseurs that formed part of our study were subjects of a series of interviews conducted over a two-year period in Australia and America. Portraits of three Australian artists (Caitlin, Miriam and Scott) and one American artist (Alberto) are reported here.

We considered all of the artists in our study, especially the four chosen for this chapter, to be exemplars of the criteria for the discerning eye. In other words, they come closest to meeting each of the 10 dimensions of connoisseurship. There were five possible designations of the extent to which the respondents possessed the dimensions of connoisseurship we have discussed. They were deemed *exceptional* if the dimension was intensely and consistently present in their interview or in the products or outcomes of their art or work. *Strong* if the dimension was perceived to be vividly present in their interview or in the products or outcomes of their art or work. They were *moderate* if their interview commentary was filled with consistent patterns or responses, but did not necessarily convey a passion or deep commitment or experience. They were *weak* if there was very little evidence of the dimension in their commentary or work. Finally, *not applicable* if there was a complete absence of any evidence or in their commentary we could not discern any evidence.

Portrait 1: Caitlin the Sculptor

Caitlin is an Australian woman in her 50s who has been working as a full-time sculptor for almost three years. Prior to her becoming a full-time sculptor, art was a hobby in which she engaged during her weekends and spare time. Previously, her employment has included work in the fashion industry which took her overseas for a number of years. She also managed the renovation of flats and houses and engaged in interior decoration of some of these residences. Before embarking full-time in sculpting, her most recent work experience was as a project manager and coordinator of Information Technology in the Australian public service.

Caitlin informed us that for as long as she can remember she has had an interest in and appreciation for different types of art including fashion, interior decoration, theater, painting and sculpture. She grew up in a large working-class family with a passionate mother who fostered in her and her siblings a great love of beauty in poetry, music and sculpture. Her mother loved sculpture and there were a couple of pieces in the family home. Yet it was fashion that interested Caitlin most during her teenage years and after she left school, she pursued a successful career in photographic modeling. Unlike some of the other artists in our study who immersed themselves in music, dance or art lessons from an early age (i.e. two of the dancers in our study started dance classes at the age of five), Caitlin took sculpture classes when she was in her 40s. She started sculpture later rather than sooner as she was the main caregiver for her son and needed the security of a full-time job. It should be noted that her great reverence for art and her awareness of its power to enrich human existence was nurtured in her early years.

Caitlin reflected that her work as an artist has certainly improved since she started and it continues to expand in different directions. She spent several years learning the basics from a very experienced sculptor and these years were instrumental for her to expand and hone her skills. An important turning point was when she developed the confidence to have some of her pieces cast in bronze

PHOTOGRAPH 5.1 The Captive

which she continues to do. Some early examples of these first pieces are shown here. The first is "The Captive" (Photograph 5.1).

She comments about this provocative piece:

> The Captive began life as a response to my personal conflicts with freedom and space. As the work took form, it acquired a far more piquant meaning, and I realized that despite the challenges we face in the free world, for many people elsewhere, oppression has a far harder physical meaning. The Captive is therefore pitched at many levels, but most particularly it is the many nameless prisoners held in dreadful circumstances in the dungeons of the disposed, stripped of the most fundamental rights, their voices unheard, hidden in the world's darkest corners. The Captive strives to give them voice.

PHOTOGRAPH 5.2 The Unnamed

Exhibiting her work at galleries was also an important developmental turning point and after experiencing her first sale she felt she had "arrived" at a level of acceptance of her work. Caitlin reflected that since this experience, she has continued to grow in confidence and the focus of her work has changed. No longer does she create what she considers to be beautiful figures (faces, bodies) but she now seeks to create work that is more connected to living contexts which form part of her "contemporary series." Two examples are shown here (Photographs 5.2 and 5.3).

The first set of figures is called "The Unnamed." Of the work she says:

> Five figures bound together in time and life called "The Unnamed" . . . it is foot soldiers of the everyday; the misfits, the beautiful, the young, and the old the young will inevitably become; the past, present and future we all share and carry with us, with silent, stoic acceptance. The subdued, uncomplaining cross-section of humanity, full of muted sound and fury that at once signifies nothing, and yet everything.

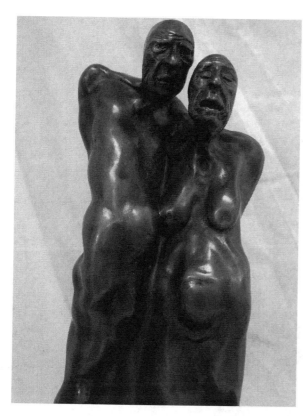

PHOTOGRAPH 5.3 Les Copains

The second is called "Les Copains" (the companions). She observes of this piece:

> Our expectations of beauty blindsight us to a deeper truth. Beyond life's transient illusion the line of time carries all spirits, all souls on regardless, without fear or favour. While we live, we learn that true friendship is never wearied by time, even though we may weary of life.

The meaning of Caitlin's work is largely intrinsic and based on what she perceives as being beautiful or in the case of portraiture capturing a certain expression or humanity. The theoretical base of her work is the human condition since she strives to show people's struggle, love and other universal experiences. In terms of how she works, she indicated that a significant metaphor that describes her work is the Myth of Sisyphus. She works on one project and tries to attain a certain level of perfection but recalls that she usually falls short then finds herself undertaking a new project.

Like the other artists in the study, Caitlin referred to significant others with whom she has great relationships (friends, family and colleagues). These significant others continue to be a source of encouragement and support.

Once Caitlin started to learn sculpture, it became a central part of her life and she sought to continue to improve her skills. Before she left her full-time public sector job to seek a more autonomous life as a self-employed artist, she used every available moment (weekends, evenings, holidays) to practice sculpture.

A chance meeting with a colleague of her sister led to her first commission. After a conversation about art and after seeing some of Caitlin's pictures, Caitlin was commissioned to create a significant religious figure (Edmund Rice— a Roman Catholic missionary, educationalist, and founder of two religious institutes of religious brothers) for his school's anniversary which is shown here (see Photograph 5.4).

Caitlin indicated that it was this work that helped her to gain her second and very substantial commission of 10 busts of winners of the Victoria Cross during the Gallipoli campaign which took one year to complete. This commission of

PHOTOGRAPH 5.4 Edmund Rice Portrait

Edmund Rice represented a significant breakthrough in Caitlin's development and recognition of her work as a sculptor.

Caitlin recognized the importance of a good grounding in the basics and the techniques governing her work in helping her develop competence leading to confidence. Apart from all of the years invested in learning her craft, and the learning through trial and error and ongoing practice, Caitlin referred to two other ways in which she sought to attain competency and become better at what she does. Caitlin said she seeks feedback on her work and has discussions about it with a small group of trusted artists and friends. She finds the exchange of ideas and sharing a valuable way of re-evaluating her work. It has been said that every piece of art is evaluated twice: once by the artist and the other by the observer. Feedback, then, is crucial to unite these two responses of art. The other way is by being aware of other artists' work and attending galleries to view it, not for the purpose of emulation but for an understanding of artistic processes. She aspires to the level of a small group of sculptors she admires for their brilliance and expertise.

Caitlin indicated that with experience she has been able to differentiate her work more easily and has become more positive about the results. As an example, she said she looks back on some of her earlier works and cringes because it is apparent to her that these early works could use improvement not only in terms of technique but also content. Another significant development is her ability to know when to stop working on a piece. Earlier in her career, she was unsure when to stop trying to continue refining a piece. It was because of her lack of experience and confidence. Later, with experience and confidence she had a much surer sense of when a piece was done. She talked about the importance of "trust[ing] your own instincts" and relying on your own judgment when evaluating the work and making decisions about its direction.

Caitlin gave two examples of the value of gaining public feedback on her work. The first was when she had a small booth in a weekend art fair where she exhibited several of her pieces. She recalls having a conversation with an elderly woman who complimented her on one of her sculptures and then proceeded to tell her what the piece was communicating. Caitlin indicated she was moved by this personal sharing and the fact that her art was able to speak to someone in an affirming way. The second example was not as positive. Caitlin attended the opening of a gallery in which she displayed several pieces (many of which were male figures in somber poses and expressions). She overhead one viewer of the public saying, "this work is so sad. The men look like they are suffering. I wouldn't want any of them in my place."

Caitlin had no difficulty in identifying artists whom she admired (both living and dead) and how she aspired to be as good as some of them, including giants in her field. At the same time, she was acutely aware how her choice of creating portraiture and figurative art lies in stark contrast to installation art, performance art and large scale public art—three forms that have dominated the art scene for some decades.

TABLE 5.2 Assessment of Caitlin as a connoisseur against the 10 dimensions of connoisseurship

Name of connoisseur: Caitlin (Stage 3)	
Dimension of connoisseurship	Assessment of the strength of the dimension
Knowledgeable perception	Strong
Experience	Strong
Competence	Strong
Framing	Strong
Desire	Strong
Understanding of practice	Strong
Aesthetic vision	Strong
Cultural awareness and reflexivity	Strong
Discipline	Strong
Identity	Strong

A tension between tradition and innovation is something that all artists are faced with according to Caitlin. As a consequence, she reflected that as she has become more experienced and confident, she has been able to take more risks in creating space to develop her own signature work. It is through risk taking that artists find a home for their work.

As discussed earlier in this chapter, we used the designations of strong, moderate, weak or not applicable to determine the strength of each of the dimensions for the participants in the sample. What follows is our assessment of Caitlin as a connoisseur (see Table 5.2).

On the 10 dimensions of connoisseurship we rated Caitlin as strong on each. We ascertained that her work is solidly within the Western, classical tradition of sculpture. This is a conscious decision on her part because she has rejected contemporary postmodern constructions of sculpture as not beautiful or meaningful in the classical tradition.

We see Caitlin as a connoisseur of substantive accomplishment in her field. She has acquired the competence and skills in the technical craft of sculpting and is now moving with increasing confidence into highly visible public works involving highly recognized leaders. However, Caitlin indicated to us that she sees herself on a continuum and positions herself on the lower end of that scale (in our reference, moving from Stage 3 to Stage 4). She is anxious to do a full life-sized figure and, at the time of writing this book, it appears she will undertake this project of a life-size sculpture of Jesus.

Portrait 2: Alberto, Artist and Jesuit Priest

Alberto is a South American artist and Jesuit priest who works in a university in the United States. He originally trained as a dancer in the Martha Graham tradition and worked as a dancer before training as a painter. Currently he works in print-making and ceramics. He works on different topics and themes and understands that they will often migrate into deeper ideas. He referred to several exhibitions he has held, some of which have showed for two years. Alberto informed us that he could not return to his native country even to attend the funeral of his father because he feared he would not be allowed to return if he left the United States. His work has been influenced by life events of hope and darkness and the massacre of 15 relatives over a decade before had taken him to some dark places. Of his work, he says he "create[s] a space to explore the ambiguity of danger and limitless imaginative depth." Much of his work is an exploration of life; a life in which he chooses to embrace hope.

He reported that he polished his technical skills in New Mexico where he worked alone in a studio for 16 hours on some days. He noted that when artists are creating an image or object they must pay close attention not only to the details of what they are doing but also the technical processes in order to achieve the overall goals. Alberto explained that different media dictate different processes. While ceramics requires more of an intuitive approach and painting is spontaneous, print-making is tedious, calculated and lengthy. After some hundreds of drawings, it is not uncommon for perhaps only five to seven drawings to be selected for the next stages of print-making. Alberto said:

> I chose print-making as primary media, not with the purpose of creating multiples, but for multiplying the possibilities of images that can be repeated; and thus, by repeating it can be reconfigured. Literally, the landscape becomes an accumulation of multiple layers of different media: ink drawing, woodblock print, digital print, stamp, silkscreen and hand painting.

Photograph 5.5 is one of a series of large prints influenced by Alberto's memories of mangrove trees of the Caribbean.

Of his work with ceramics (see Photograph 5.6), Alberto said it consists of two dimensions. The first is the ceramics itself and the second is using ceramics as a mixed medium. He says:

> The significance of creating art through ceramics is that each piece is the materialization of the centrifugal force of the wheel and of the centripetal force of the artist . . . Both forces constitute the container. Moreover, the spiral movement is the key force of the universe materialized in each object. This materialization of the force into the object connects to my inner experience and idea of the folding and unfolding universe.

PHOTOGRAPH 5.5 Mangrove Trees of the Caribbean

Alberto is a recognized artist in the United States and South America. At the time of our interview with him he was working on two big commissions. Alberto informed us of his love of learning about other cultures. In one of his recently completed projects he created an interfaith place to meditate and pray at his university. It was designed for Buddhists, Jews and Muslims so they would have a sanctuary for prayer, spiritual activities and meditation within a Catholic university. The multi-faith room includes design elements that represent all of the major religions of the world. Alberto used a variety of materials such as wool, glazes, pigments, sand, clay and gold leaf to "create a habitat for the encounter with the divine." Moreover, he said that he "created a space with symbols that speak to a universal audience because they are common to different cultural and religious traditions." Among these symbols are the tree of life (the main decorative motif of the room; see Photograph 5.7) which is a universal symbol that "speaks

PHOTOGRAPH 5.6 Ceramics

deeply about life, tradition, relationships, and spiritual growth." Alberto says that the tree of life

> is a "cosmic tree" that all mystics must climb to understand the divine. With care and nurturing, a tree will continue the growth of new life for many generations. It has been said trees are the earth's effort to speak to heaven.

Alberto noted that an artist can recognize what may be invisible to others. Art has no morality. Art can integrate reality. Art is a whole way of recognition. Art, according to Alberto, is not entertainment. It has a social function. It should not be conditioned by any political or religious agendas. It is not a tool to illustrate the values of the establishment. For the most part, it is about resisting.

Alberto's religious perspective was evident when he observed to us that "Art is a spirit. Art is not a human product. Art is a being that comes through artists. It's a living force." Alberto felt that we live in a world that is not appreciated. We like fast products. His students were "a bunch of people deeply connected with devices." He commented that when people observe his work they don't see the labor he puts into it. "They don't go deeper, to see, to feel. Society is very superficial and most people have no idea of the joy of creating. They live in a bubble and they are interested in accumulating privilege. There's no room for funky spaces or poor people."

PHOTOGRAPH 5.7 Tree of Life window

Alberto observed that he became more "whole" as a person when he went back to his childhood since it enabled him to become more honest and transparent with himself and realize he does not need to prove anything to anyone. He now sees himself as more contemplative and has become more selective in the tasks he undertakes.

Alberto's insights about educational leadership were instructive. He was one of a small number of artists we interviewed who work in an educational institution. His commentary about leaders at the top was harsh. He saw such leaders as too much into themselves and too interested in foreseeing mistakes and preventing problems. Leaders were often out to acquire privileges. "They think they deserve their authority," he observed. His judgment was that power comes from privilege that creates a world the size of oneself. As a consequence, people draw into themselves and in the end they have to create alliances to survive.

Alberto opined that leadership should be free from notions of commodification and that leadership should be viewed as service and that power was not part of privilege. Education is about becoming human and about people "doing things." He asked rhetorically, "What kind of leadership comes from just the content?" If that was what educational leadership was all about he said, "We get a robot" and "we don't need a leader."

TABLE 5.3 Assessment of Alberto as a connoisseur against the 10 dimensions of connoisseurship

Name of connoisseur: Alberto (Stage 3)	
Dimension of connoisseurship	Assessment of the strength of the dimension
Knowledgeable perception	Strong
Experience	Strong
Competence	Strong
Framing	Strong
Desire	Strong
Understanding of practice	Strong
Aesthetic vision	Strong
Cultural awareness and reflexivity	Strong
Discipline	Strong
Identity	Strong

We see Alberto as an experienced and well-recognized artist and connoisseur (see Table 5.3). We deemed he is strong on all of the dimensions of connoisseurship. One illustration that stands out is his strong cultural awareness regarding and responsiveness to people of different faiths and denominations. This awareness manifested itself in his creative work. Not only has Alberto acquired technical skills and competence in his field, but in our interview with him, he demonstrated a discerning eye in his outlook on the social, aesthetic and political context of art. (Our assessment is that he is close to moving into Stage 4.)

Portrait 3: Miriam—Choreographer, Community Arts Leader and Humanist

Miriam is both an artist and a leader and her portrait could have easily fitted next to other leaders' portraits in the chapter that follows. However, we decided to include her in this chapter, alongside fellow artists, because the focus of the portrait explores her creative dance project.

Miriam is a qualified English and drama teacher who has worked in a number of capacities including supply (substitute) teaching in a high school, teaching belly dancing to women, lecturing at a university, and running arts-based adult education programs for community-based organizations. It is her work as a freelance community arts educator/community cultural development worker/creative producer/leader who created and ran a dance project inclusive of women with and without disabilities that provides a context in which to understand her work as a connoisseur. At the time of the interview, the dance project had ceased operation as Miriam said she felt "completely burnt out as if I had given all of myself away to others." Currently she is exploring a new creative way of working with voice that involves individuals rather than groups of people.

For some eight years, Miriam was successful in receiving funding to offer a dance project to women in her local community. The dance project was open to all women with diverse abilities and disabilities (including carers/support workers of the women who had disabilities). It incurred no charge to participants and no auditions were required. The socially inclusive dance project consisted of weekly dance classes that culminated in a yearly dance performance open to the wider community. Unlike some forms of dance such as ballroom dancing, belly dancing and ballet that both prescribe and limit specific movements, Miriam views dance very broadly; it is based on creative movement that builds upon individuals' everyday movements so that they become performative.

She said that in the first weeks of a program, she goes through a whole broad set of activities to help her understand how each individual moves to a range of different stimuli and what they can do and where they can be extended. Much of this time is devoted to moving with participants, observing them, not just with one's eyes but with all of the senses to get a feeling for where they are at. For those women who have severe disabilities, Miriam offers strategies to help develop their own movement vocabulary. As she said, "It has to be authentic to the person." For those participants who wish to challenge themselves, she invites them to expand their way of moving creatively so they can find ways of expressing themselves more broadly.

Over the weekly dance classes, she and her co-facilitator work one-on-one with individuals and with groups to help them workshop ideas and themes that then form part of the end-of-year performance. Workshop ideas emerge from the personal qualities, abilities and interests of participants so that their way of moving inspires the direction of each piece. She said she works "very intuitively" to get a sense of what is emerging from the workshops so that connections can be made and a performance program can be developed. She said:

> Life is a performance, the everyday acts that we do, the way we move, the way we relate to each other, the everyday actions that we do can well be performative. It's really about taking those, putting them together, merging

them together in ways that are interesting artistically and presenting that to an audience . . . the whole package, lights, sound, costume make it extraordinary.

A driving force behind Miriam's vision for the dance project is political; her inclusive project is a statement against disability-based segregation. Dance, for her, is a vehicle for personal transformation and social change. She commented that her project has been transformative for both participants and the audiences who attended the annual performance. For participants, her 10-month project provided a safe and creative space where they felt valued and their creative contribution was acknowledged. She also commented that:

> the connections that were made between participants through the creative process were deep and profound. This aspect of the project enabled greater acceptance and compassion of and for one another. This is how differences between people can be valued—through developing respect for difference as something that is valuable . . . The creative process within performing arts lends itself beautifully to practices and approaches that develop connections between people without relying on word-based language.

For the audiences who attended the annual free yearly performances, it was an educative and transformative opportunity that challenged the perception of what dance is as well as what an inclusive project can achieve. Miriam said that in society there is a preconception that we should expect little from people with disabilities, yet audience feedback to all of her shows has been outstanding. Audience members have commented they were "Blown away by the performance." One of the authors of this book had the privilege of attending an end-of-year performance some years ago, and found it to be thought-provoking, deeply moving and beautiful.

In terms of what Miriam believes is an outstanding project, she said it begins with respect; respect shown by the leader/facilitator for participants demonstrated verbally and non-verbally. She used words such as "empathy," "self-awareness" and "love." Facilitators need to not only work with participants where they are at, but show empathy and support their personal empowerment and quest for creativity. Facilitators need to "be aware of their own thoughts, feelings and behaviors and to take responsibility for these . . . [in order to] . . . maintain integrity within themselves." Facilitators need to bring to their work kindness and acceptance—"love of humanity" that works with the best in all people.

During the life of the dance project, Miriam worked in isolation and was the only person in her state to offer a socially inclusive program for women with multiple disabilities. She secured the funding, liaised with service providers of disability to locate participants, and was the co-facilitator and creative producer during the project's life. She said this was important as she is a person who has a need for autonomy and freedom. Yet, she commented that in retrospect she may have been able to cope better with stress if she had an outside colleague/mentor with whom she could have confided and talked things through during some of the difficult times. Some of the challenges she faced ranged from the stress involved in applying for funding to run the program every year and uncertainty about receiving it, challenges with participants who found it difficult to commit to the weekly sessions of the 10-month program (due to mental health problems and other difficulties), and persons/organizations in the disability sector who were not fully supportive of the program and the consistent commitment required to achieve the best possible outcomes for all participants. She commented on the inflexibility of the disability sector characterized by structure and standardization that clashes with flexibility of the arts.

Miriam described her work as the project's creative producer and co-facilitator as a collaborative journey of learning with and from participants. She said, "I'm enabling people to discover something that's already within them and for me that's a glorious thing." She said she has felt inspiration "to be part of the life of the ordinary person who doesn't identify as an artist discovering and expressing their creativity."

We deem that Miriam is a connoisseur (see Table 5.4). Her approach to working with participants is based on a discerning eye that is intuitive, aesthetic, and a sensitive celebration of the human spirit. In developing and running a transformative dance program for women of varying abilities, she showed a

TABLE 5.4 Assessment of Miriam as a connoisseur against the 10 dimensions of connoisseurship

Name of connoisseur: Miriam (Stage 3)	
Dimension of connoisseurship	Assessment of the strength of the dimension
Knowledgeable perception	Strong
Experience	Strong
Competence	Strong
Framing	Strong
Desire	Strong
Understanding of practice	Strong
Aesthetic vision	Strong
Cultural awareness and reflexivity	Strong
Discipline	Strong
Identity	Strong

sophisticated level of cultural awareness and responsiveness. We rated her in Stage 3 and "strong" on all dimensions.

Portrait 4: Scott, Actor and Director

Since the mid-1970s, Scott has been involved in the theater business as an actor and director. He has also worked as a teacher, lecturer, writer, and for eight years held the position of artistic director and CEO of a Brisbane-based theater company. He has won numerous awards for both acting and directing due to his sustained contribution to the arts in Queensland.

Scott indicates that he rarely auditions anymore. He sees his strength in ensembles and in collaboration. He said he "builds things" and that he is "a change agent." He does premiere works and views himself at his best when starting with a "blank sheet." He indicates that he never starts by saying, "I have to create." His response to an artistic challenge is to focus on solutions and to create sustainability. "I don't manage very well. I'm a builder. I'm always looking for challenges."

Regarding the medium within which he works, he said that "any genre limits the expression of anything." Yet it also has strengths. He sees that technology has brought with it advantages; not only in terms of responsiveness through communication but also advances can be felt directly in sound and lighting. When discussing the production of a play, Scott said that it is important to turn perceived liabilities into assets. Not only that, but "creativity should be joyful." He indicates that what you are asking actors to do is to self-actualize. "Leadership is not standing on some high place and calling people to you. It's about getting down and going to them." He reported that there is "a lot of mythology surrounding performance." However, what needs to be done is to create common ground: "you need to express your skills and ask actors to tell you about their skills."

Reflecting on his work as a director, he said he never abandoned a play despite encountering difficulties, especially if money had been invested in it. He identified five key questions that need to be asked before putting on the play: "What is the play? Where is it going to be performed? When is it going to be performed? How will it be performed? and Why?" Ultimately, Scott said, "the task is to do your best." He said that a play is about building something and within a play are only three essential things that frame the work: an actor, a space, and an audience. He said "there is no right or wrong way. What happens is what is."

Scott explained that given the nature of actors they are most often of the mind that their responsibility is to make a play work even under the most impossible of circumstances. He facetiously called this "turd polishing," observing that "a good actor makes it happen when everything else is going wrong," adding, "Anyone can act when things are going right."

According to Scott, theater has to have a purpose. "Theater is ridiculous if it has no purpose. A lot of theater is bourgeois. I've never subscribed to that." Scott indicated that the purpose of artistic expression is to provoke change by viewing ordinary situations from extraordinary angles. In referring to the artistic process of direction, he says that one builds a play from a brief. The brief varies in complexity and specificity. Some are more open-ended than others. Working from the brief, there has to be a vision of what it should be but not in tactical terms. One begins with a collaboration in which the director, actors and significant others construct something like a virtual house. They do so until the texture and details are clear. The task of the actor is to live in the house in every detail.

Within this strategic process of direction, Scott indicated that issues emerge along with the construct. Some actors are seen to rattle the cage of directors and sometimes when it works there is no reason for why it worked. Scott referred to this situation as the "aesthetic realm." Within the interrogation of ideas in constructing this virtual house, good ideas will survive and bad ones will not. He said, "Some things can work and you don't know why." A true collaboration means that everyone has a role to play and is encouraged to express themselves. This is not the case with cooperation. In this latter case individuals tend to hold back.

Scott indicated that his own satisfaction comes from the construction and collaboration part of directing, which he views as essentially "puzzle solving." Not only that, he said, "I really love the company of actors [because] theater people have a particular sense of history." He likes being thrown a curve ball because it is challenging. He confesses that to be successful, one has to have "a real love of audiences and treat them with respect. Audiences move us to be inspired and to be clever . . . They want us to be passionate and understanding." He observes that, "passion is in short supply at the public level." Yet audiences want to see actors act with pleasure. Scott said, "we deal with people's stories [because] the story is the most important thing."

He says that his passion for theater was fueled by an accident as a young adult and he has had to work very hard to restore the full use of his body. He wanted to be liked and performing was a way to achieve that. However, he reflected that if that passion for performance cannot be sustained he will stop acting (and has done so for several years).

Scott says that theater involves an aesthetic response, not an intellectual response. He went on to say that "an aesthetic response is the most truthful . . . the body has an innate sense of truth. It is the basis for all sub-text." For Scott, performance is a lie which exposes a greater truth. It is only "the uncreative [who] do the same thing twice."

On all 10 dimensions of connoisseurship, we rated Scott as "strong" in Stage 3 (see Table 5.5). He is not only a very experienced actor and director but an accomplished one who has received the respect of his colleagues, peers and the

TABLE 5.5 Assessment of Scott as a connoisseur against the 10 dimensions of connoisseurship

Name of connoisseur: Scott (Stage 3)	
Dimension of connoisseurship	Assessment of the strength of the dimension
Knowledgeable perception	Strong
Experience	Strong
Competence	Strong
Framing	Strong
Desire	Strong
Understanding of practice	Strong
Aesthetic vision	Strong
Cultural awareness and reflexivity	Strong
Discipline	Strong
Identity	Strong

profession at large. Scott has used his discerning eye to read and interpret situations and in some cases turn around what might appear to be limitations into assets. His close work with actors has seen him develop collaborative working relationships so that the experience is not only joyful for everyone involved, but enables the actors to be the best they can be. Ultimately, he sees the creative experience of theater as needing to be provocative and meaningful for the audience. For these and other reasons, we see Scott as a connoisseur of theater who demonstrates aesthetic, social and political sensibilities.

Summary

This chapter has recounted four portraits of artists, each of whom has demonstrated he or she is on the continuum towards connoisseurship. All were at Stage 3 in their respective fields. Connoisseurship is a personal quest to increase one's competence and understanding in a chosen field or medium. Though there are some common dimensions and characteristics of connoisseurs, there is no standard or "normal" way connoisseurship is attained. It is a highly individualized and personalized journey. The timetable for its attainment is not standardized either. Connoisseurship is intimately connected to a person's growth and development and the interaction of life experiences with that growth.

IMPLICATIONS FOR POLICY AND PRACTICE

Advancement of Expert Knowledge is Part and Parcel of Connoisseurship

Typically a career educational leader who is upwardly bound thinks about advancement principally in terms of climbing a career ladder based on expanding hierarchical positions in an organization. Connoisseurs are not principally motivated by this ideal. Rather they are motivated by personal ideals and goals that are anchored in advancing their status and power based on acquiring expert knowledge and not on bureaucratic upward movement. Appeals to develop connoisseurship must therefore be couched in these terms rather than in the usual ideas of gaining more authority through the formal organizational apparatus.

Key Chapter Ideas

• As an Evolutionary Process Connoisseurship Can Be Mapped

Structured interviews with artists did reveal that their evolutionary journey could be mapped, that is, located on a continuum of development by identifying the distinctive stages of that development. The stages are not precise delineations but general approximations of their location on an evolutionary continuum. Even at Stage 4 there is no lid or cap to the continuation of expertise or competence in any respective field.

• Connoisseurship is Not Role Dependent nor Role Bound

The status of connoisseurship is not dependent upon a person being in a particular role, nor is it defined by an organizational role. Roles are simply boundaries in organizational space, while the competence a connoisseur possesses may reside but may also exceed or overlap into other areas. Connoisseurs are defined by their competence but not necessarily by their roles.

References

Clough, A.H. (Ed.). (n.d.). *Plutarch's lives* (J. Dryden, Trans.). New York: Modern Library.

Cuban, L. (1976). *Urban school chiefs under fire*. Chicago: University of Chicago Press.

English, F.W. (2006). Understanding leadership in education: Life writing and its possibilities. *Journal of Educational Administration and History, 38*(2), 141–154.

Jung, C. (1958). *The undiscovered self* (R.F. Hull, Trans.). New York: A Mentor Book.

Lawrence-Lightfoot, S. (1983). *The good high school: Portraits of character and culture*. New York: Basic Books.

Lawrence-Lightfoot, S. & Hoffman Davis, J. (1997). *The art and science of portraiture*. San Francisco: Jossey-Bass.

Ribbins, P. & Sherratt, B. (1997). *Radical educational policies and conservative secretaries of state*. London: Cassell.

Schama, S. (2006). *The power of art*. New York: HarperCollins.

Wolcott, H. (1973). *The man in the principal's office: An ethnography*. Prospect Heights, IL: Waveland.

6

PORTRAITS OF CONNOISSEURS OF LEADERSHIP PERFORMANCE

I have no sympathy with the belief that art is the restricted province of those who paint, sculpt, make music and verse . . . the material used is only incidental . . . there is an artist in every man [sic].

(Henri, 2007, pp. 223–224)

WHAT THIS CHAPTER IS ABOUT

In this chapter, six educational leaders are sketched out who are in various stages of connoisseurship. They include Australian and American women and men who are both site and system level educational administrators/leaders currently at work in both nations' schools. Some of these leaders are quite experienced while others are more towards the initial stages of learning their roles and gaining competence and confidence in fulfilling them.

Specifically, this chapter addresses the following points:

- As educational leaders gain competence on the job, their field of vision and their ability to engage in finer-grain differentiations in the work environment expands, though not as a "standard" process nor on a uniform timetable.
- The development of job/role differentiation is highly personal and context dependent.
- Growth towards connoisseurship rests on the acquisition of "tacit" knowledge of which a leader may not always be fully aware or able to consciously recount.

Six Portraits of Educational Connoisseurs

As we discussed in Chapter 2, there are three types of connoisseurs. The first is a *connoisseur of leaders*, a person who is able to recognize and discern greatness in others' performance. A good example here is a scholar or researcher of leadership or in the field of the arts, an art critic. The second is a *connoisseur of leadership performance*, a person who has mastered his or her craft. Thus, this person is a connoisseur in action. The third is a *leader connoisseur*, a person who is both a connoisseur of leaders and a connoisseur of leadership performance. The portraits we offer in this chapter are all connoisseurs of leadership performance.

There are six portraits: two Australian leaders (Robert, Matthew) and four U.S.-based leaders (Tanya, Templeton, Julia and Donovan) presented in this chapter. Similar to the portraits of artists presented in the previous chapter, the six leaders are considered against the 10 dimensions of connoisseurship.

Portrait 1: Robert, Primary School Principal

Robert has been a school principal for seven years and prior to that worked as a deputy principal for seven years. Typical of most school principals, he began his career as a teacher. His desire to work in school administration was fueled by an observation that he could do it better than some of his contemporaries. In other words, it is an "anti-model" that has guided his philosophy and practice. Robert referred to a noble friend, colleague and mentor who has been a source of inspiration and support to him. He and his mentor have a similar outlook when it comes to education. He commented on the value of engaging in conversations with his learned friend and appreciating being challenged by someone who holds an alternative view to the technical-rational perspective that has dominated school leadership in Australia for decades.

Robert has spent most of his principalship at his current school. The school is 16 years old and was one of the first new schools in the area. It started with 256 students and enrollment is now close to 700. A characteristic of the school is its distinctive inclusive ethos. According to Robert, a number of the students who attend have struggled in other schools and parents have chosen this school for its reputation to cater to the needs of children who have previously had difficulties with social skills. A key challenge for the school is how to redistribute its finite resources so that all students can achieve a worthwhile and equitable education.

As a leader, Robert sees himself as a person who "leads conversations regarding learning" with his staff. He uses a team-based approach with staff so that teachers are aware of what is happening in the school and "everything is on the table." An advantage of utilizing teams is the different strengths that teachers bring and the different solutions that are generated.

Robert talked about the need to enliven teachers by providing a vision, map, and steps of how to get there. Action research, as an inquiry-based learning strategy, is promoted in the school and teachers are encouraged to use it to evolve and improve practice. Robert said that teachers are "change weary" and part of his way of helping them was to translate big ideas into smaller ideas that are more accessible and easily understood. He stressed the importance of having a big picture knowledge of teaching and learning, curriculum, management, finances, technology, working with parents, and small and big P politics.

A strong belief that Robert held was the need for school leaders to "establish the circumstances." By this phrase he meant that every question impacting upon the school sits in a context of where the school is going (i.e. the vision, the values and beliefs). For this reason, it is vital to have a vision with the values and beliefs as a moral compass so that some things are not compromised and alignment is present in decision-making.

Outstanding practice for Robert was viewed as the ability to work around a whole range of issues and be able to participate in them not only at their smallest point but also at their largest point. This is a way of seeing both the big picture and the small details at the same time. He developed this perspective based on an early teaching experience when he was asked to convene a major sporting event. He reflected that a significant learning was that he was able to adopt both a strategic view by observing the overall activity but at the same time could focus on the smallest moment and detail. This moving in and out of the big picture to the minute details of the event was instructive in his understandings. He described this process as being in the trenches but also ensuring you can see the whole field.

Making discerning decisions is also part of the work of school leaders in addition to keeping the balance between what is and what should be (and should not be). Robert said that much of leadership is concerned with being thoughtful and mindful and realizing you will not have all of the answers. Yet, it is incumbent on leaders to be well read, understand national drivers and imperatives of education, and actively seek out research in the field. As he said, it is critical to have a handle on what is going on in education (both nationally and state wide). Robert is one of a small but growing number of school principals in Australia who has studied for and been awarded a Doctor of Education. In terms of himself as a leader, he conceded that competence exists on a continuum. He reiterated that leadership is a continual quest of knowing what needs to be known and what does the evidence say. Not to be open to learning is likely to have detrimental effects on children's learning.

Robert lamented that the dominant view of good leadership is that it is tied to school performance via test score results. There is an assumption that good leadership must be part of this type of school performance yet this may not be the case. Uppermost in Robert's mind is a schooling experience that produces joyful children who are comfortable and happy coming to school.

We consider Robert to be a connoisseur of leadership performance on all of the 10 dimensions and in Stage 3 (see Table 6.1). Robert not only has mastered

TABLE 6.1 Assessment of Robert as a connoisseur against the 10 dimensions of connoisseurship

Name of connoisseur: Robert (Stage 3)	
Dimension of connoisseurship	Assessment of the strength of the dimension
Knowledgeable perception	Strong
Experience	Strong
Competence	Strong
Framing	Strong
Desire	Strong
Understanding of practice	Strong
Aesthetic vision	Strong
Cultural awareness and reflexivity	Strong
Discipline	Strong
Identity	Strong

the craft-centered skills of being a principal, but he has incorporated creative responses which have moved his school into a different realm than simply reproducing state-designed visions for education. Robert has a strong identity and a strong desire to push forward. He is very reflective and has read widely in the field. He has demonstrated cultural awareness as his school serves the culturally different learner, students who have previously had social and other difficulties in other schools. Moreover, he demonstrated this awareness by insisting that a school leader should possess both a mastery of the essential small skills and, at the same time, be able to engage in larger and more far-reaching conversations. Within this context, Robert has found generalizations within specifics, that is, locating essentially localized responses in larger data sets.

Portrait 2: Matthew, Education Manager of an Arts Organization (Previously a Primary School Principal)

Matthew commenced his career in teaching and after 18 months became an acting principal of a small school (i.e. fewer than 10 children) in far Western Queensland. After this initial foray into the principalship, Matthew applied for and was successful in securing a principalship at a slightly bigger school in Western Queensland where he worked for two years. Following this was a secondment to work as an education officer for an arts organization. This opportunity made him realize that leading and working in the arts was where he wants to be. Currently, Matthew is employed within this same arts organization as an education manager who manages staff, organizes community workshops, and provides education programs to students in primary schools across the state of Queensland. Although Matthew is no longer a school principal, he maintains his connection to schools through the various education programs that his organization offers and visits schools from time to time. Matthew said his ambition is to become a general manager of a major performing arts company.

Matthew reflected that a point of commonality between his current position and that of his work as a principal is that both jobs involve working closely with and leading people. In the school context, it was teachers and groundstaff, while the staff he leads in the arts organization are mainly artists. The challenge back then was to lead teachers who were older and more experienced than he was. He said the challenge now is to lead artists who have skill sets that he does not have. A key point of difference between the two contexts (schools and the arts organization) is the latter affords greater opportunity for creativity, flexibility and responsiveness, while the former is a structured affair. After catching up with a former school colleague, it reinforced to Matthew how the system saps it out of you. His colleague said to Matthew, "you're pretty lucky to have a job that gives you goose bumps every day." Matthew agrees and said how working in the arts is a lifestyle decision.

It was through training and practice that Matthew developed competence as a school leader. He said he developed through trial and error, learning on the job and through mistakes. One of the important things he learned early in his career was to approach others and always ask for assistance. Because he was located in a rural school where the nearest school was over 150 km away, he learned to pick up the phone and use it. Reflecting on his current position, he regretted that early in the job, he did not ask for help as he was scared of looking foolish and asking a silly question. He said he is more confident in the position now and sees himself as "an education leader in the arts."

Matthew is keen to find a mentor and mentioned how important it is in the fickle world of the arts to know people. At the time of the interview he had applied to participate in a special Australian-based week-long residency program concerned with arts leadership. This program provides mentors for its participants. In his current job, Matthew commented that there are only four other people who hold a similar position in Australia and because of the nature of the industry he did not think it would be possible to contact these people for advice and guidance. However, he made contact with others occupying a similar job to himself in the United Kingdom and United States and spent a day with a person from a company in each country to share and learn more about leading arts-based organizations. Unlike managers of other arts-based companies, Matthew has an education/teaching background.

Matthew reflected on himself as a leader in both contexts. In the schooling context, he was principal for 3.5 years and this experience was based in small schools. He acknowledged that while he developed quickly over that time he had much more to learn. He noted that as a principal he was more of a manager than a leader, but after a while he was able to lead rather than maintain the status quo. His current job provides him with the scope to be more of a creative leader who takes risks. For instance, he said how important it is to be willing to let go of concerns of failure and how you cannot be a creative leader in the arts unless you are willing to make mistakes. Matthew has great respect for artists in the field and is inspired by the artists he employs who do not always know when their next job is coming yet their passion for their work is ever present.

A critical incident and turning point for Matthew during his time in the principalship took place when he attended a principal conference that attracted over 500 principals across the state of Queensland. The Minister of Education was due to give a presentation at the conference at a particular time but was running late because of flight delays. One of the convenors of the conference was keen to pass the time until the minister arrived and approached Matthew to come on stage and sing a song. This convenor had seen Matthew sing karaoke some six months before (at a pub at the end of a principals' conference) and thought it might be entertaining. Matthew agreed to do it and later received much praise from other principals. One principal said that he showed "passion by making a fool of himself." However, Matthew said it showed a willingness to have a go and take a risk.

Another critical incident that helped Matthew grow as a leader in the context of his current position concerned work he carried out for an under-privileged Aboriginal community in Queensland. The idea was that he and his team would work with the community not only to improve attendance rates of children but also to help them develop an interest in and deep appreciation of the arts. As it turned out, not one child was willing to perform. Matthew acknowledged a lack of cultural awareness on his part helped to explain the limited participation of the children. Subsequent visits to the school (and the employment of an Aboriginal artist to support the program) have made this program very effective. For instance, some 45 children performed in the program three years after the first program. A key learning for Matthew from this experience was "to ask those in the know and ask what to do."

Matthew referred to the members of his current team within the arts organization. While three of these members are senior to him, there is no sense of hierarchy in how the team works. Matthew noted that all members respect each other and their position and negotiation is the main way in which the team operates. He said that an important skill leaders demonstrate is to allow input from others and give credit where it is due. Thus, a true leader is seen to channel the strengths of everyone to achieve a positive outcome. Matthew lamented that there was not a chance to work this way when he was principal in small schools. In the broader communities in which he worked as a principal, he was often the only person with a higher education background and was looked upon as *the* "community leader."

Arts organizations like schools have not been exempt from financial cutbacks and have been expected to operate within tight fiscal constraints. Matthew commented on an arts director in Australia who moved his organization away from artistic integrity towards commercialization. Such a move comes at a cost.

TABLE 6.2 Assessment of Matthew as a connoisseur against the 10 dimensions of connoisseurship

Name of connoisseur: Matthew (Stage 3)	
Dimension of connoisseurship	Assessment of the strength of the dimension
Knowledgeable perception	Strong
Experience	Strong
Competence	Strong
Framing	Strong
Desire	Strong
Understanding of practice	Strong
Aesthetic vision	Strong
Cultural awareness and reflexivity	Strong
Discipline	Strong
Identity	Strong

We consider Matthew is a connoisseur of leadership performance and strong on all dimensions (see Table 6.2). Matthew is one of the strongest Australian leaders we interviewed in our study on cultural awareness. He exhibited a clear sense of personal identity and a desire to excel. Time after time in the interview he gave examples which exhibited an awareness of gradations and differentiations which were the "discerning eye" of the connoisseur. He also demonstrated "tacit knowledge" quite beyond the formal experience of his short time as a school principal. He is in Stage 3.

Portrait 3: Tanya, Veteran Elementary Magnet School Principal

Tanya is a veteran elementary magnet public school principal in a large suburban school system. A magnet school is one with a theme and attendance is voluntary and open to parents who want to enroll their children in a school centered around that theme. Her school has an outstanding reputation as a warm and caring place with excellent parental rapport. But it was not that way when Tanya arrived eight years ago.

Tanya came to her magnet school (hereinafter referred to as Magnolia Elementary School) following a principal who had been fired. This principal had barricaded herself in her office behind a huge desk. Her use of spatial relationships clearly communicated to staff, parents and others she did not seek any kind of personal relationship with them. She was cold and standoffish. Her door was almost always closed and there was no window in it.

Tanya had been an assistant principal and a principal for 10 years prior to coming to Magnolia. The environment she left and the one she entered were stark contrasts. She used adjectives to describe her initial entry to Magnolia as "dark, wounded" and trying to get a reaction to anything was like administering CPR. She recalled, "Where I found life I grabbed it and nurtured it. I looked for any chance to draw on the strengths of the staff." She mentioned that she found a teacher of French who displayed leadership skills and a passion for the school. Though she was only beginning to imagine transitioning to a leadership role, this teacher needed someone to believe in and responded positively to Tanya's belief in her. Tanya held on tight and formed a collegial and collaborative relationship with this young leader and anyone else who was open to change.

She recalled her all-out efforts to change the culture at Magnolia, remarking, "When I got here I was disciplined about it, setting a tone. Every single time you interact with others, you are putting yourself out there. Every single time you do that. That is contributing to the definition of the school." She changed the furniture in the principal's office and had a window installed in her door. She got rid of the massive desk and obtained a smaller one along with a conference table and chairs. She rearranged the room so that parents and teachers could easily make eye contact with her as they passed by, easing accessibility. She paused and considered this change, saying, "The public perception of you is everything. You are either working to rewrite what their perception of you is or you are reifying what is."

As the culture of the school changed she had teachers come to her office and told her what a difference it was to work at the school than before. She paused and said, "When people say they love working here that matters to me."

Tanya's examination of herself indicated that she has solid "people skills" and that she has learned how to frame and reframe problems. "I do have a sense of how to word something. The ability to say what needs to be said, to change the wording to create a different effect." Tanya thought about the pressures upon principals today:

> It seems now that everything we hear about people is what they are not doing. We need to send this person to the behavior workshop. It's all about bearing down on people for what they are not doing instead of tapping into their strengths.

Tanya looks in the classroom to see if her teachers still have that "thrill" with teaching and, if not, "figure out what's missing. If people are important we can figure it out. If you're not happy we can figure out why. Teaching is the hardest job there is."

Tanya credits her passion for nurturing to her own childhood. She was the daughter of teenage parents. Her father was 19 and her mother was 17. They divorced early and Tanya recalls being chronically short of money and living in an extremely volatile home environment. Both of her parents went through a number of failed relationships but they both were hard workers. She credits her work ethic to that example. But her need for a warm and nurturing home was marked by its absence more than anything else. She remembers having the home lights turned off because bills were not paid and a variety of shady characters she encountered in her parents' friends and relationships. Her father died very young at 48 by committing suicide (Tanya is now 47). Her mother has had a long history of depression and multiple suicide attempts, one resulting in a long-term stay at a residential treatment facility. This experience has given her a passion for creating a nurturing and protective environment at Magnolia and explaining to her staff how some of their children are suffering and require greater compassion and caring. This early period of her life also prompted her to develop her intuitive skills about people, something which she feels is one of her strengths as a school leader and which is also a requisite for a leader of a school that must attract enough enrollment to stay viable in a competitive environment.

Tanya is single and she reflects upon the fact that she is not likely to have children of her own. She is wistful about that, saying that "When I see some people put pictures of their kids on Facebook with their backpacks on ready for school it does have an effect on me." She sees her "kids" as administrative interns she has mentored and them getting jobs themselves as educational leaders in their own schools as her contribution.

Tanya is also a school site leader who can battle central system fads and mandates if necessary. She explained that her school district had adopted a packaged literature program and decreed that it would be used by all teachers in the system. Tanya had an outstanding teacher whose scholarship and skills were far superior to the adopted books and teaching methods. Tanya would not force this teacher to change to the adopted program, saying that if she did she would lose an outstanding teacher whose skill level surpassed the level of competence required to implement the district program. Then, at principal meetings, some principals were given certificates for achieving high "fidelity checks" and insuring that the district program was being implemented in their schools. Tanya's choice was to support her teachers and their judgments, especially if they were getting the same or better results than the district's program.

While Tanya has other school leaders she admires, especially a colleague principal who has been an elementary, middle school and high school principal and still has "the heart of leader," she worries about her own continuing passion for her work at Magnolia. Everything is running very smoothly. Teachers transfer into her school to be part of its ethos and work with her and become part of the faculty. While Tanya confesses she has grown enormously in her emotional skills and her ability to handle tough human interpersonal matters, she muses, "Now I'm a bit slower to respond to some questions. Now my answer to some questions is, I'd like to think about that." Tanya has made other changes as well. When asked about her public face she commented:

> I don't go in on the social stuff anymore (with the staff). I might go to the Christmas party. I still exercise every day. I see a therapist from time to time. When they need me I can be strong for them. Today people get more from me than they did 17 years ago.

As she thought her tenure as principal at Magnolia, Tanya reflected on it, saying:

> I feel good where I am. I'm grateful for where I am. I'm proud of what we did. Everything is kind of good. But what have I really done? I need to figure out how to light the fire again, or I need to go where that may be. The longer I stay here the more I lose my confidence. Other leaders had that dazzle point. It was successful but nobody is going to write a movie about it.

TABLE 6.3 Assessment of Tanya as a connoisseur against the 10 dimensions of connoisseurship

Name of connoisseur: Tanya (Stage 3)	
Dimension of connoisseurship	Assessment of the strength of the dimension
Knowledgeable perception	Strong
Experience	Strong
Competence	Strong
Framing	Strong
Desire	Strong
Understanding of practice	Strong
Aesthetic vision	Not applicable
Cultural awareness and reflexivity	Strong
Discipline	Strong
Identity	Strong

When Tanya was asked what kind of advice she would give to someone considering educational leadership today she nodded, smiled and leaned forward in her chair, "Hang on. It's a wild ride. It's crazy how it evolved. If it's not working hang on. You're going to grow."

We see that Tanya is strong on nine of the 10 dimensions of connoisseurship of leadership performance (and not applicable on aesthetic vision) (see Table 6.3). She is in Stage 3. Over many years as an experienced school principal and assistant principal, she has worked very hard to develop a supportive, nurturing and learning focused school where both children and staff are happy and working well. Her excellent communication and interpersonal skills have enabled her to build solid collaborative relationships with staff and to win the trust and support of her school community. While she was able to reflect on her own and the school's achievements, she was acutely aware that the time was quickly approaching when she would need to leave the school and seek out new challenges.

Portrait 4: Templeton, School Superintendent

Templeton is a middle-aged African American school superintendent. While outwardly appearing confident, jovial and engaging, he described himself as "a painful introvert" which he learned to mask. Templeton thought about it and remarked, "I know that code switching is an important part of what I do. I have to size up situations quickly and determine what hat I have to wear." Templeton was an only child raised by his mother with his grandmother a constant contributor to his value system in his formative years. He reflected that while he always wanted to be an educator (at one time he toyed with law, however) his own school years were not marked by any academic brilliance. He did well enough in the school subjects he enjoyed most, but just "got by" in others. However, he did score above average on most standardized tests.

Templeton became a middle school language arts teacher and later a high school English teacher. His principal encouraged him to pursue a master's degree in school administration and he became an assistant principal in a split assignment between an elementary and a high school. Reflecting on this first position and his feelings about it, Templeton commented, "Your scope is so small. You go in thinking you can change the world right away. What I learned is it's not that easy." He resented this first assignment but later admitted it provided him with experience at two job levels simultaneously. He later became a high school principal and then earned a promotion into the central administration, ultimately becoming a school superintendent in seven years while also earning his doctorate.

When interviewed for this book Templeton had spent 16 years in school administration. He paid his dues. He thought back and mused:

> What I learned is that I speak less than I used to speak. I do a lot more analysis. I don't let my guard down with the wrong people. I'm careful

about what I say and how I say it because whatever you say once may be repeated. I'm wary of conversations with those who have ulterior motives. I'm more thoughtful about my position. Things used to be black and white and now I live in the land of gray. And I've learned that the higher you go the smaller my circle. I'm a lot more careful of who I befriend. As I was climbing anyone could mentor me. Now I want people who can help me in specific aspects of what I'm doing. I'm a lot more cautious because the funnel is smaller. There's a lot of stress in my position.

As a minority male Templeton is "always concerned with the achievement gap" and other social justice issues. His work orientation is grounded in trying to eliminate disparities with minorities and students who have been marginalized. Thinking back he admitted he was not always encouraged to move in an upward direction when he was at school and that forced him as a school administrator to ensure that those who want a chance get one. "I always pull for the underdog. I want them (the students) to feel satisfied once they leave school."

From the position of the superintendent Templeton noticed that academic success for students looked different. His role of ensuring academic achievement has meant he has to navigate his Board of Education and mitigate some of the big issues that could torpedo his career and his legitimacy. He paused and smiled, "Much of what I've accomplished is not because I'm brilliant. It's my work ethic and my competence is in being able to legitimize my work and have credibility with the folks I serve."

Templeton admires leaders who can pull people together, "take folks from different perspectives, ideologies and reach a middle ground." He has been able to connect with people who have been overlooked. In describing metaphors which would apply to himself, Templeton paused,

> I'm like an onion. I have multiple layers. I'm complex. I can project and be a mirror. I'm a situational leader who can adapt and meet the needs at hand. Sometimes I make the decision and other times I say these are the options and let's talk about it.

When asked how he sized up other leaders and their competence Templeton said:

> I watch leaders in their element. The principals don't come to my office, I go to their schools. I want them to walk me around their schools and tell me what they see in the classrooms. I want people who can adapt and be multi-dimensional. I want them to be abreast of the research and strategies for improving outcomes for students.

He also explained that if every time he called a school the principal always answered the phone, then he knew they were not out in their buildings. This was a very worrisome sign for him as it indicated there was a lack of leadership.

Templeton took the converse position in describing a school and a school leader who was incompetent. He observed that a poor leader was simply working in "unorganized chaos" (he approved of organized chaos). He noted that there would also be a lack of collaboration with the faculty and staff and a culture that came across as toxic. Whereas a competent leader was one who kept his/her community actively connected to the school and the principal's vision, the incompetent principal saw his/her community as one to be manipulated and kept at bay.

When asked about the public aspect of his job, Templeton reflected that he didn't realize until he was in the seat of superintendent how political the superintendent's position really was. In former roles he had been isolated and insulated from this public aspect of the job. In reality, he said, "I'm the CEO of the largest employer in the area."

Near the conclusion of the interview Templeton paused,

> I'm a cheerleader for the underdog. It is the responsibility of educators that marginalized groups are looked after and elevated. I was the little black boy from the housing projects. I was discouraged from applying for fellowships. Social justice is my number one theoretical lens. I talk to our leaders and ask questions all the time.

An example of Templeton's concern and his decision on a seemingly trivial matter was the superintendent's responsibility to call a snow day, that is to cancel school because of weather. On a particularly volatile day, Templeton called for a delay in school opening rather than be closed and then sent the students home with early dismissal. When questioned about this apparently contradictory decision (because if he had sent students home early anyway, why was school not closed altogether?), Templeton answered his critics by saying that for some of his children, school was the only warm place they would have that day and the only place where they could have a meal. Without that they would have been confined in a cold location with nothing to eat. He silenced his critics with his compassion.

Templeton made meaning of his work by commenting:

> It's based solely on outputs. It's the benefits to children. Nothing excites me more than to hear a former student talk to me about something which was born out of the vision I generated, when they say I did what I did because of you. Students have an uncanny ability to tell the truth.

TABLE 6.4 Assessment of Templeton as a connoisseur against the 10 dimensions of connoisseurship

Name of connoisseur: Templeton (Stage 3)	
Dimension of connoisseurship	Assessment of the strength of the dimension
Knowledgeable perception	Strong
Experience	Strong
Competence	Strong
Framing	Strong
Desire	Strong/exceptional
Understanding of practice	Strong
Aesthetic vision	Strong
Cultural awareness and reflexivity	Strong/exceptional
Discipline	Strong
Identity	Strong/exceptional

Here is how Templeton was rated by us in this interaction (see Table 6.4). We rated him at Stage 3, strong on seven dimensions and strong/exceptional on three dimensions. He is clearly moving into Stage 4. Templeton was an experienced school administrator. Because he was an introvert he had been prompted to be extremely aware of his own feelings and perceptions about his job and about himself. He had overcome initial shyness and learned to mask his own sense of loneliness. He learned early, as many successful African Americans do, how to "code switch" to fit in and swim in the mainstream without losing his personal identity. He clearly brought his compassion and his dedication to the plight of minority children to his job and to the decisions he made in the role of superintendent. He was unusually sensitive, perceptive and resilient. He was a "quick study" not mired in any ideology that made him blind to situational leadership requirements. He was well on the road to become a leader connoisseur.

Portrait 5: Julia, Educational Consultant

Julia is a middle-aged Native American educational consultant. She had a long career in the field, beginning as a special education teacher, serving as a principal then an administrator in the State Department of Education, worked with a middle-sized national consulting firm and recently launched on her own consulting company. Her tribe is one of the dominant Indian groups in her state, with a long history of land cultivation and farming.

Julia's childhood was diversified. Her mother's side of the family were land owners. Her father's side were sharecroppers. To help with the family's farming Julia's mother dropped out of school in the tenth grade. But she retained a passion for education which she instilled in Julia insisting that she attend college. The other aspect of Julia's childhood was the family's focus on Christianity and church affairs and the establishment of Native American churches in adjacent counties.

Julia's father was a gifted student. He graduated class Valedictorian of his high school and money was raised for him to attend college. But when he got there he was only given two options because he was an Indian. He could be a teacher or a farmer. Everything else was closed to him. As a result he left college and began driving an ice cream truck. He worked his way to up to top levels of management and became a respected citizen of his community. Julia's parents were divorced fairly early in her life.

Julia was the first grandchild to attend college. Because her father had experienced segregated schools he did not want his children to have to attend them as well. He moved the family to a white neighborhood where Julia was at times the only Native American student in her classes. She was exposed to Native Americans and Native American culture on the weekends, however. Later her family moved back to a Native American community where Julia attended the once segregated school that her father attended. Although schools were desegregated, most students in attendance were from the local community and therefore most of the students were Indians. Here she was called a "white Indian" and she remembered having the same book in the ninth grade she had had at the white school she attended in the fifth–sixth grade. She did not realize at the time that white schools passed on their used textbooks to Indian schools when they were no longer deemed good enough for them to use. Julia later reminisced that the discrepancy between white schools and Indian schools marked her insights into how to navigate both worlds which has become her life story and her work.

Julia's selection of teaching special education students began when she began playing with her mother's youngest sister who had an intellectual disability. Julia remembered teaching her how to count and read. This also created within her a passion to help those in need, something which has always been strong within her orientation to work and to education. She got her first taste of prejudice when her former white teacher was involuntarily transferred to her school where she was a teacher. She observed that her former teacher treated Indian students as inferior and less intellectually able, something she had not experienced before when she was a student in this teacher's class where the students were majority white.

Reflecting on her growth as a leader she indicated that maturity is evolutionary. "We are all gifted with certain strengths," she told us, "as we grow older those areas mature. Age brings wisdom." When asked about her own abilities as a leader she explained:

One of my strengths is being able to connect and interact with people no matter where they came from. I felt comfortable in an all white world, the native world and in between. I was put in front of groups to bring folks together.

She recalled having this ability at a young age in 4-H (a national youth agricultural and farming group for young people) when she was seven or eight. The leader of her 4-H group observed her bringing people together and empowering others. While she recognizes her own growth is on a continuum, she indicated there really was no end to it. She emphasized the importance of being challenged to step outside of her comfort zone. It was important for her to be continually challenged in order to keep growing. She recalled many instances where because of circumstances on the job and the guidance and friendship of significant others in her professional life, she was pushed to mature:

I've been thrown into situations where I had to leverage the strengths I had. I was totally terrified of the first time I had to speak to the state board of education. I received some coaching from others and then each time I spoke it got easier.

Julia reflected much about the fact that leadership is directly connected to a person's core identity. "Leadership is leadership of self," she observed. "It's your maturity and your integrity. You have to become confident in who you are. You have to have empathy. It's more than just skills." Her conceptual framework for leadership, not surprisingly, was that leading one's self is integral to leading others. She said:

It's bringing diverse differences together and finding that common need and bringing unity. That piece falls into people leadership, having compassion, being able to see outside of where I walk in my own moccasins. I can read a situation and understand what people are thinking and approach it accordingly. If all you have are the skills, you are just doing that, you are not really leading.

When Julia encounters problems or moral dilemmas:

I go back to self. I re-examine every situation where something has been questioned. I may not have made a good decision and I go back to self. I weigh it against my values and about what is right and what is appropriate. If it aligns with my core beliefs I'm good with that decision.

In her career she admits to being a perfectionist. Her work is never good enough. She says her husband says she goes to extremes on this. Making a difference with those decisions and understanding its impact sustains her. "If I can sleep at night I've made a good decision," she added, "especially if it's been made for the better of the community."

Julia does recall having some significant professional mentors. Her first principal was especially important as he enabled her to understand the importance of consistency and the necessity of having structures for discipline in place. She also learned a great deal about forming teams, about being able to assess where people are at and what is meant by empowering others. She described herself as a servant leader.

When queried as to how she knew if a school was led by a competent leader, Julia responded:

> It doesn't take long for you to assess if it's an effective school. The leader creates the culture, you feel that culture. There has to be a sense of purpose, emotional intelligence and from that you derive their motives. They have to know how to listen and communicate well. If a school is unfocused it can't be led well.

She reiterated a common theme, "You can't lead others unless you can lead yourself. Otherwise the school is a ship without a rudder."

Julia's theoretical base for her work involved thinking about three important circles. At the core is her own identity. The outer circles or layers are the external events and the challenges she has faced. "Maybe it's all interchangeable," she mused, "You can't separate all those things because it's all integrated." When prodded to think about her own evolution Julia found it hard to trace. But she observed that a key crossing for her occurred in 2001 when her mother was killed in a car accident. "She was at the core foundation of my being and I had to look to self. I went into a group of other leaders that became a personal journey. They were diverse around religion, sexuality, ethnic origin." She had never been put in a group like that before. She crossed the threshold. "I internalized it because I was on my own. It was a turning point. It was about self."

Based on our interview with Julia, we deem her to be strong on seven of the 10 dimensions and strong/exceptional on three: "understanding of practice," "cultural awareness and reflexivity" and "identity," and in Stage 3 (see Table 6.5). Julia is a very experienced and competent educator, having been a special education teacher, school principal, system administrator and now consultant where she provides high level advice and support to schools and school systems. As a Native American Indian, Julia spoke of her ability to walk and work across different worlds: the white world, the Native American world, and the world in between. Moreover, she recognized how important it is for leaders to find unity and common ground when they work with people from diverse communities. In addition to her sharpened sense of cultural awareness, she had a clear view of herself as a person and a leader; not only her strengths and limitations, but also the centrality of knowing and leading oneself if one is to be able to lead others.

TABLE 6.5 Assessment of Julia as a connoisseur against the 10 dimensions of connoisseurship

Name of connoisseur: Julia (Stage 3)	
Dimension of connoisseurship	Assessment of the strength of the dimension
Knowledgeable perception	Strong
Experience	Strong
Competence	Strong
Framing	Strong
Desire	Strong
Understanding of practice	Strong/exceptional
Aesthetic vision	Strong
Cultural awareness and reflexivity	Strong/exceptional
Discipline	Strong
Identity	Strong/exceptional

Portrait 6: Donovan, New Elementary School Principal

While a career teacher and school administrator, Donovan is enjoying the first four months of a principalship in a rural area in the American South. He could have bypassed being a principal (called a head teacher in many parts of the world), but being in charge of a school was always something he wanted to do. The school he now leads has over 77% on free and reduced lunch which is a measure of the poverty level of students that attend. A large number of his students do not speak English. Many are from Mexico and an unknown number are from families where the parents are undocumented adults (illegal immigrants).

Donovan grew up in a household in which his mother was a kindergarten teacher and his father a mathematics professor at a nearby state public university. He has four older sisters. His regular church attendance as a youngster and his mother's involvement with the Civil Rights Movement took him into homes of African Americans where he was a witness to extreme deprivation and poverty first-hand. It made a lasting impression on him. He has a lot of memories about encountering extreme levels of poverty as a teenager.

From an early age he was a "defender of the underdog" and recalled "fights in high school where he was protecting a friend being picked on." He covets being a "voice for the voiceless" and sees his role at his school as doing that since the number of undocumented parents deprives them of any rights of citizenship and other perquisites of being legal.

Admitting he was not a serious student in school until college, he finally found something that ignited his passion which was the study of history and economics and he got serious about academics for the first time. He drove a school bus for 10 years and learned that he loved working with children. When he was turned down for admission to the prestigious Johns Hopkins University in Maryland he determined to go into teaching, eventually going so far as to earn a master's degree in ESL (English as a Second Language). He traveled to the Czech Republic and taught at university level there, moving back to the United States to teach ESL at two high schools and then going to work for the local diocese educating future priests. Later he worked with migrant students, some of whom did not read beyond the fifth grade level and were already 17 years old. This was challenging but eventually he moved up the career ladder and into a central office administrative role as director of ESL for a large school district.

Central office administrative work was not where his heart was and so he applied for an assistant principal's position so he could put in his time and become a principal. He was successful within less than two years and now finds himself with a huge instructional challenge in a rural school which by state standards is rated very low in performance on the state metrics which include student scores on standardized tests.

Donovan followed a long-term principal who had deep roots in the community, but had drifted in its focus when that leader was transferred to another school. He sees his first task as bringing all the teachers and staff back into the fold and doing it in a collaborative way. At first he admitted he was uncomfortable delegating tasks, but eventually he had no choice as the job grew ever larger. He confessed that early on he thought he could do it all and knew it all. But the longer he toiled the more he realized that "you have to get people around you who shore up your weaknesses and build on your strengths."

Donovan also learned that in making decisions some people are not going to be happy and that pertains even if the leader doesn't make a decision. "You can disturb people making a decision," he mused, but that also "brings comfort. People like to know someone is in charge."

Donovan was asked about how he thought about the establishment of competence as a leader. He responded that competence was

> something that takes a long time to earn and is quick to lose. You demon-
> strate it day after day. You can show competence in one thing, incom-
> petence in another. It's a totality. When competence is really good it becomes
> excellence. It's an analytical process.

When queried about how he made decisions as to whether a school was good or not, Donovan thought about it and remarked:

> There's something to be said about how you are greeted and how you are
> welcomed, and things you see as you go through classes. It's also the level

of student engagement. It's student talk versus teacher talk. I like to see a lot of student talk that is focused.

When Donovan paused to think about the challenges of the politics of the principalship he said, "You have to develop relationships with central office. They have to cover your back. Your job is to be an advocate for your school and your community. Politics do matter."

As for the theoretical base for his job Donovan observed that his school community was one that was critical, especially with so many parents who were undocumented:

> You know so many don't have the social capital as the middle class that you have to improve school from the outside. You have to have the community involved. We have a dual language school and you have to have the support of the home. An early childhood program is essential. Words only go so far with parents. What you have to have is a total body of work on which they can judge you.

When asked how he has been able to get parents involved in the school, Donovan said flatly, "You have to feed them. If you feed them they will come out."

Donovan recalled he had had several fine mentors in the past. One former mentor taught him that "details matter. You can skate along with the big picture but sooner or later the details will get you." Another mentor taught him the value of silence. In conferences she would simply listen and eventually people kept talking to fill in the silence and revealed their agendas. Finally Donovan said:

> My Dad was an incredibly ethical person. He always did the right thing in his mind. I always respected him. He taught me that hard work and curiosity can carry you a long way because while having a high IQ is good, curiosity means you are going to continue to learn.

Then he paused and remarked, "As a principal you are learning at twice the normal speed."

Donovan's rating on the 10 dimensions of connoisseurship of leadership performance were strong on six dimensions and moderate on four; he was just beginning his career as a principal and his field of vision was beginning to be differentiated (see Table 6.6). He was beginning to define his own competence and move confidently into his new role and for this reason we placed him in Stage 2. He exhibited a growing understanding of the politics of leadership and the criticality of connecting with his school community. He had a deep understanding of and commitment to social justice stemming from his early

TABLE 6.6 Assessment of Donovan as a connoisseur against the 10 dimensions of connoisseurship

Name of connoisseur: Donovan (Stage 2)	
Dimension of connoisseurship	*Assessment of the strength of the dimension*
Knowledgeable perception	Strong
Experience	Moderate
Competence	Moderate
Framing	Strong
Desire	Strong
Understanding of practice	Moderate
Aesthetic vision	Moderate
Cultural awareness and reflexivity	Strong
Discipline	Strong
Identity	Strong

childhood experiences with his mother in the Civil Rights Movement. He was perfectly matched to the clientele of his school, a segment of society which lived on the margins and shadows as illegal immigrants. He spoke passable Spanish and could communicate with students and parents.

Summary

This chapter presented six portraits of educational leaders we deemed to be connoisseurs based on our 10 dimensions, including knowledgeable perception, experience, competence, framing, desire, understanding of practice, aesthetic vision, cultural awareness and reflexivity, discipline and identity. While each of the individuals had different life experiences, competence in different fields and disciplines, and strengths in particular areas of practice, common to all of them was a "discerning eye" that enabled them to make sense of themselves, their professional practice, and the broader aesthetic context.

IMPLICATIONS FOR POLICY AND PRACTICE

The Inward Journey of an Educational Leader is More Important Than the External Career Ladder Advancement to Attain Connoisseurship

Many educational leaders focus rather exclusively on bureaucratic advancement in the hierarchy of their school systems. If they are conscious of their own internal development it is usually in relation to this advancement, that is, the development of internal differentiation is seen as a necessary factor in the attainment of external recognition. The development of connoisseurship reverses this process. To attain connoisseurship the emphasis is placed first on sculpting the internal self by engaging in conscious shaping activities and these are not connected necessarily to role advancement in the administrative hierarchy. The development of strong internal competence and the capability of engaging in finer and finer grain judgments regarding practice is not dependent on bureaucratic role advancement, but is rather independent of it.

Key Chapter Ideas

- ### Connoisseurship is a Journey Into the Self

The six portraits of educational leaders in both Australia and America clearly reveal that the advancement of competence supporting connoisseurship is a journey into self. It is a journey sometimes based on failure and it is deeply reflective and highly idiosyncratic in nature. The regulator of connoisseurship is the motivation, discipline and willpower of the leader and how the leader compels himself/herself to continually re-examine their own performance in light of feedback from persons in their immediate work environment.

References

Henri, R. (2007). *The art spirit*. New York: Basic Books.

7

CONNOISSEURSHIP VS. CORPORATE MANAGERIALISM

If you want to understand the sciences and . . . by 'understanding the sciences' I mean both the context of discovery and the context of justification—then you have to turn to the arts and the humanities, i.e., you have to abandon these artificial classifications most philosophies and 'rational accounts' are full of. A really comprehensive world view absolutely cannot do without the poets.

(Paul Feyerabend, 1991, p. 148)

WHAT THIS CHAPTER IS ABOUT

This chapter draws upon the biographical and archival data gathered on connoisseurs from a variety of fields, such as the arts, history and leadership (Chapters 1–2) and in international educational contexts before the 21st Century (Chapter 3). It then distills the information learned in the interviews of school leaders in Australia and America (Chapters 4–6) and compares it to the dominant management model in schools today, a derivative approach called *managerialism* (Gunter & Thompson, 2010). The main focus of managerialism is efficiency, that is, cost containment and/or reduction. To attain low costs the role of management is rooted in top-down authority and a penchant for total control of the work and the worker. Dissent in any form is ruthlessly suppressed or eliminated. One result has today been called the rise of "ed-bizspeak," a lingo that involves a penchant for quantification and the use of numbers "without social conscience" (Emery & Ohanian, 2004, p. 13).

Introduction

An alternative vision to the conceptualization of the field of educational adminis-tration/leadership is long overdue (Bolton & English, 2010; Culbertson, 1988; Ehrich & English, 2012, 2013; English, 1994, 2008; English & Papa, 2009; Foster, 1986; Hodgkinson, 1996). Leadership connoisseurship offers one promising con-ceptual alternative to this problem. Such an approach does not erase the long affiliation with the dominant behavioral social science methods that remain firmly entrenched in our texts and research traditions, but rather seeks to restore to that tradition much older and more humanistic perspectives anchored in the aesthetic, humanistic and emotional dimensions of human thought and action. Depending upon how this perspective is implemented such a view may not be radical, but rather restorative since before the establishment of educational administration in the United States in colleges of education at the beginning of the 20th Century, formal studies exploring leadership were anchored in the arts, humanities, theology and religion before school administration was considered "scientific" (Culbertson, 1988; English, 1994, 2008). If, however, the idea is to completely re-order the field around a new locus, then it may be considered radical in that context.

Similarly, it is instructive to note that in the early 1980s, a group of lead-ing scholars in public administration gathered together in Blacksburg, Virginia, and issued *The Blacksburg Manifesto*. They contended that the original founding of their field represented "a misapplication of the tenets of managerial or adminis-trative science onto government" (Evans & Wamsley, 2007, p. 200). These fellow academics called for a reconceptualization of the policy process to be located in the public interest, as opposed to the idea of privatization and marketization advanced in business administration. The writers of *The Blacksburg Manifesto* viewed public administration

> as a calling to service of one's fellow citizens—a moral enterprise [embracing an] empowered citizenry as partners in the governance process [and] agential leaders whose authority is derived from their civic virtue, their sense of vocation, and their experience in administration.
>
> (Evans & Wamsley, 2007, p. 200)

A similar reconceptualization is advocated in this chapter.

A Contrast Between Connoisseurship and Corporate Managerialism

In order to clarify the dimensions of connoisseurship and how they pose an alternative to the dominant "managerialist" mindset of the field of educational leadership today, we have identified 20 dimensions that attempt to highlight our understanding of the significant focal points of difference. These focal points have been derived from our interview data, the wider academic literature and research, and popular pieces of opinion which are cited in previous chapters of this book. While it is probably the case that ideologically "pure" personifications of either perspective exist only in the abstract and real persons may have some of the perspectives of both categories, we believe that by posing them as clear oppositional points greater clarity can be gained in understanding the differences between them. The purpose of the contrast is thus primarily heuristic.

The tenets of managerialism are very real and pervasive, not only in the United States but also in the United Kingdom, Canada, parts of Europe and Australia (Gunter, 2002). Managerialism is positioned within a designated socio-political space that is fluid and dynamic, a social field where actors, agencies and groups compete for legitimacy and power in a bid to extend their own agenda, to curtail or subdue agendas they deem threatening, and to extend their influence (Bourdieu & Wacquant, 1992). It is within this concept of a field that managerialism rooted in rational choice theory has been implemented rather ruthlessly. Clarke, Cochrane and McLaughlin (1994) paint a picture of the struggle:

> Managerialization constitutes the means through which the structure and culture of public services are being recast. In doing so it seeks to introduce new orientations, remodels existing relations of power and affects how and where social policy choices are made.
>
> (p. 4)

Leaders embodying managerialism need no special sensitivities, talents nor aesthetic sensibilities to run schools. They don't have to be connoisseurs because connoisseurship is not required or valued in this workplace. What is valued is conformity and adherence to the marketplace and its dynamics based on rational calculation and Simon's (1947) "economic man," a vision of human decision-making that eliminates human subjectivity and emotion in the pursuit of an ideology masquerading as science.

Simon (1947) put it bluntly:

> Procedures are termed "good" when they are conducive to the attainment of specified objectives, "bad" when they are not conducive to such attainment. That they are, or are not, so conducive is purely a matter of fact, and it is this factual element which makes up the real substance of an administrative science . . . To illustrate: In the realm of economics, the proposition "Alternative A is *good*" may be translated into two propositions, one of them ethical, the other factual: "Alternative A will lead to maximum profit." "To maximize profit is good." The first of these two sentences has no ethical content, and is a sentence of the practical science of business. The second sentence is an ethical imperative, and has no place in any science.
>
> (pp. 249–250)

The elimination of ethics occurs when science is defined by Simon in purely economic terms. Bourdieu (1998) pointed out the fallacy of this argument when he wrote:

> Economics is, with a few exceptions, an abstract science based on the absolutely unjustifiable separation between the economic and the social which defines economism. This separation is the source of the failure of any policy that has no other end than to safeguard "economic order and stability," the new absolute [which is] a failure to which the political blindness of some is leading us and of which we are all the victims.
>
> (p. 51)

No more poignant reminder of Bourdieu's (1998) warning occurred in 2015 when Janet Yellen, U.S. Federal Reserve Chairwoman in a speech to the Citizens Budget Commission of New York, reminded the financial titans of Wall Street:

> It is unfortunate that I need to underscore this, but we expect the firms we oversee to follow the law and to operate in an ethical manner. Too often in recent years, bankers at large institutions have not done so, sometimes brazenly.
>
> (McGrane, 2015, p. C5)

Leadership is about enlisting persons to a common cause and that only occurs, especially in public service, because of "a willingness to subordinate immediate personal interests for both ultimate personal interest and the general good, together with a capacity of individual responsibility" (Barnard, 1938, p. 293). While intelligence is required in this enterprise, "Inspiration is necessary to inculcate the sense of unity, and to create common ideals. Emotional rather than intellectual acceptance is required" (Barnard, 1938, p. 293).

We have used the arts as a reference point in constructing an alternative view, one which we have asserted is restorative, that is, it returns and reinvigorates concepts of leadership practice so that the whole human being, rational and emotional, is fully considered in leadership discourse. Barnard (1938) underscored this restored balance when he said:

> I believe that the expansion of cooperation and the development of the individual are mutually dependent realities, and that a due proportion of balance between them is a necessary condition of human welfare. Because it is subjective with respect both to a society as a whole and to the individual, what this proportion is I believe science cannot say. It is a question for philosophy and religion.
>
> (p. 296)

TABLE 7.1 Comparison of connoisseurship model of leadership to managerialist model

Dimension	Connoisseurship model	Managerialist model
1. Highest value/ purpose of leadership	Human fulfillment	Efficiency
2. Major view of leadership	Artistic performance, a bodily experience	Economically defined on mind/body dualisms—the body is viewed as inferior
3. Enactment of leadership	Reflexivity	Measurement
4. View of ambiguity	Accepted as part of developmental process	To be eliminated to attain greater control
5. View of creativity and imagination	Organic—part of the evolution towards artfulness	Mechanistic—narrowly defined and evaluated in refinement processes
6. View of risk taking	Integral to work	Minimized, controlled
7. Approach to work	Joyful, imaginative	Routinized, standardization
8. View of competence	Workmanship pride, craft competence	Prescribed skills for standardized tasks
9. Values	Morality and ethical matters most important in communal values	Technical efficiency within role standardization
10. Power	Referent power, bonding based on enhanced competence	Legal and bureaucratic refuge
11. View of people	People are the ends of all means	People are means to ends
12. Understanding of practice	Endless possibilities, artful performance, pursuit of beauty	Best practice defined as means to the lowest cost; utilitarian based
13. Identity	Development of self and personal fulfillment beyond organizational role— becoming more human	Confined to organizational role, other aspects not considered relevant for work
14. View of change	Open to new ways of thinking and doing— openness and readiness to learn—never complacent— positive view of disruptive ideas and processes	Centered on "smooth" operations, skeptical and resistant to disruptive ideas or processes which challenge the basis of control
15. Ethics	Central to locating and defining acceptable means to ends	Defined by questions of legality and economic results

continued

TABLE 7.1 Continued

Dimension	Connoisseurship model	Managerialist model
16. Emotion and intuition	Essential to leadership and to the human condition	To be subordinated or eliminated to rational calculation
17. Cultural awareness	Expert knowledge located in context and awareness of limitations of that context	Monocultural—unaware of cultural biases
18. Framing	Multiperspectival—open to alternatives and alternative interpretation—understands limitations of framing	One system model based on unilateral forms of power and control—no understanding of limitations of framing
19. Responses to challenges or threats	Positive reaction—can negotiate new terrain because of deep knowledge of the field and its traditions	Threatened—revert to tried and true and old solutions—defenders of the orthodoxy
20. Working relationships	Providing space for individual and team contributions—respecting idiosyncratic responses	Rigidly defined as either totally individual or totally team centered, no flexibility, cannot match structure to task and human talent

We now contrast this perspective with the rational choice model of leadership which we have sought to change in conducting the study behind this book. Behind that contrast is a remark by Nolan Bushnell, a U.S. business entrepreneur who founded a famous restaurant chain:

> Business is a good game—lots of competition and a minimum of rules. You keep score with money. Fair dealing can be important in the business world . . . but fairness per se—in the sense of everyone getting his or her just desserts—rarely is. Markets are engines of efficiency, not fairness. In fact, a generous helping of greed may be good in business.
>
> (Blinder, 2012, p. A19)

The next part of the discussion contrasts the connoisseurship model to the managerialist model according to the 20 dimensions of leadership (see Table 7.1).

Dimension 1: Highest Value/Purpose of Leadership

The connoisseur of leadership views human fulfillment as the barometer of human efficacy. This purpose was reinforced by Maria Montessori whom we discussed in Chapter 3:

> The subject of our study is humanity; our purpose is to become teachers. Now, what really makes a teacher is love for the human child; for it is love that transforms the social duty of the educator into the higher consciousness of a mission.
>
> (Montessori in Montessori Australia, n.d., p. 3)

Montessori meant the extent to which one's essential humanity is affirmed and also benefits children. It is also about attaining a personal sense of achievement in the knowledge that a person has worked to his/her full capacity and that this effort has not depended on the domination or denigration of others. Therefore, a connoisseur of leadership takes a human-centered and principled approach to leadership which is not dependent on work hierarchy and superior/subordinate relationships or an underlying coercive climate based on centralized, top-down forms of authoritarian control. Human fulfillment and the development of the highest form of professional competence is the principal motivation behind connoisseurship.

In the discussion in Chapter 4 between artists and educational leaders, interview data reinforced the idea that those leaders in education are involved with the development of the full range of human capabilities and so they must also be developed in their own capacities, including recognizing the importance of emotion and creative expression. One cannot easily develop in others what one does not possess or recognize himself/herself.

Robert, an Australian seasoned principal, insisted on being able to perceive both the big picture and the details at the same time (Chapter 6) so that he could engage in meaningful conversations about change and understanding that he would not have all the answers. He lamented that definitions of good school leadership were tied to measures of performance defined by test scores. A good school in Robert's mind was a place that produced joyful children who were happy and wanted to come to school. This was also the objective of the international educational leader Tsunesaburō Makiguchi of Japan whom we studied in Chapter 3.

The managerialist model is the principal perspective of economics and for-profit business models. It is the engine of the dominant forms of managerial accountability at work in so-called "reform" initiatives proffered by the dominant neo-liberal think tanks in the United States and many governments around the world today (see Ball, 2009; Mullen, Samier, Brindley, English & Carr, 2013). To implement a managerialist model requires what has been termed "creative destruction" of all forms of monopoly on the belief that such situations inhibit a consumer from maximizing choice in a free market.

Adherents of managerialism envision schools existing in a social space where they must compete for resources and students in the arguable belief that such competition will produce the most efficient (cheapest) and effective form of education possible. The tenets of this perspective have been roundly criticized by Gunter (2002), Bottery (2004), Anderson and Pini (2011), Ravitch (2010, 2012), Kimber and Ehrich (2011), and English (2014).

The primary motive of leadership in managerialist thinking is political, that is, to create a social space where an individual can optimize economic and other life decisions without restrictions. It has little to do with ethics or humane or aesthetic perspectives outside of those that support economic and political choices. The notion of social justice, the perspective that some persons must have some restrictions placed on their choices to support others having a fuller range of choices is not considered legitimate by managerialist true believers. Theirs is a world of power and authority dominated by capital (materialist, social, cultural) in all of its forms (Bourdieu, 1999).

Dimension 2: Major View of Leadership

The perspective undergirding this dimension of connoisseurship rests on the understanding that "leadership is a type of bodily practice or performance that helps leaders to foster a capacity to read, register and feel compassion . . . [providing a] capacity for openness and learning" (Sinclair, 2005, pp. 403–404). This requires a sensitivity by leaders to spatial relationships and to the presence of others and to their own presence in the world (Ropo & Parviainen, 2001).

Tanya, an experienced American magnet school principal, recounted that in assuming leadership of a school with a troubled history of failed leadership, she took every opportunity to "draw on the strengths of the staff" (Chapter 6). She recast her office to be less foreboding and open to conversation and she worked at every exchange with teachers, students and parents to set a tone for the school that was welcoming and positive. She recalled, "When I got here I was disciplined about it, setting a tone. Every single time you interact with others, you are putting yourself out there. Every single time you do that. That is contributing to the definition of the school" (Chapter 6).

In contrast, the managerialist model rests on the familiar mind–body dualisms anchored in ancient Greek thought, but which subordinates human emotion and the so-called non-rational to a realm of secondary importance in decision-making. Specifically the body is inferior to the mind and, in early Christian thought, the seat of Satan and sin. The body is the source of corruption. In some forms the body in aesthetics is considered the source of all wisdom because it never lies. This is especially true for dance, the mother of all the arts (see Ehrich & English, 2013).

Dimension 3: Enactment of Leadership

Enactment refers to the doing of leading. It is the acting or performing of leading. The connoisseur leader is able to engage in *reflexive thinking*, which Bourdieu (1990) defines as the capacity to think about how one is thinking instead of thinking about how one has accomplished or completed designated tasks which is the managerialist ideological model. *Reflexive thinking* is meta-cognitive analysis, a step beyond being locked in the usual cognitive maps of problem solving. *Reflexive thinking* examines how problems have been conceptualized and framed. It exposes the frame itself to scrutiny and inquires what has been included and excluded in its purview.

The Australian principal Robert envisioned enactment as the ability to work around a whole range of issues and be able to sort them out simultaneously as one of seeing both the big picture and the small details of the same picture at the same time. He indicated that a significant personal learning was that he was able to adopt both a strategic and tactical view by observing the overall activity but at the same time focus on the smallest detail. This moving in and out of the big picture to the minute details of the event was instructive in his understandings. He described this process as being in the trenches but also ensuring you can see the whole field.

Managerialist model enactors rarely ever question the basis of their own assumptions and limitations. Many are theory averse and merely "practicing practice" instead of being consciously aware of any larger narrative that defines their efforts and being able to relate one to the other. It can be argued that without this capacity practice is not going to be improved or changed significantly. Shils (1968) said it succinctly, "no great ideology has ever regarded the disciplined pursuit of truth . . . as part of its obligations" (p. 73).

Dimension 4: View of Ambiguity

Ambiguity refers to the idea that there is no one answer to any problem and there can be multiple meanings or intentions. Eisner (2002) made this point on more than one occasion in reference to the arts since the arts have a tolerance for multiple solutions and open-endedness when it comes to creation. An important finding of our empirical work with artists (discussed in Chapter 4) was their willing and even enthusiastic embrace of ambiguity. Caitlin, the sculptor, said, "ambiguity is part of the process; a challenge, sometimes you play with the clay; that's when you come up with the answer when you are not thinking about what you are doing." Greg, a writer, remarked, "You have to have an open attitude towards ambiguity. You define it positively. It can suddenly become a tool or medium you use for the benefit of an audience." Sandra, a senior education officer, also noted that "you expect the unexpected. There are no two days the same. There's no real routine."

In contrast, the managerialist model seeks to eliminate ambiguity to attain greater control because ambiguity is seen as an unbridled source of variance and hence a threat to the authority of management. It is the epitome of the maximum of the tenets of machine bureaucracy, "When in doubt, control" (Mintzberg, 1983, p. 180). The source of anxiety of the *managerialist* is the future, because "the future is the most ambiguous and unknowable medium in man's [*sic*] cognitive world" (Rokeach & Bonier, 1960, p. 367).

Dimension 5: View of Creativity and Imagination

Similar to Dimension 4 (view of ambiguity), the connoisseurship model maintains that creativity and imagination are central to the work of artists and, we would argue, to the work of educational leaders. Both creativity and imagination enable a stance towards artfulness and actions that are born of limitless possibilities and directions (Marcellino, 2006). As Eisner (2002) maintains, change developed from any imaginative venture will not be linear or tidy, nor will it be prescribed. Scott, the actor and director who admitted he considered himself a change agent, said he liked it best when he started a production with "a blank sheet." The challenge he pursued was to "focus on solutions and to create sustainability." For him, "creativity should be joyful."

In contrast, the managerialist model holds a view of creativity and imagination that is narrowly defined and evaluated. Since it is centered on measures of efficiency, cost is the principal means of assessing the efficacy of change. Measurability is a second important criterion. Administrative control only exists in the eyes of the managerialist if it leads to improved predictability and greater outcomes at reduced cost. Since managerialism is an ideology there is little use for experimentation and innovation because control is more equivocal and less certain with the unknown. The only controllable measures are those which are well known and well established. For this reason, "change," if it comes at all, is most likely going to look like what already exists though it may be given a new name to connote something different. In contrast, Donovan, a new elementary school principal, whose school served a large majority population of disadvantaged students, remarked, "Hard work and curiosity can carry you a long way because while having a high IQ is good, curiosity means you are going to continue to learn."

Dimension 6: View of Risk Taking

Risk taking is part and parcel of the arts. It is represented in the quest of the artist to connect what is linked but not normally considered connected. This is what may be startling about art. Oscar Wilde said that this was the purpose of art, that is, prompting the viewer to think again about what he or she thought they already "knew" about something. Our connoisseur educators embodied risk taking.

Matthew recalled having to perform on stage in front of his peers at a conference to fill in time for a late education minister and later being praised for it as many senior educators declined the opportunity, fearful that they would make a fool of themselves. Matthew also recounted an incident involving work he carried out for an under-privileged Aboriginal community in Queensland. The original concept was that he and his team would work with the community not only to improve attendance rates of Aboriginal children but also to help them develop an interest and deep appreciation of the arts. As it turned out, not one child was willing to perform. Matthew confessed to a lack of cultural awareness on his part because of the deep reservation within the Aboriginal community about bringing shame to one's family if there was failure. Subsequent visits to the school (and the employment of an Aboriginal artist to support the program) turned the program around. Three years later there was a healthy involvement of Aboriginal children in this same program.

Another kind of risk was taken by Templeton, the American school super-intendent who delayed calling a snow day in order to enable some of his less privileged children to come to school and get warm and to enjoy a hot meal. For this decision he faced some internal criticism but his commitment to the well-being of all of the children in his school system protected him from it.

In the managerialist approach risk taking is minimized. Leaders become risk averse, believing that taking of such risks will do damage to the "bottom line," that is, their test score results which is the business equivalent of their profit margins. For example, Silverman (2015) examined the behavior of the leadership of some of the giant food companies such as Campbell Soup, Kraft Foods and others in the wake of new consumer demands for healthier products. In the past such companies were generous with sugar and salt in their products because they were cheap and commanded "fat profit margins" (Silverman, 2015, p. 7). However, as market share began to decline because of new consumer demands for healthier food, the leadership at these companies chose to engage in cost-cutting measures to retain their profit margins instead of increasing their knowledge of the market and researching potentially new products to appeal to this shift in consumer perspective. An expert in the food industry characterized these types of decisions as myopic, in which "it encourages everybody to trade off current sales for future sales" (Silverman, 2015, p. 7).

Dimension 7: Approach to Work

The artists and leaders spoke of the intrinsic satisfaction of doing their work, whether it was creating a piece of art, choreographing a dance or theatrical performance, or writing a piece of prose. The leaders were no different; and their enjoyment of their work was closely connected to children's enjoyment and achievement. All of the study's participants demonstrated a passion to "make a difference" in their own respective contexts. James Watson, a geneticist who shared the Nobel Prize for determining the double helix structure of the DNA molecule, remarked, "The highest goal—in science or life—isn't simply to win. It's to become the best at something that's really difficult; it's to reach beyond your level of ability and come out on top" (Ames, 1997, p. 30).

In contrast the managerialist approach is to routinize as much as possible in an effort to exert control and precision in the workplace. In the managerialist model "thinking, direction—even purpose—must be provided from outside or above" (Mintzberg, 1983, p. 177). The consequence is that the meaning of the work itself is compromised or even destroyed. "Organizations have paid dearly for these attitudes in the various forms of worker resistance—absenteeism, high turnover rates, sloppy workmanship, strikes, even outright sabotage" (Mintzberg, 1983, p. 178).

Dimension 8: View of Competence

Competence on the job is the bedrock of connoisseurship. Everyone we interviewed was on the continuum towards connoisseurship and following a personal quest to become more competent. It was an internal quest not motivated by external demands or rewards. The relationship to intrinsic job satisfaction is paramount. The quest for competence is central to the identity of the artist and the leader, perhaps best exemplified in the concept of the "flow experience" described by Frase (2006) as "a distinct state of consciousness that integrates high but effortless concentration, intrinsic motivation, loss of awareness of self and time, facile response to challenge, and feelings of competence and freedom" (p. 399). Flow has been described as "the key to intrinsic motivation" in which "the experience itself is so enjoyable that people will do it even at a great cost, for the sheer sake of doing it" (Frase, 2006, p. 399). James Barber (1983) described a leader with a drive towards competence as an "active positive" by saying that such a leader displays

> a congruence, a consistency, between much activity and the enjoyment of it, indicating a relatively high self-esteem and relative success in relating to the environment . . . he [sic] sees himself as developing over time toward relatively well defined personal goals—growing toward his image of himself as he might yet be.
>
> (p. 9)

In contrast the managerialist approach is limited by the fact that central to managerial control is to simplify or to "de-skill" competence. "De-skilling" is also the means to lower the costs of specialization in order to hire workers who have only minimal skills and to pay them less. Proposals to de-professionalize preparation of educational leaders are examples of de-skilling that place limits on the development of competence. When the Broad Foundation and Thomas B.

Fordham Institute (2003) gave their ideological blast at educational leadership and advocated replacing school leaders with former admirals and generals, business leaders from the private sector and former lawyers, their rationale was that a school superintendent didn't have to know much about the technical aspects of teaching and curriculum, they just had to know how to lead despite the fact that even in business when those who did not understand how a business really worked, their record was dismal. A survey of American business conducted in 2003 and published in *The Economist* indicated that when the CEO was an outsider his or her *average* tenure was reduced by three years. The advice was "pick someone from the same or at least a similar industry. Considerable research suggests that at least part of an individual boss's performance depends on context: the industry, the company, the culture in which he [sic] is used to operating" (A Survey of Corporate Leadership, 2003, p. 13).

However, this is a form of de-skilling a job in order to eliminate competence in a field from blocking the entrance of those who do not have such competence. Chester Finn (1991), a long time advocate of de-skilling of educators who once wrote, "any well educated adult of sound character, who knows a subject and is willing to try teaching it to children, should be considered a candidate for entry into the classroom" (p. 268) also said in the same book *We Must Take Charge*:

> I see impressive potential in ideas such as private contracting with schools for educational services . . . As for involvement of businessmen (and women) we should welcome them to the conference room, particularly when they do not check their bottom-line orientation at the door.
>
> (p. 233)

Dimension 9: Values

Connoisseur leaders are first and foremost concerned with values and ethical actions. Values are those beliefs that provide humans with a moral compass regarding decisions about life and professional practice. Ethics involve ways of adhering to those values so that they are not compromised. Beck and Murphy (1997) identify two perspectives on ethics. The first perspective is that ethics "are embodied in rules, ideas, and ideals that transcend individual preferences and can guide objective decision making and problem solving" (p. 33). Such principles can be derived from rigorous rational thought. The second approach is that "ethics is less about making decisions using objective principles and more about living morally in specific situations" (Beck & Murphy, 1997, p. 33). The first approach uses reasoning as the major means by which ethical principles are discovered. The second way stresses *ways of seeing* and this is centered on "developing acute moral perception, of understanding persons and context, and of cultivating virtues" (Beck & Murphy, 1997, p. 34).

Our view of leader connoisseurship stresses *ways of seeing* as the means to discern what is value-driven and ethical. Robert developed a way of seeing by observing some overall activity at the "big picture" level but then was able to move in and out of the smaller levels of details. He derived his understanding of an activity through this procedure. It was a *way of seeing* for him. Tanya aggressively sought out teachers and staff to draw out their strengths in order to transform her school. Tanya's work at school transformation was based on an overall value of finding people who were interested in change. Templeton similarly had an overarching value-based way of seeing that recognized a good leader was one who could bring diverse people and their differing ideologies together in a cohesive working group. Julia felt that "leadership is leadership of self" and not vested in principles outside of human beings.

Managerialist values are about efficiency and, as Usher and Edwards (1996) note, "efficiency has no end" because it is a teleology, that is, true by definition. Managerialists are about making efficiency the be all and end all of *good* administration. As an ideology centered on the tenets of neo-liberalism, it "is predisposed to conserve what exists, to resist change, and to support the community or societal traditional ways" (Wallace, 2008, p. 229). We are reminded here of an insight from T.B. Greenfield:

> great art is moral. It is an ethical statement about the world, and that is what makes it great. Gobs of spit may besmirch it, but not deny its message. Art and ethics are ultimately united. So too the individual and his understanding of the world are ultimately united with ethics.
>
> (Greenfield & Ribbins, 1993, p. 271)

Dimension 10: Power

Leader connoisseurs envision power as a means to diffuse throughout the system as the means to move a school or a school system forward. In this sense it is close to *empowerment*. Our educational leader connoisseurs had a realistic view of power. For example, Donovan told about his political work in developing relationships with the central office so that his back "was covered" in case his work at his school was challenged. Using the French and Raven (1959) typology of power, it was also clear that connoisseurs rely on expert power centered on their growing competence as well as referent power based on their own personalities. For example, Julia recalled that during her early adolescence, when she was a member of the young person's agricultural club called 4-H, she could bring people together and empower them. She later described herself as a servant leader. Robert Greenleaf described one of the facets of a servant leader as a person to whom potential followers turn, regardless of the leader's formal status in the organization. Greenleaf observed:

We say now that no one should be made a supervisor to whom the workmen [*sic*] do not go for guidance and counsel before any designation of supervisory status is made. In a conference, it is not always possible to spot the boss. If he [*sic*] is wise, he knows how to drive hard with a light hand. His organization will work with zeal and inspiration and never be conscious of his direction.

(Frick, 2004, p. 113)

The managerialist leader, on the other hand, operates best from a base of legitimate power vested in its bureaucratic position and employs both reward and coercive powers to ensure compliance (French & Raven, 1959). A good illustration of referent power was provided by Miriam (Chapter 5, community arts leader). She had no legitimate power or formal role; she was a grassroots leader who used referent power to build strong connections to the women in her dance project.

Dimension 11: View of People

Leader connoisseurs see people as the end of their efforts to improve education. People are not the means to ends but they are the ends. Connoisseurs do not see people to be manipulated to fit into some sort of system. They are able to step outside of the system, that is, any system including any system of governance and, in the case of schools, outside the school. Connoisseur educational leaders see the artifices of schooling but can still work within them and know how to bend the rules to create good working relationships. Tanya was able to change the culture of her school. She learned how to frame and reframe problems through her linguistic skills. She lamented how her own school system practiced deficit thinking in trying to change human skills so that they improved. Tanya was a nurturing school leader and her school was a nurturing place for teachers and staff. She protected her teachers and enabled them to avoid system compliance when she felt their responses were more adept than those advocated by system administrators.

Templeton's practice of *code switching* to survive in the dominant white culture provided him with practice of being in the system while actually being outside of it. He used his knowledge to make room for cultural and racial differences in the system he led. He actively worked to create improved sensitivity of his school principals to the needs of minority students and he intervened in the system to help them in his abbreviated school hours when he had to call school off because of snow. For Templeton, students came first and the effectiveness of the system came second since the system should serve students.

Managerialists, on the other hand, place their priority on the system. Running a "tight ship" is paramount to their view of order. Contrast Templeton's view with one advocated by Andrew Grove (1983) in his text *High Output Management*:

your task is to find the *most cost effective* way to deploy your resources—the key to optimizing all types of productive work. Bear in mind that in this and in other such situations there is a right answer, the one that can give you the best delivery time and product quality at the lowest possible cost. To find the right answer, you must develop a clear understanding of the trade-offs between the various factors—manpower, capacity, and inventory— and you must reduce the understanding to a quantifiable set of relationships.

(p. 10)

Grove's advice means people are the means to attain organizational ends. Grove sees control as manipulative and creates the means to force compliance through "free-market forces, contractual obligations and cultural values" (p. 145). By "cultural values" he means creating an environment in which "all share a *common* set of values, a *common* set of objectives, and a *common* set of methods" (p. 147). This is Weber's (1930) *iron cage* with velvet bars. It is extreme work standardization where differences are erased in the pursuit of efficiency.

Dimension 12: Understanding of Practice

The artists and educational leaders we interviewed were aware of the traditions regarding behavior, both real and expected, in their fields. They understood the expectations of accomplishment. For example, the Australian principal Robert espoused a perspective that outstanding practice for him was his ability to place the smallest point in the large picture, to grasp both simultaneously in the process of having conversations with his faculty. Templeton talked about the difference between a school which was "organized chaos" and one in which it was "unorganized." Julia spoke of a leader being able to create a culture based on his/her "emotional intelligence" and one who knows how to listen and communicate well, and remarked, "If a school is unfocused it can't be led well." Donovan recalled a former mentor telling him that "details matter."

For the artists, Caitlin spoke of acquiring the insight within her practice of knowing when to stop working on a piece and trusting in her own instincts about that. Alberto polished his skills working in a studio for 16 hours on some days. He emphasized the criticality of mastering the technical skills involved and he understood that different media required different processes. Miriam honed her skills in being able to work with women with disabilities and coming to understand what kinds of movements were possible based on their disabilities. Scott, the actor and director, acquired a sensitivity regarding what was possible within different theater genres but at bottom theater had to have a purpose. The world-class cellist János Starker remarked that:

Great teachers are people who care for the individual and are willing to spend a lifetime learning every aspect of their art so that they can transmit the message of the great composers. A great teacher finds limits unacceptable and will even set unreasonable goals for students who are able to handle the challenge.

(in Ames, 1997, p. 31)

Managerialists may be as personally driven as their connoisseur counterparts but they have less of an understanding of the limits of the organizational medium in which they work. They question the organization's roles and purposes less, if at all. They are less apt to see individual competence as starting with themselves and more apt to stress compliance with the rules and roles in which they work as the key to excellence. "Excellence" is about making what exists run better. They don't push the limits of the school, they push only within the limits. For managerialists, excellence means efficiency.

Dimension 13: Identity

In Chapter 6, Julia observed that, "Leadership is leadership of self." As such it is directly connected to one's identity. Julia went on to say that identity was related to "your maturity and your integrity. You have to become confident in who you are. You have to have empathy. It's more than just skills." Here we see Mead's (1934) view that there is the "I" of identity and the "me" of identity. In Julia we see this relationship. The "I" part is what she views as herself apart from interactions. It's her integrity. The "me" part is building confidence and that is related to the views of others. She confessed to being "totally terrified" when she had to speak to the State Board of Education and "each time I spoke it got easier." When she encounters a moral dilemma which would be the "me" part in a situation with others, she returns to the "I" part and searches for congruence.

Similarly Caitlin the sculptor learned to trust her own instincts as she gained experience in her craft which was her "I" as an artist. Public feedback was also important for her identity in the "me" part. She felt reinforced when she received positive affirmation of her work.

In contrast, Templeton, the African American school superintendent, indicated that he was "like an onion. I have multiple layers." He said he could project and also then be "a mirror." He was adept at situational leadership which was the "me" part of his leadership. The "I" part was that he was "a painful introvert."

The *managerialist leader* submerges his/her identity in his/her organizational role and it becomes his/her identity. One is the other. There is no separation and no stepping outside of it. He/she is largely externally motivated to rewards and sanctions supplied by the bureaucracy in which he/she resides. In this case Mead's "I" and "me" are identical. The core of the *managerialist leader* is blind acceptance of the norms and expectations imposed on him/her from top down. He/she would be a person most likely to "pass the buck" as a decision strategy if he/she was uncomfortable in having to render a decision (English & Bolton, 2008).

Dimension 14: View of Change

The artists interviewed almost universally looked at change as a necessary part of their growth and development. For example, Scott, the actor and director, indicated that one of the purposes of artistic expression is "to provoke change by viewing ordinary situations from extraordinary angles." The educational leaders interviewed had two perspectives on change. The perspectives revolved around their core values, those values they held most dear about the role of education in the lives of children. Nearly all viewed the current neo-liberal assault on public education with disdain, even contempt. They saw it as harmful, even destructive. Yet, change that they endorsed and that coincided with their view of the purpose of education was viewed as a positive thing. Robert saw teachers as "change weary," mostly from types of accountability politics currently in force. Tanya was disdainful of change that worked on the weaknesses of people instead of their strengths.

At the policy level, the managerialist approach to change is to disrupt current procedures so as to be able to offer alternatives that create competition among schools for scarce resources. At the school site level, managerialists are uncomfortable with change, especially when such changes may introduce instability in the organization because it is harder to maintain managerial control. Change brings about major anxieties in this regard. Managerialists are most comfortable in completely closed systems. By closed is meant the authority system in place remains intact. Leaders comfortable in closed systems have also been shown to be both rigid and dogmatic in their thinking (Rokeach, McGovney & Denny, 1960, p. 194).

Dimension 15: Ethics

Ethics has been described as what we ought to do (Plato) and how we should live our lives. Not surprisingly, at its core is our relationships with others (Singer, 1993). A connoisseurship model of ethics is one that prizes relationships with others as it adheres to human-centered values such as those espoused by Erich Fromm (1995) in his classic text, *The Art of Loving*. Fromm describes brotherly love (which underlies all other types of love) as including "the sense of responsibility, care, respect, knowledge of any other human being, the wish to further his [sic] life" (p. 37). Thus a connoisseurship model connects the ethical values of brotherly love to leadership since ethics and leadership co-constitute each other. This view lies in stark contrast to the managerialist model that falls heavily upon legal protocols, policies and procedures that legislate how leaders should work with others. At best, managerialism suggests a minimal approach, focused on economic results without any sense of the centrality of the human being.

All of the artists and educators we have classified as on a continuum of connoisseurship displayed moral convictions and ethical dimensions to their lives and leadership roles. Caitlin described one of her early sculpted pieces as representing conflict between freedom and space. Alberto searched for symbols that were universal and would speak to individuals of different cultural and religious traditions. Alberto was keenly aware of the social function of art. Miriam worked with women with disabilities in a socially inclusive dance project. Scott, the actor and director, indicated that an aesthetic response was the most truthful because the human body has an innate sense of truth. These illustrations demonstrate ethical sensitivities to moral truths and dilemmas in human relationships.

Among the educators, Tanya worked extremely hard to change the culture at her school. She recounted that "Every single time you interact with others, you are putting yourself out there. Every single time you do that. That is contributing to the definition of the school." Tanya was extremely focused on being congruent with the value she placed on collaboration and creating an atmosphere of cooperation. Templeton, the African American school superintendent, had to engage in "code switching" so he could function in a white world but he never strayed from his values of fighting for the underdog, declaring "I'm a cheerleader for the underdog. It is the responsibility of educators that marginalized groups are looked after and elevated."

In contrast, the managerialist view of ethics is that all transactions revert to economic models in which ethics are simply *what works at the moment* to satisfy immediate short-term goals. The economic circumstances of managerialism make it susceptible to corruption. For example, Florida state school superintendent Tony Bennett had to resign from office when it was revealed that as former Indiana state school superintendent, he had intervened in the state's grading system for schools in order to ensure that a wealthy Republican donor's charter school improved its ranking. This donor had given more than $2.8 million to Republicans and that included $130,000 to Bennett himself (LoBianco, 2013). Clearly the neo-liberal agenda anchored in rational choice theory is one that is dominant in both Indiana and Florida. Henry Giroux (2011) had written about this takeover of values and ethics when New York Mayor Michael Bloomberg appointed Cathie Black, a former media magnate, as Chancellor of the New York City Schools. Black had no educational credentials or preparation. She had never been a teacher or worked in a public school. She was placed as head of the most prominent American urban school system by neo-liberal politicians espousing business techniques as the solution to education's problems (Giroux, 2011). Black's lack of knowledge and her incompetence as an educator resulted in top flight administrators leaving the school system. That brought about her swift firing by Mayor Bloomberg within months after taking the job. Black had no credentials nor any moral vision for the school system. The only morality in business is the "bottom line." The continued emphasis only on profits as the barometer of success in a study of corporate fraud found that from 1978 through 2002 "federal regulators initiated 585 enforcement actions for financial misrepresentation by publicly traded companies, naming 2,310 individuals and 657 firms as potential liable parties" (Cools, 2005, p. B2). The "bottom line" here was that fines were levied against these firms of $15.9 billion dollars and 190 corporate leaders received jail sentences.

Dimension 16: Emotion and Intuition

The artists in our sample were more forthcoming in using emotive language to describe what they do and how it made them and others feel more so than the leaders. A good illustration of this was provided by Miriam, the dancer/choreographer, and Scott, the artistic director. Miriam referred to the power of dance to create emotional connections between dancers and she admitted that she works "very intuitively" to derive a sense of what is emerging from her workshops. Scott underscored the centrality of the aesthetic dimension within theater. While the leaders in the sample did not use this type of language, there was recognition of the place for feeling and emotions. Here Bernard said, "Being a leader is as much about the heart as it is the head."

We have previously discussed in this book the importance of emotion in leadership. Intuition is also an indispensable aspect. Intuition frequently involves tacit knowledge, the ability to know and understand without being conscious of it. A startling account of intuition as aesthetic vision is attached to a poem, *Eureka*, by poet and writer Edgar Allan Poe in the year 1848, the penultimate year of his life. Poe was ridiculed for this poem which no one could make much sense of at the time. However, Marilynne Robinson (2015) notes that only with 21st Century physics could one come to appreciate this futuristic vision in which:

> *Eureka* describes the origins of the universe in a single particle, from which "radiated" the atoms of which all matter is made. Minute dissimilarities of size and distribution among these atoms meant that the effects of gravity caused them to accumulate as matter, forming the physical universe . . . space and "duration" are one thing, that there might be stars that emit no light, that there is a repulsive force that in some degree counteracts the force of gravity, that there could be any number of universes with different laws, simultaneous with ours, that our universe might collapse to its original state and another universe erupt from the particle it would have become, that our present universe may be one in a series.
>
> (p. 4)

Robinson (2015) notes that, "Poe had neither evidence nor authority for any of it. It was a product, he said, of a kind of aesthetic reasoning, therefore a poem" (p. 4). Intuitive insights of the kind which were behind Poe's *Eureka* indicate that truth and accuracy can be determined in other ways besides cool calculation.

Dimension 17: Cultural Awareness

Cultural awareness includes all facets of culture such as gender differences and racial biases. It is concerned with a person being able to step outside of his/her own culture and see how the biases of that culture enable blind spots to exist in a person's ability to see clearly what is really at work in his/her own field of vision. The imposition of a majoritarian culture founded on white supremacy and the elevation of white models of beauty have marginalized people of color around the globe. West (1999) has documented how even the dominant figures of the European enlightenment such as Montesquieu and Voltaire, Hume and Kant all held racist views of black people and these views were accepted "without their having to put forward their own arguments to justify it" (p. 82).

Furthermore, the prevalence of white (Greek and Italian) statues with the anatomical features of classical antiquity were the foundation of classical aesthetic ideals and, as a result, "the black presence, though tolerated and at times venerated, was never an integral part of the classical ideals of beauty" (West, 1999, p. 85). Blackness then became the antithesis of what was considered beautiful and the epitome of ugliness.

The difficulty of working through these traditions by people who live on the cultural margins is illustrated by two women in higher education, one in New Zealand and one in the United States, who found inspiration and validation to persist in their respective institutional settings because of the life examples of Gloria Anzaldúa, Octavia Butler and Frida Kahlo (Santamaria & Jaramillo, 2014). We have previously written of the life and work of Frida Kahlo in Chapter 2 and so the reader is familiar with her story. Gloria Anzaldúa was an American Chicana, a bisexual, sixth-generation Tejana ranchero. She created her theoretical perspective called *mestiza consciousness* and she promoted leadership around the concepts of social justice, equity and access. Octavia Butler was an African American woman who was the first to be recognized as an accomplished author in the science fiction genre. She was the first sci-fi writer to receive the MacArthur Foundation Genius Grant.

The nature of cultural awareness is illustrated when Santamaria and Jaramillo describe the influence these three women (Anzaldúa, Butler and Kahlo) had on them as they were growing up. From Lorri Santamaria:

> when I discovered Gloria Anzaldúa's writings . . . I knew I was finally home. Anzaldúa and I shared multiple ethnic identities from the start and feminist underpinnings as I dug further; however, the ways in which she taught me to think about work that transcends physical borders was precious. Her work and life example taught me to commit. Commit to your cause, love your work, flow, and grow. And so I did and still do.
>
> (Santamaria & Jaramillo, 2014, p. 326)

From Nathalia Jaramillo:

> I hold Frida Kahlo deep and close to my heart. Her art and willingness to delve into the sacred realms of personal experience and pain and her reflections on the US-Mexico border helped me to find the courage to undertake deeper analyses of my social formation . . . She was such a dynamic woman, always challenging tradition and norms, yet she did not deny emotion—love, pain, and longing—in the construction of her womanhood.
>
> (p. 330)

The importance of cultural awareness is a critical attribute of modern connoisseurship in leadership. In our interviews Matthew told his story of his initial failure to understand the cultural norms of Aboriginal people and how he corrected his own ignorance by involving them in an artistic project designed to improve school attendance. Templeton, the African American school superintendent, recounted his own treatment in school when he recalled, "I was a little black boy from the housing projects. I was discouraged from applying for fellowships. Social justice is my number one theoretical lens. I talk to our leaders and ask questions all the time." Alberto described his work on creating an interfaith room for worship at his university that included all of the elements from the major religions of the world which created "a habitat for the encounter with the divine."

Dimension 18: Framing

Framing refers to the manner in which a leader chooses to define problems and issues upon which followers and potential followers might find connection. John Gardner (1990) defined the underlying living tissue behind framing when he observed:

> we want meaning in our lives. For many this life is a vale of tears; for no one is free of pain. But we are so designed that we deal with it if we can live in some context of meaning. Given that powerful help, we can draw on the deep springs of the human spirit to bear with the things we cannot change, to see our suffering in the framework of all human suffering, to accept the gifts of life with thanks and endure life's indignities with dignity.
>
> (p. 189)

Artists are constantly engaged in framing and reframing issues. Miriam framed her work and her mission as bringing kindness and acceptance to the women who had physical and intellectual disabilities in her dance program. She attributed it to a "love for humanity." Caitlin's quest was framing certain expressions of humanity and human struggle in her sculptures. In framing his work Scott indicated that there were only three things that were essential: an actor, a space and an audience. Everything else just happened.

Tanya framed her work at Magnolia as one in which she wanted to create an environment where teachers and students could pursue a joyful and positive experience, an experience which drew upon the strengths of that staff. She felt satisfied "When people say they love working here that matters to me." Templeton framed his work as one in which he toiled to eliminate disparities with minorities and students who had been marginalized, remarking, "I always pull for the underdog. I want them (the students) to feel satisfied once they leave school." Julia likewise framed her work as bringing people together to work in teams on mutual problems. A good decision for her was one that had "been made for the better of the community." Donovan's early life experiences also made him a defender of the underdog. He observed poverty first-hand. He too found framing his job as one of creating a collaborative work environment and learned how to delegate tasks and because he found that he could improve school solely from the inside he had to form partnerships with the community and get it involved in the school.

For the managerialist framing is much simpler. It's already been done by the system itself. Problems are externalized and defined by "outcomes" and all else is sacrificed for those outcomes. The *North Carolina Standards for School Superintendents* (North Carolina State Board of Education, 2007) is replete with a managerialist frame of reference. For example, one of the philosophical foundations for the standards is: "School district leadership does not require doing all tasks by oneself, but it does require creating systems and processes where all tasks can be accomplished at high levels of proficiency" (p. 1).

This so-called "philosophical foundation" was written by Frederick Taylor in 1911. It is an example of founding a system into which people must "fit in" and where leadership can only come from "system men." Another philosophical foundation stipulates that "Within a school district, there are nested leadership systems. . . . To be successful, the superintendent must ensure these systems are aligned and are mutually supportive of one another" (p. 1).

Once again this is placing primary allegiance on systems as opposed to people, structure over talent and motivation to create "smooth" hierarchies in clean chain of command lines of authority which promote accountability and efficiency, the watchwords of managerialism.

Dimension 19: Responses to Challenges or Threats

Artists look forward to challenges. School leaders are more circumspect as their organizational setting is somewhat different and they are more dependent on positional roles and authority in a bureaucracy. Artists typically have more independence in facing and responding to challenges. Caitlin looked at challenges as an emerging sculptor and the risks she took to grow. She works in the space between tradition and innovation and finds it easier to occupy that space as she grows more experienced. Similarly Alberto has created a space to explore the ambiguity involved with his previous life of darkness and the loss of family members in conflict. He works to find hope and embrace it. He laments that some viewers of his art have no idea of the joy in creating it where "there's no room for funky spaces or poor people." Miriam worked in a space where her commitment to social inclusion challenged designated social judgments about how to accommodate differences among people, especially those who are physically disabled. She positions her work as a statement against disability-centered segregation. Scott saw challenges as a form of "puzzle solving" and remarked that "Some things work and you don't know why."

Matthew's challenge was to lead teachers who were much older than he was as a principal. He confesses he did not have as much flexibility as he would have liked to meet those challenges. He was aware of how the school system sapped the creative energy from him and reduced a leader to a more compliant sort. Tanya responded to a challenge to her desire to create a different school culture by working with everyone and anyone whom she found responsive, irrespective of how long they had been at her school. Templeton confronted the challenges of his job by becoming more introspective and more thoughtful, even though he was a painful introvert. He found the challenges of being superintendent learning to understand that his circle of friends grew smaller, to becoming sensitive to the personal agendas of people who befriended him and he understood that some of the hard and fast positions he took before had become more nuanced after he confronted them. Julia faced her foremost challenge when her mother was killed in a car accident. Her mother occupied a central place in her own identity and she had to return to that self for a renewed understanding of who she was and wanted to be. Donovan was still coming to grips with the challenges his rural school faced with so many undocumented immigrants and the extent of poverty and deprivation in his community being served by the school. In the beginning he thought he had enough energy to do the whole job by himself, but found he had to delegate some tasks in order to survive.

Managerialists confront challenges by working to extend their control of the uncertainties in organizations. They typically see challenges as those directed at their ability to control sources of variance and uncertainty. Instead of trying to understand they seek to control and suppress sources of instability. They find solace in quantification because it eliminates the need to become emotionally involved in decision-making contexts. Emotion is a source of great risk because it lacks rational control and cannot be reduced to cool calculation. Quantification is seen as a detached means of control and retaining authority and power in a bureaucratic organizational structure.

Dimension 20: Working Relationships

The ability to work with people and get the most from them in building a cohesive organization applied to only some of the artists interviewed. Artists who work alone, sculptors and painters for example, do not usually require colleagues to engage in their work. However, Scott, the actor and director, spoke about seeing himself as a "builder" and not a "manager." He said, "leadership is not standing on some high place and calling people to you. It's about getting down and going to them." He emphasized the importance of creating common ground for everyone and "you need to express your skills and ask actors to tell you about their skills." Miriam, the choreographer, worked with each woman in her group. She studied what each could do and the movements that came naturally to them. "It has to be authentic to a person," she said. As a leader Miriam displayed empathy and even love. She was there to encourage her dancers' personal empowerment.

The educational leaders in our sample referred to the importance of reaching out to others and developing good working relationships with them. One example was Robert who described himself as a person who "leads conversations regarding learning" with his staff. He also indicated a preference for using teams as a means of ensuring as many people as possible are involved and active in issues arising in the school. Other leaders referred to working both individually and in a team situation with staff as a way to harness the special talents of the staff and at times to build their capacity. Tanya invested enormous personal energy into building collaboration among her teachers and creating a nurturing climate. She saw the effort as one in which her school was defined and it centered on how people felt about working there. Templeton's view of a competent principal was a person who didn't see his/her community as one to be manipulated; rather, it was one characterized by collaborative and mutually respectful relationships. Julia spoke passionately about bridging diverse differences and finding a common need among people upon which to create a positive working group. She indicated that it was the leader's responsibility to create the culture of a school, one that was positive and could be felt as having a sense of purpose. In her view focusing the work of the school and leading were synonymous, one required the other. Donovan, the new principal, had already learned the importance of having people around you who can shore up your weaknesses and build on your strengths. He indicated he valued colleagues who were not his clones.

Managerialists envision relationships as economic transactions. Altruism has little place in their orientation to work. To motivate people to work they resort to rewards and punishments and economic incentives, essentially to selfishness and fear. David Sloan Wilson, a distinguished professor of biology and anthropology, studied the biological basis for altruism in humans. He advanced the proposition that if a group was composed mostly of individuals out for themselves and engaged in activities of self-advancement, the group as a whole suffers in its ability to survive. On the other hand, if there are altruistic persons in the group, its solidarity and performance will be enhanced and become better *as a group* (Orr, 2015, p. 27). Managerialist thinking has little place for altruism. It is not quantifiable nor easily assessed in typical on-the-job evaluations common in most bureaucracies (if it is included at all).

Summary

These, then, are the 20 dimensions of a model of connoisseurship which has emerged from the work thus far in Australia and the United States. There is much more to know and understand. Both authors believe that with further refinement and empirical analysis, the total number of categories is likely to be condensed as there are possible overlaps and duplications in what has been a preliminary and largely descriptive inquiry. The initial approach we have taken in identifying these 20 dimensions of connoisseurship has been to cast a wide net so as to avoid missing any potential elements. Refinement and further study is warranted to put a finer point on the findings reported in this book.

Key Chapter Ideas

There are three major ideas in this chapter:

1. Connoisseurship Represents a Break with the Dominant Tropes of the Field

The long tradition of a search for science in educational administration came to fruition in the 1960s and continued for over 30 years. It began to wane and yield when it failed to deliver on its promises of making management into a respectable and empirically based scientific discipline. But we are still living within its traditions and the master tropes it left behind as a residue continue to dominate how both practitioners and professors think about, write about, and practice administration in our schools. We have called this amalgamation a blend of behaviorism and structural functionalism. It is heavily laced with traditional quantitative social science methods largely derived from classical psychology and sociology.

As our work in the arts in educational leadership came into sharper focus it became clearer to us how our thinking and our research differed from what we and others had done before and eventually how it broke with the dominant tropes and traditions in our field. We believe the concept of *connoisseurship* represents a distinctive break in outlook and with implications for changes in the practice and preparation of educational leaders for our schools. We see this break as long overdue and the need to engage in a corrective course of action imperative.

We believe that as the concept of a *connoisseur educational leader* is explored in greater detail that it will force a reconsideration of the de-humanizing check lists of disembodied skills and dispositions so common in leadership licensure criteria and preparation programs at the present time. We have no need for cookie-cutter leaders or cookie-cutter schools. We have a great need for schools where children are treated with respect, dignity and integrity in regard to their common humanity and, like Tsunesaburō Makiguchi, we want schools to be joyful places for all children. That too many are not such places and seem unlikely to become such places is deeply disturbing.

2. Connoisseurship is Restorative of Humane Practice in the Schools

At stake in the current political environment surrounding education is the concept of a disinterested professional public service to continue to shape leadership thought and practice on behalf of all children. We see traditional modes of domination and subordination based on social class, race, gender and sexual orientation continued and reinforced with the neo-liberal antidotes of reduction in public funding of schools and in the privatization of education at all levels. We view this shift with great concern not only for the continued gaps in wealth and privilege which are accompanying the widening cleavage between the haves and the have nots, but in a threat to the very foundation of an effective and workable democracy which benefits all citizens irrespective of their economic, social and cultural capital. The artistic base of connoisseurship rests firmly on the individualism and integrity of all human beings, a deep respect for a common humanity, and a trust of the emotional and visual manifestations of the human experience which are non-linear and in many respects non-quantifiable.

We see in *connoisseurship* the possible re-emergence of a human-centered leadership practice in the schools. Such a practice flies in the face of the pervasive domination of business practices in schools and colleges. Mark Burstein (2015), president of Lawrence University and himself a recipient of an MBA from the Wharton School of Business cautioned:

> Strategies from the business world can help us streamline our institutions, but we must take care that the tools we borrow not jeopardize the values of the academy. If business concepts dominate our thinking about the future, we will have lost our way.
>
> (p. A48)

Further we see the connoisseur educational leader as focused first on human relationships and in the highly personal and individual recognition of the differences in our teaching staffs and our students. An educational leader who is a connoisseur is not likely to be the equivalent of a factory foreman or woman supervising monotonizing and robotizing scripted classroom lessons.

3. Connoisseurship is a New Perspective in a Contested Field

The concept of connoisseurship is presented as both a developmental one and also one which is crystallized in a line of argument we advance in this book.

We understand and agree with Wacquant's notion (1992) that professional fields are dynamic, fluid and contested and within any field there is a theory of practice peculiar to the logic of that field. Ideas are advanced and/or attacked as various individuals, groups and/or agencies seek to expand their sphere of influence. The core of that influence is the authority to dominate the discourse about what is and is not legitimate to discuss, who is empowered to speak, and what topics are appropriate to consider as serious.

IMPLICATIONS FOR POLICY AND PRACTICE

If the Status Quo is Not Questioned it Becomes Normative and Excludes Real Alternatives

Famed organizational interventionist Chris Argyris (1972) of Harvard observed over nearly a half-century ago that "Descriptive theories about the present state of the universe inevitably become normative if someone suggests or assumes that they are or should continue to exist" (p. 116). The work undertaken in this book began as a way to seriously question the continued viability and reliance on the *managerialist* ideology which now dominates the political and policy discourse for educational leadership. The co-authors and researchers fervently believe that this ideology undermines the democratic nature of public education and serves to reinforce existing social divisions between the economic haves and have nots in our countries. The simple fact is that efficiency is the mantra of the *managerialist* ideology for education. We posit that the notion of *leadership* as *connoisseurship* is about fulfilling human potential which may not always be efficient. *Connoisseurship* is about becoming more human and humane and where humans are both the means and the ends of education.

References

A survey of corporate leadership: Tough at the top (2003, October 25–31). *The Economist* (special insert 1–22).

Ames, J. (1997, September/October). Advice from the masters. *Indiana Alumni Magazine*, 30–31.

Anderson, G.L. & Pini, M. (2011). Educational leadership and the new economy: Keeping the "public" in public schools. In F. English (Ed.), *The SAGE handbook of educational leadership* (2nd ed.) (pp. 176–194). Thousand Oaks, CA: Sage.

Argyris, C. (1972). *The applicability of organizational sociology*. Cambridge: Cambridge University Press.

Ball, S. (2009). Privatising education, privatising education policy, privatising educational research: Network government and the "competition state." *Journal of Education Policy*, *24*(1), 83–99.

Barber, J.D. (1983). *The presidential character: Predicting performance in the White House.* Englewood Cliffs, NJ: Prentice-Hall, Inc.

Barnard, C. (1938). *The functions of the executive.* Cambridge, MA: Harvard University Press.

Beck, L.G. & Murphy, J. (1997). A framework for thinking about ethics and ethical leadership. In L.G. Beck & J. Murphy (Eds.), *Ethics in educational leadership programs: Emerging models* (pp. 31–76). Columbia, MO: UCEA.

Blinder, A.S. (2012, October 2). The case against a CEO in the oval office. *The Wall Street Journal*, A19.

Bolton, C. & English, F.W. (2010). De-constructing the logic/emotion binary in educational leadership preparation and practice. *Journal of Educational Administration*, *48*(5), 561–578.

Bottery, M. (2004). *The challenges of educational leadership.* London: Paul Chapman.

Bourdieu, P. (1990). *In other words: Essays towards a reflexive sociology.* Stanford, CA: Stanford University Press.

Bourdieu, P. (1998). *Practical reason: On the theory of action.* Stanford, CA: Stanford University Press.

Bourdieu, P. (1999). *Acts of resistance: Against the tyranny of the market.* New York: The New Press.

Bourdieu, P. & Wacquant, L.J.D. (Eds.). (1992). *An invitation to reflexive sociology.* Chicago: University of Chicago Press.

Broad Foundation and Thomas B. Fordham Institute (2003). *Better leaders for America's schools: A manifesto.* Dayton.

Burstein, M. (2015, March 2). The unintended consequences of borrowing business tools to run a university. *The Chronicle of Higher Education*, *LXI*(25), A48.

Clarke, J., Cochrane, A. & McLaughlin, E. (Eds.). (1994). *Managing social policy.* London: Sage.

Cools, K. (2005, March 22). Ebbers Rex. *The Wall Street Journal*, B2.

Culbertson, J.A. (1988). A century's quest for a knowledge base. In N.J. Boyan (Ed.), *Handbook of research on educational administration* (pp. 3–26). New York: Longman.

Ehrich, L.C. & English, F.W. (2012). What can grassroots leadership teach us about school leadership? *Haldiskultuur-Administrative Culture*, *13*(2), 85–108.

Ehrich, L.C. & English, F.W. (2013). Towards connoisseurship in educational leadership: Following the data in a three stage line of inquiry. In S. Eacott & R. Niesche (Eds.), *Empirical leadership research: Letting the data speak for themselves* (pp. 165–198). Niagara Falls, NY: Untested Ideas Research Center.

Eisner, E. (2002). *The arts and the creation of mind.* New Haven, CT: Yale University Press.

Emery, K. & Ohanian, S. (2004). *Why is corporate America bashing our public schools?* Portsmouth, NH: Heinemann.

English, F.W. (1994). *Theory in educational administration.* New York: HarperCollins.

English, F.W. (2008). *The art of educational leadership: Balancing performance and accountability.* Los Angeles: Sage.

English, F.W. (2014). *Educational leadership in the age of greed: Requiem for res publica.* Ypsilanti, MI: NCPEA Press.

English, F.W. & Bolton, C.L. (2008). An exploration of administrative heuristics in the United States and the United Kingdom. *Journal of School Leadership*, *18*(1), 96–119.

English, F.W. & Papa, R. (2009). *Restoring human agency to educational administration: Status and strategies.* Lancaster, PA: ProActive Publications.

Evans, K. & Wamsley, G. (2007, August). Blacksburg manifesto in the *International Encyclopedia of Public Policy and Administration.* Retrieved from http://www.cpap.v.edu/current/manifesto.pdf.

Feyerabend, P. (1991). *Three dialogues on knowledge.* Oxford: Basil Blackwell.

Finn, C. (1991). *We must take charge: Our schools and our future.* New York: The Free Press.

Foster, W. (1986). *Paradigms and promises: New approaches to educational administration.* Buffalo, NY: Prometheus Books.

Frase, L. (2006). Flow theory. In F. English (Ed.), *Encyclopedia of educational leadership and administration. Vol. 1* (pp. 399–401). Thousand Oaks, CA: Sage.

French, J.R. & Raven, B. (1959). The bases of social power. In D. Cartwright (Ed.), *Studies in social power* (pp. 150–167). Ann Arbor: University of Michigan Institute of Social Research.

Frick, D.M. (2004). *Robert K. Greenleaf: A life of servant leadership.* San Francisco: Berrett-Koehler Publishers, Inc.

Fromm, E. (1995). *The art of loving.* Glasgow: Thorsons.

Gardner, J.W. (1990). *On leadership.* New York: The Free Press.

Giroux, H. (2011). Business culture and the death of public education: Mayor Bloomberg, David Steiner, and the politics of corporate "leadership." *Policy Futures in Education, 9*(5), 553–559.

Greenfield, T. & Ribbins, P. (Eds.). (1993). *Greenfield on educational administration: Towards a humane science.* New York: Routledge.

Grove, A.S. (1983). *High output management.* New York: Vintage Books.

Gunter, H. (2002). *Leaders and leadership in education.* London: Paul Chapman.

Gunter, H. & Thompson, P. (2010). Life on mars: Headteachers before the national college. *Journal of Educational Administration and History, 42*(3), 203–222.

Hodgkinson, C. (1996). *Administrative philosophy: Values and motivations in administrative life.* Oxford: Elsevier Science Ltd.

Kimber, M. & Ehrich, L.C. (2011). The democratic deficit and school-based management in Australia. *Journal of Educational Administration, 49*(2), 179–199.

LoBianco, T. (2013, July 29). Tony Bennett, former Indiana school superintendent, changed top GOP donor's school's grade. *Huffington Post*, 1.

Marcellino, P.A. (2006). Creativity, in management. In F. English (Ed.), *Encyclopedia of educational leadership and administration* (pp. 232–233). Thousand Oaks, CA: Sage.

McGrane, V. (2015, March 4). Yellen scolds Wall Street on culture, ethics. *The Wall Street Journal*, C5.

Mead, G.H. (1934). *Mind, self and society from the standpoint of a social behaviorist.* Edited by C.W. Morris. Chicago: University of Chicago Press.

Mintzberg, H. (1983). *Structure in fives: Designing effective organizations.* Englewood Cliffs, NJ: Prentice-Hall, Inc.

Montessori Australia (n.d.). A biography of Dr Maria Montessori. Retrieved from http://montessori.org.au/montessori/biography.htm.

Mullen, C., Samier, E., Brindley, S., English, F. & Carr, N. (2013). An epistemic frame analysis of neoliberal culture and politics in the US, UK, and the UAE. *Interchange, 43*(3), 187–228.

North Carolina State Board of Education (2007). *North Carolina standards for superintendents.* Raleigh, NC.

Orr, H.A. (2015, March 19). The biology of being good to others. *The New York Review of Books, LXII*(5), 27–29.

Ravitch, D. (2010). *The life and death of the great American school system: How testing and choice are undermining education.* New York: Basic Books.

Ravitch, D. (2012). *Reign of error: The hoax of the privatization movement and the danger to America's public schools.* New York: Alfred A. Knopf.

Robinson, M. (2015, February 5). On Edgar Allan Poe. *The New York Review of Books, LXII*(2), 4–5.

Rokeach, M. & Bonier, R. (1960). Time perspective, dogmatism, and anxiety. In M. Rokeach (Ed.), *The open and closed mind* (pp. 366–375). New York: Basic Books.

Rokeach, M., McGovney, W.C. & Denny, M.R. (1960). Dogmatic thinking versus rigid thinking: An experimental distinction. In M. Rokeach (Ed.), *The open and closed mind* (pp. 182–195). New York: Basic Books.

Ropo, A. & Parviainen, J. (2001). Leadership and bodily knowledge in expert organizations: Epistemological rethinking. *Scandinavian Journal of Management, 17,* 1–18.

Santamaria, L.J. & Jaramillo, N.E. (2014, August). Comrades among us: The power of artists as informal mentors for women of color in academe. *Mentoring and Tutoring: Partnership in Learning, 22*(4), 316–337.

Shils, E. (1968). The concept and function of ideology. In D. Sills (Ed.), *International encyclopedia of the social sciences. Vol. 7* (pp. 66–85). New York: The Macmillan Company.

Silverman, G. (2015, March 17). FT big read consumer trends. *Financial Times,* 7.

Simon, H. (1947). *Administrative behavior.* New York: The Free Press.

Sinclair, A. (2005). Body possibilities in leadership. *Leadership, 1*(4), 387–406.

Singer, P. (1993). About ethics. In *Practical ethics* (2nd ed., pp. 1–15). Cambridge: Cambridge University Press.

Usher, R. & Edwards, R. (1996). *Postmodernism and education.* London: Routledge.

Wacquant, L.J.D. (1992). Toward a social praxeology: The structure and logic of Bourdieu's sociology. In P. Bourdieu & L.J.D. Wacquant (Eds.), *An invitation to reflexive sociology* (pp. 1–59). Chicago: University of Chicago Press.

Wallace, J. (2008). At the service of the (restructured) state: Principal's work and neoliberal ideology. In E.A. Samier & A.G. Stanley (Eds.), *Political approaches to educational administration and leadership* (pp. 223–239). London: Routledge.

Weber, M. (1930). *The Protestant ethic and the spirit of capitalism.* London: Allen & Unwin.

West, C. (1999). *The Cornel West reader.* New York: Perseus Books.

8

LEADING BEAUTIFULLY

The Cosmogony of Connoisseurship

The concept of 'leading beautifully' brings our attention to that often un-articulated, but nonetheless powerful aspect of how leaders embody their role. Leading beautifully speaks to a quality of being—one honed through the development of self-mastery, and quickened through the congruence of one's acts with their 'measured' expression. It also alerts us to the possibility of a leader's goals being directed towards the best of human purposes.

(Ladkin, 2008, p. 40)

WHAT THIS CHAPTER IS ABOUT

This chapter is the capstone for a presentation regarding connoisseurship as leadership performance and as a perspective to restore the human side of educational leadership to at least an equal partnership with the intellectual and cognitive side. This perspective can be encapsulated succinctly in the concept of *leading beautifully* instead of what is the dominant catchphrase in management today, which is *leading effectively*. The idea of "effective" is the embodiment of only the cognitive side of leadership. It is the child of *rational choice theory* which is the hegemonic ideology of business, banking and commerce and an increasingly destructive one for organizations which deliver public services. As an ideology, *effective leadership* is linked to quantification of activities and an elimination of those that cannot be quantified. Goals or activities which cannot produce measurable results are recast (reduced in complexity) or dropped altogether. It is a *minimalist* approach to leadership because its view of humanity erases emotion and context and with it decision relevancy and significance (see Kenneth, Hamm, Grassia & Peterson, 1997).

Pierre Bourdieu (1999a) summarized this situation accurately when he observed:

> Economists have sufficient specific interests . . . to make a decisive contribution, whatever their emotional responses to the economic and social effects of the utopia that they dress up in mathematical reason . . . Cut off . . . by their generally purely abstract and theoretical intellectual training from the real economic and social world, they are, like others in other times . . . particularly inclined to take the things of logic for the logic of things.
>
> (p. 101)

No better example of the de-humanization of leadership can be found than the current North Carolina Standards for Superintendents (North Carolina State Board of Education, 2007), which declared, "Leadership is neither a position nor a person. It is a collection of practices that must be embedded in all job roles at all levels of schools and the school district" (p. 1). This is rational choice theory personified. It is Frederick Taylor's proclamation in 1911 in *The Principles of Scientific Management*, "In the past the man [*sic*] has been first. In the future the System must be first" (p. 7).

This chapter explores the roots of connoisseurship in craft knowledge and what it can offer to the practice of leadership in schools. It then provides a synthesis of the major ideas and research generated from the study, represented in Table 8.1. The chapter closes with an exploration of how preparing leader connoisseurs could change the traditional manner of training leaders in university settings and how that would alter the regnant practices and approaches in use today. At its core, however, is the juxtaposition of connoisseurship as a completely different cosmology regarding educational leadership. Previous works on the arts in educational leadership have always had to work themselves back from the margins into the dominant discourse. Connoisseurship is more than that. It is a re-ordering of the cosmology of the field itself, a kind of fundamental shift in the core vision for its purpose. Zabel (2015) captured our intent when he observed, "Artists can illuminate truth, offer transcendent experience in a far too literal world, challenge us to feel, and connect us to our common humanity" (p. 1).

Introduction

The concept of leadership as connoisseurship opens up an expanded perspective on the nature of leadership as aesthetic performance. The shift in re-visioning the nature of educational leadership moves from notions of "effective" leadership embedded in what Kimber and Ehrich (2011) called a workplace governed by "contractual accountability driven by the market" (p. 179) and one that de-professionalizes teaching and privatizes public goods and services by redefining citizens as customers, to one which is involved with "leading beautifully."

The proposal to engage in this more inclusive perspective is not original with the co-researchers of this book, nor is it confined to educational leadership. Chester Barnard (1938), a prescient management thinker, formerly President of the Rockefeller Foundation and President of the New Jersey Bell Telephone Company, spoke of "the executive arts" in his classic work *The Functions of the Executive* (p. 222), and commented:

> It is the function of the arts to accomplish concrete ends, effect results, produce situations, that would not come about without the deliberate effort to secure them. These arts must be mastered and applied by those who deal in the concrete and for the future.
>
> (p. 290)

There have been other views and proposals to move the field more in this direction in the past as well, before the research framing this book (see Greenfield, 1975, 1986; Heilbrunn, 1996; Maxcy, 1991; Samier, 2011; Starratt, 1993).

Forces to Confront in Proposing a Change

As we consider how the field of educational leadership may be redefined to improve its efficacy and capacity to make a difference, two rather immediate obstacles present themselves. The first is the "democratic deficit" and the second is the presence of "passive evil."

The Democratic Deficit and the Hollow State

The current emphasis on the marketplace and market forces as the alleged self-correcting mechanism to promote efficiency in educational schools and institutions have led to severe social consequences and the presence of a "democratic deficit" (Kimber & Ehrich, 2011, 2015). This negative condition has been defined as: (1) the weakening of professional accountability; (2) the ignoring of the roles and values of public employees; and (3) the emergency of the "hollow state." The "hollow state" consists of "the removal of public goods and services from the public sector and the reduction of citizens to customers or clients" (Kimber & Ehrich, 2011, p. 180). Bourdieu (1999b) also lamented the hollowing out of the public responsibility of the state to its citizens:

> it is impossible to understand the present state of affairs without taking into account the wholesale conversion to neoliberalism that began in the 1970s . . . it was accompanied by a destruction of the idea of public services . . . they identify "modernization" with the transfer into the private sector of the public services with the most profit potential and with eliminating or bringing into line subordinate staff in the public services, held responsible for every inefficiency and every "rigidity."
>
> (pp. 182–183)

The neo-liberal idea that the marketplace can correct its own deficiencies is belied by the startling fact that since the year 2000, the U.S. Federal Government has had to take action against 2,163 corporations for legal infractions and shoddy business dealings and practices. Among the most notable was a fine of $17 billion against the Bank of America, $1.2 billion to Goldman Sachs and $300 million against Standard Chartered. In 2014 the U.S. Justice Department collected $5.5 billion in direct payments from successful prosecutions and another $2.6 billion by other federal agencies (A Mammoth Guilt Trip, 2014, p. 21). While the state is being hollowed out from serving the poor, the rich are taking advantage with massive cheating and tax avoidance schemes. It was revealed that HSBC Bank had set up secret accounts in its Swiss Unit to help wealthy Americans, dictators, arms dealers and rock stars avoid taxes and even advised clients on how to avoid taxes in their home countries (Letzing, 2015).

The Presence of Passive Evil

The second destructive force released in the arena of educational administration and leadership is that of "passive evil" (Samier, 2008, p. 3). "Passive evil" exists when leaders become "neither moral nor immoral actors [but] . . . moral mutes" (Menzel, 1999, p. 521). This condition arises when administrators cease asking moral questions which are sacrificed to economic imperatives, measures of efficiency and other benchmarks of alleged productivity. Administrative moral evil has been defined as "the violation of moral rules causing harm to organizational members, clients, and society in general by virtue of administrative powers over resources, influence, and decision-making" (Samier, 2008, p. 4).

No more dramatic evidence of this "passive evil" could be found than in the recent widespread Atlanta (Georgia) Public Schools (APS) cheating scandal. After several years of suspicious test score rises in the school system, a statewide investigation in 2011 revealed that 185 teachers and administrators in APS in 44 schools "participated in cheating on the 2009 Criterion-Referenced Competency Tests. The inquiry formed the basis for the criminal charges brought against the educators March 29, 2013" (*Atlanta Journal-Constitution*, February 12, 2015, p. A6). This same report called the situation in APS an example of "organized and systemic misconduct" (Jarvie, 2015, p. A5) in 44 of 56 schools in the district.

During a lengthy trial, "More than 130 witnesses told a story of a school system run amok, with employees engaging in or condoning behavior that compromised the educations of untold numbers of children" (Tagami & Cook, 2015, p. A1). The prosecution of the Atlanta educators "characterized the Atlanta public schools as a pyramid system designed to create a false impression of academic success, with teachers and administrators routinely cheating, lying and stealing" (Jarvie, 2015, p. A5).

Some of the behavior revealed in testimony was that one teacher left the answer sheets "on a table in her classroom and instruct[ed] an aide to correct any wrong answers" (Cook, 2015, p. B2). Another witness indicated that an elementary school principal had a student report to her that a teacher had given him the answers on the test but that she "brushed the boy aside and kept walking" (Tagami & Cook, 2015, p. A6). A teacher told of another school principal who threatened her to engage in cheating when she was admonished with the phrase, "Wal-Mart's always hiring" (Tagami & Cook, 2015, p. A6). Wal-Mart is a U.S.-based discount store which has had a reputation for low paying wages for its employees and a long history of pay discrimination practices against its female employees. As a result it is always hiring new sales clerks. In the end eight former educators in Atlanta were sentenced to prison sentences, financial penalties and 1,000 hours of community service. The presiding judge said of the Atlanta mess that it was "the sickest thing that's ever happened in this town" (McWhirter, 2015, p. A3). The concept of connoisseurship with its roots in the arts and humanities needs to be restored to its place in enabling leaders involved with moral and ethical issues the means to confront conditions within the pervasive marketplace model based on rational choice theory which eliminates moral issues from even being considered. This was underscored when Lori Revere-Paulk, a former math coach in APS who became a whistleblower and was demoted as punishment, later observed as fellow teachers were facing severe prison sentences, "That's kind of hard because a lot of teachers had pressure to do things. But as an adult, you have to know right from wrong" (Tagami & Cook, 2015, p. A6).

The Restoration of Arts-Centered Leadership Research

The research behind this study of leadership supports the restoration of the view of educational leadership as one involving an ethical, humanist and aesthetic perspective. It includes and builds upon prior inquiry on "arts informed research in educational administration" (Baskwill, 2008, p. 37). Specifically the concept of "activist professionalism" (Sachs, 2000, p. 81) can be applied to the work of school leaders who work in concert with teachers, students and members of the wider community, and it is based on eight principles:

- Inclusiveness rather than exclusiveness
- Collective and collaborative action
- Effective communication of aims and expectations
- Recognition of the expertise of all parties involved
- Creating an environment of trust and mutual respect
- Being responsive and responsible
- Acting with passion
- Experiencing pleasure and fun.

(p. 87)

Behind these eight principles lies the idea that humans are not only concerned with logic and economic calculations, but also with emotionality. James Barber (1983) wrote of U.S. presidents:

> Every story of Presidential decision-making is really two stories: an outer one in which a rational man calculates and an inner one in which an emotional man feels. The two are forever connected. Any real President is one whole man and his deeds reflect his wholeness.
>
> (p. 4)

The presence of emotionality in decision-making is one of the reasons that the building of trust is essential in leadership. The construction of trust is part of what Weick (1993) called *sensemaking*, in which an individual's *personal cosmogony* (see Armstrong, 2005) is involved. A person's *personal cosmogony* represents his/her core values and comes into play as a person confronts ethical or moral dilemmas in a leadership role. Harding and Pribram (2004) add this note to the presence of trust:

> The circulation of emotion produces in and between people connection, ruptures, depends on responsibilities, accountabilities, and so on . . . [When] people care—they are invested. If people care, certain effects are produced; they feel and act in certain ways.
>
> (p. 879)

Any model of leadership which does not deal with the emotional side of decision-making may severely miscalculate not only the nature of the decision but its impact. For example, Groopman's (2007) analyses of how physicians engage with patients indicates that in the training of doctors, there are few lessons learned from medical school in how to deal with their own emotions in diagnosis and prescription. Horton (2007) commented about this issue:

> Disclosing uncertainty and error will demand a deep change in medicine's attitude toward emotion. Most physicians fail to recognize, let alone analyze, their own emotional states in clinical encounters. This repression of feeling misses an important variable in the assessment of a patient's experiences and outcome. The emotional temperature of the doctor plays a substantial part in diagnostic failure and success.
>
> (p. 18)

In contrast to physicians, artists are more comfortable with their own emotions and use them to stimulate their vision and creativity. For example, Alberto, one of the artists in our sample, referred to art as a medium in which deep human experiences resided. He spoke about art being a spirit that comes through artists, and referred to it as "a living force." The next part of this chapter looks more closely at what is meant by *leading beautifully*.

Leading Beautifully: The Realm of Aesthetics in Providing an Alternative Leadership Model

Current functional skill-based definitions of leadership present images of leaders as "disembodied beings," automatons without hearts or souls (Sinclair, 2005). The sources of such lists reside chiefly in rational choice theory, economics, and behavioral research studies that, while they may include some leadership content activity such as visioning, planning, alignment and creating efficient groups of teachers conversing about student achievement, fail to define performance of the leader beyond a sort of simple accumulation of tasks. Leadership is thus not "superb" or "beautiful," it is only "effective" or "adequate" in comparison to how it has been defined.

The minute one wants to deal with leadership beyond "ticking the boxes" of the lists of functions and skills, then we enter the realm of describing it from the arts and aesthetics. Connoisseurship is not a skill, though it embodies skills. It is located in practice and it includes feelings, perceptions, emotions, intuition and morality. Connoisseurship in leadership is *practice plus*. It lies at the heart of performance. While functional leadership practice can perhaps deal with the question, "What is it that leaders are expected to do?" it fails to describe how well they may do it. It fails to deal with such critical issues as leader credibility and authenticity. The "what" and "how well" dimensions of leadership reside in different realms, one in science and the other in the arts.

In their book *The Leadership Paradox*, Deal and Peterson (1994) describe two types of school principals: engineers and artists. The engineers are those excelling in what would be called *managerialist* aspects of leaders. They prefer goal-directed activities, timelines, clear delineation of lines of authority and run a "tight ship." In contrast are the artists:

> Artist-principals seek to define reality, capture and articulate symbols that communicate deeply held values and beliefs, and engage people in ritual, ceremony, theater, and play. Their primary motivation is to instill a deep sense of meaning that makes school a place of the heart, as well as of head and hands. Artistic principals tell stories, talk expressively about teachers and students, articulate and exemplify values in their own everyday behavior, create heroes and heroines, and make memos and meetings fun—even musical.

(p. 8)

We suggest that the arts and aesthetics are sources for repositioning the content of educational leadership, a position also advocated as early as Collingwood's (1938) *The Principles of Art* and later by Jones (2006) and Barry and Meisiek (2010).

One of the advantages of aesthetics as a field in which to locate educational leadership is that in aesthetics there is a central place for human emotion (Harris, 2006). We agree with Fineman (2000) that organizations can be understood as *emotional arenas*. This view of organizational life posits that emotion is recognized and performed for specific audiences. For principals "this audience is a particularly wide and diverse one, encompassing staff, pupils and the wider community" (Crawford, 2009, p. 129). On first blush this perspective may be at odds with the overly rational-technical models that dominate the skill check lists so popular with accrediting and licensing agencies for school leaders, for as Baskwill (2008) reminds us, "The expression of emotion is not readily endorsed or exercised in Western society. In this cultural climate, it is particularly difficult to express the emotional turmoil that is part of the day-to-day reality of the principalship" (p. 40). However, Zorn and Boler (2008) warn us that "Emotion matters in educational leadership because leaders, teachers and learners understand and enact their roles of subordination and domination significantly through learned emotional expressions and silences" (p. 148).

Paraphrasing Hansen, Ropo and Sauer (2007), Bathurst, Jackson and Statler (2010) argue that aesthetics "focuses primarily on that which is dynamic and sensate within relationships" (p.313) and "allows for imagination and tacitly-held beliefs to be expressed" (Adler, 2006, p. 491). Bathurst et al. (2010) also considered beautiful leading as "leading aesthetically" and employed the work of Roman Ingarden (1975) to describe aspects of such leading. We review these now.

Presencing and concretization. This aspect of beautiful or aesthetic leading is one in which the leader engages in *presencing*, which is the creative engagement that allows the work undertaken "to unfold within the contingencies imposed by the environment, and the skills of the artist" (Bathurst et al., 2010, p. 316). This leadership attribute is also connected to *concretization* which deals with how the leader and his/her decisions or actions are perceived by followers (Bathurst et al., 2010). Of key importance is to have a sense of how much change or stress followers can handle. There is obviously no science to this judgment.

Bathurst et al. (2010) provide as two examples the aesthetically aware leader's sense of timing, that is, when to make a decision or take an action. This involves knowing when to intervene in an unfolding event and either let it take its course or to take control of it and direct it. This aesthetic awareness is critical, especially if the event in question is non-linear or not logical. It involves what some have called "deliberate deferral" (Tichy & Bennis, 2007, p. 318).

Backward reflexivity. The leader leading beautifully understands that the present is connected to the past and that these linkages will be extended into the future (Bathurst et al., 2010). The key issue is an awareness and acknowledgment that contemporary organizational arrangements are "temporal," that is, the leader sees all three of these tenses simultaneously in *social time* and envisions himself/herself able to make sense of all three in a kind of "co-presence" (Hepburn, 2002, p. 27).

Form and content. Beautiful leadership finds the leader grasping the interplay between form and content (Bathurst et al., 2010), the ideal and the real in a kind of "dialectic interplay between subjective and objective elements in human experience" (Langer, 1962, p. 13). This balance between form and content enables leaders to situate the local and immediate to the global and longer term flow of events (Eisner, 2002).

Myth-making. By myth is meant a narrative that informs and supports a flow of events that provides overall meaning for the participants and sometimes creates special designations for terms that come to have special earmarks for organizational participants (Bathurst et al., 2010). The importance of stories and slogans that capture these important benchmarks are part of leading beautifully. Paul J. Keating (2011), former prime minister of Australia, described *myth-making* eloquently when he said:

> it is important that we are able to see the world as it really is—to have a wider comprehension of it; see it in a framework . . . because once you have a picture, you are able to get the coordinates of your circumstances right. The latitude and longitude by which we focus on a problem, but problem in context, in a framework or wider picture.
>
> (p. 581)

Connoisseurs who are leaders have developed a fine-tuned capability of using their intuition based on tacit knowledge of how their schools and school systems function. They are at home in comprehending and working in a realm of "feelings, desires, tastes, and passions" (Strati, 2010, p. 880). Connoisseurs differ from ordinary leaders who may not feel comfortable working in these realms and who may believe that showing emotion is a sign of weakness in a leader.

Artists are more at home in dealing with personal realms of imagination, taste, feelings and matters of their own identity than school leaders. Artists are more open to learning and, as Wenger (1998) notes, "learning transforms who we are and what we can do [and] is an experience of identity" (p. 215). As school administration has become re-centered in managerialism around accountability, machine metaphors and rational choice theory anchored in economic models, school leaders may be reluctant to stray very far from them in their day-to-day roles in schools.

We found, however, that an educational leader who is a connoisseur is able to span both worlds and not only make sense of them but integrates them in a way that produces a healthy place for teachers and students to live and work. The educational leader who epitomizes this capacity was Templeton, the African American school superintendent who understood the conditions of the home life of much of his minority student population when he called a snow day with restricted hours when the school would be open so that the students would have a warm place to come to for part of that day and a hot meal, perhaps the only one they would receive that day (see Chapter 6).

Connoisseurship's Roots in Craft Knowledge

Artistic judgment is not a matter of science, rational choice theory and/or behaviorism which have little place for the qualities rooted in aesthetics. We are not the first researchers who have taken issue with the paucity of knowledge regarding leadership which is inclusive only of social science and its attendant disciplines (see Bolton & English, 2010; Duke, 1986; Greenfield, 1975; Hansen et al., 2007; Heilbrunn, 1996; Kelehear, 2008).

For example, we agree with Blumberg (1989) who posited that educational administration is essentially a craft. He differentiated between a science and a craft by noting that "Craft aims to produce a specific result be it a physical product or performing ability through the development of skills built up through practice" (p. 28). Here are the characteristics Blumberg (1989) identified with a craft. The parallelism to connoisseurship and the elements of it are striking. Essentially, if educational leadership is viewed from this perspective as a kind of "craft" then leaders would have:

- Developed a kind of "nose for things"
- Have a sense of what constitutes an acceptable result in any particular problematic situation
- Understand the nature of materials
- Know administrative techniques and having the skill to employ them in the most efficacious way possible
- Know what to do and when to do it
- Have a sense of "process," being able to diagnose and interpret the meaning of what is occurring as people interact in any problematic situation.

(p. 47)

While we concur that educational leadership embodies craft knowledge, like Eisner (2002) we also agree that when the educational leader encounters novel situations, craft knowledge is not enough. When a leader confronts the unexpected it is then that craft knowledge must be augmented by an aesthetic and creative response and move beyond the leader's current repertoire.

The development of these capacities is an example of "tacit knowledge" (Polanyi, 1967), especially when Blumberg (1989) talks about "developing and learning to trust one's sixth sense" (p. 176). Such a sense is one involving aesthetic awareness and qualitative judgments which "are often unpredictable, are non-prescriptive and can be performed with such skill and grace that . . . the experience can justifiably be called aesthetic" (Kelehear, 2008, p. 240). It is to this realm that we now turn.

What Can a Connoisseurship Model Offer the Field for a More Powerful Exemplar of Educational Leadership?

Based on our research reported thus far and logical extensions of it and the findings in the larger literature we posit that these new dimensions constitute a fundamental cosmological shift in the field, away from scientism, behaviorism and structural-functionalism as the dominant perspectives to a more humane and human principled discourse. It is not only a restoration but potentially a re-centering. In this sense it is radical. And by radical we mean from the Latin *radicalis* or *radix* (Barnhart, 1995, p. 631). Its original Latin meaning was *a root* as in a plant or *that upon which is fixed or rests* (Andrews, 1854, p. 1963).

A Final Synthesis of the Dimensions, Frames and Stages of Connoisseurship

A final synthesis of the research of this book is now presented in Table 8.1. This table shows *the 10 dimensions* which were discussed in Chapter 1 and were applied to the life of the art connoisseur Bernard Berenson. Following is the connoisseurship model that identifies 20 core leadership dimensions (Chapter 7). The final two columns are Eisner's (2002) seven epistemic frames (Chapter 4) and seven ways in which leaders developed a discerning eye that emerged from our empirical study (Chapter 4).

Table 8.1 indicates that there are many facets of connoisseurship and many of them overlap or extend a dimension slightly more than others. But they all coalesce around common themes. There are glimpses of many of these dimensions in the leadership literature across many years, from a different perspective in the classic book by Douglas McGregor (1960) *The Human Side of Enterprise* which examined the *Theory Y* leader to James McGregor Burns' (1978) *transformational leader*; Jerry Starratt's (1993) *The Drama of Leadership*; Terry Deal and Kent Peterson's (1994) *The Leadership Paradox*; Thomas Sergiovanni's (2000) *The Lifeworld of Leadership*; Peter Gronn's (2003) *The New Work of Educational Leaders* and Neil Cranston and Lisa Ehrich's (2007) *What is This Thing Called Leadership?* All of these sources contain elements of connoisseurship identified in this book. It is our hope that this text based initially on the work of artists has created a clearer picture of an alternative we believe is long overdue. It is not only an alternative view of leadership, it is a change in the cosmogony of thinking about leadership. *Leading beautifully* is in a different realm altogether than *leading effectively*. The former concept pushes the arc of leadership to new heights. The latter concept suffices with only the effort to reach specified objectives. The idea of performance incorporates and exceeds any notion of objective statements of possible outcomes. It is *leadership plus*.

TABLE 8.1 A synthesis of the dimensions, frames and ways of developing connoisseurship

Ten dimensions of connoisseurship	Connoisseurship model of leadership	Eisner's seven epistemic frames	Seven ways of developing the discerning eye
1. Knowledgeable perception	View of change; power	More than one answer; imagination is given license	Emerges from hard work; emerges from increasing differentiation; utilizes benchmarking
2. Experience	View of risk taking; responses to challenges or threats; view of ambiguity	More than one answer; artist composition of relationships	Developmental, evolutionary and dependent on others; emerges from hard work; emerges from increasing differentiation; dependent on feedback and public recognition
3. Competence	View of competence; working relationships	Work should be flexibly purposive	Developmental; evolutionary and dependent on others; emerges from hard work; results of personal efforts to attain competency; outcome of increasing differentiation; dependent on feedback and public recognition
4. Framing	Purpose of leadership; major view of leadership; framing	More than one answer; imagination is given license; non-quantifiable, non-literal and non-linear representations are central	Outcome of increasing differentiation; utilizes benchmarking
5. Desire	View of creativity and imagination; emotion and intuition	Intrinsic satisfaction matters	Result of personal efforts to attain competency; result of increasing differentiation of work
6. Understanding of practice	Enactment of leadership; under-standing of practice	More than one answer; artist composition of relationships	Emerges from hard work; out of increasing differentiation; feedback and public recognition; utilizes benchmarking
7. Aesthetic vision	Values	Imagination is given license; form and content inter-penetrate; non-quantifiable, non-literal, non-linear reps are central; more than one answer	Result of increasing differentiation; utilizes benchmarking

continued

TABLE 8.1 Continued

Ten dimensions of connoisseurship	Connoisseurship model of leadership	Eisner's seven epistemic frames	Seven ways of developing the discerning eye
8. Cultural awareness and reflexivity	Ethics; cultural awareness; view of people	More than one answer; form and content inter-penetrate	Result of increasing differentiation
9. Discipline	Approach to work	Work should be flexibly purposive	Emerges from hard work; result of personal efforts to attain competency; outcome of increasing differentiation; feedback via public recognition; utilizes benchmarking
10. Identity	Identity	Artist composition of relationships	Begins in early childhood; result of personal efforts to attain competency; outcome of increasing differentiation; dependent upon feedback via public recognition; utilizes benchmarking

A Composite Portrait

These are the final descriptors of the concept of a leader of connoisseur performance as linked to Table 8.1. An individual who is on the continuum of connoisseurship as a leader is defined by a desire to attain a high level of competence far beyond his/her peers, to develop the broadest and most in-depth perception of the context in which his/her leadership is to be expressed. A connoisseur of leadership performance fully understands the matter of framing problems, that problem solving is dependent upon how a problem is framed or posed. A connoisseur of leadership performance enjoys areas of ambiguity because this is where creativity and innovation can be exercised and exhibited. They understand the limits of practice and how practice is defined within a larger field of logic which may not always be logical to a person outside that field. A connoisseur of leadership performance grasps the limitations of quantification and measurement. What may be measured is not always the most important variable or dimension of leading. They know that there are always many answers to questions and they often eschew the easy or most traditional or conventional ones in favor of a search for one that may be "crazy." Connoisseurs of leadership performance possess a strong sense of personal identity, they are extremely disciplined in their approach to work and they work very hard and have done so for a long time. These educational leaders value difference and they are culturally sensitive. They are not afraid to use their imagination and buck tradition when it is necessary. Moreover, they value experience and work at integrating that experience into advanced levels of performance. Paul Feyerabend (1995) wrote about how discoverers, inventors and thinkers put together their source of knowledge. He said that the most important criterion was "the changing ability of the professional to deal with his [sic] surroundings; it uses the *schooled eye*, the *practised hand* of the artisan, the navigator, the artist and it develops with his craft" (p. 17). Our research echoes many of these same insights.

Summary

This concluding chapter brought together all of the data and evidence to present a picture of the connoisseurship of leadership and what it means for a connoisseur of leadership performance to lead beautifully. It is our position that the connoisseurship model better fits the requirements of the day for a complete education of what has been called "the whole child." The penchant for test, test, test as the sole benchmark for determining leadership efficacy not only misses the mark with leadership, but is singularly destructive and detrimental to the education of the young, not to mention teachers and support staff in the schools. Perhaps the restoration of the arts and humanities in the preparation of educational leaders in which the heart as well as the head find recognition and training will mark a turning point in the dreadful landscape which is unfolding before our eyes. That we have "out there" current educational leaders in both countries, Australia and America, on a continuum of connoisseurship represents the untapped human resources that will be needed to restore the balance which is so desperately needed to re-engage learners and their teachers in what should be a joyful experience.

IMPLICATIONS FOR POLICY AND PRACTICE

The Preparation of Educational Leaders Will Have to Be Re-Professionalized Around a Broader Array of Fields to Prepare Leadership Connoisseurs

The dominant selection of courses in U.S. universities remains locked in rational choice theory and economics. A review of the courses in the top-ranked American educational leadership programs (Bolton & English, 2010) revealed all in the thraldom of rational choice theory aping the top-ranked business school curriculums. In only one top-ranked educational leadership program was a non-rational course required for graduates. T.B. Greenfield summarized this phenomenon:

There are ways of understanding and expressing knowledge that are powerful, satisfying and important, but non-rational—ways that are essentially cast within an artistic, literary, historical, philosophical even journalistic mode. A mode that is descriptive, withholding judgement, though moving towards it, moving to insight.

(Greenfield & Ribbins, 1993, p. 254)

Thirty years later former Australian Prime Minister Paul Keating (2012) told a Sky News reporter in a televised interview, "the arts are important to me . . . I often say to people, the Australian economy was reformed off the back of Gustav Mahler, Anton Bruckner, and Mr. Shostakovich."

We are not suggesting that courses in the social sciences be dropped from the curriculum that seeks to prepare educational leaders. We are strongly advocating that the curriculum and the courses be modified and re-balanced, that courses which are based on a study of literature, the arts, philosophy, music, theology, be mixed in with this curriculum, especially at the doctoral level. Any curriculum that alleges its aim is to bring an educational leader into a school that is concerned with *the whole child* must be prepared to examine *the whole human being* and that, as Greenfield remarked, is, "If you would be a leader, first lead yourself" (Greenfield & Ribbins, 1993, pp. 254–255).

We imagine all kinds of outcries over this, that such courses are "not practical," but we would reply that they are among the most practical of all courses for leading a moral enterprise which is a school. T.B. Greenfield replied to the same question when he responded, "I think the most valuable form of training begins in a setting of practice, where one has to balance values against constraints—in which one has to take action within a political context" (Greenfield & Ribbins, 1993, p. 257).

Many professors at current institutions are former school practitioners. And while their experience in practice makes their perspectives contextualized, they often do not think outside of that context and they do not perceive how laws and regulations define what is thinkable and what is not. In short, they are not *reflexive* about our discourse. They are products of the system *as it exists*. What is always "practical" is the present and not the future. Many do not have the epistemological lenses to probe deeply about practice, to question why we do what we do and why we don't do what we do not. In short, as Frederick Taylor (1911/1967) desired, they come from the system and their perceptions fit that system. What constitutes change is simply tinkering. We can't keep cranking out future leaders who will do little but perpetuate the status quo. Current practice, as we understand it and exemplified in the national school leader standards, is little but a reflection of that existing practice (Sperville, 2014). Its shortcomings have been documented in the research and literature of the field since T.B. Greenfield issued his first critique in 1974 in Bristol, England (Greenfield & Ribbins, 1993, p. 229).

To move in this direction we need different eyes. We need to see differently. That has always been the function of the arts, to make us see anew.

One way is to examine leadership outside institutional arrangements, outside bureaucracies. We have called that "grassroots leadership" (Ehrich & English, 2012). Grassroots leadership is different. Foster (1986) observed that:

> Leadership can spring from anywhere . . . it derives from the context and ideas of individuals who influence each other. Thus, a principal may at times be a leader and at other times, a follower. A teacher may be a leader, and the principal a follower.
>
> (p. 187)

Foster (1986) went on to say, "Leadership is an act bounded in space and time, it is an act that enables others and allows them, in turn, to become enablers" (p. 187).

Gloria Steinem characterized this division as *corporate leadership* versus *movement leadership*. The latter type of leadership requires the ability to persuade and hand out orders. There's no role in an organization to require obedience. There's no legal authority to fall back on. *Movement leadership* requires inspiration and because of creating common bonds it becomes the basis for trust and for coalitions to develop (Steinem in Bennis, 1989, p. 159). Collaborative leadership is emotional.

It is our position that the preparation of school leaders must undergo a shift, a re-centering from values of conformity and compliance to ones which emphasize diversity, collaboration, coalition building, the creation of schools as places of learning and joy, and not mindless drudgery. The routinization of learning coincides with managerial rigidities often encapsulated in standards which are disembodied skills and categorical attributes. The construction of such standards for school leaders amounts to a ruthless quest for conformity and in itself is a denial of the importance of context and even the need for leadership. If the creation of managerial control of schools involves doing the same things and it is expected that by so doing some sort of "excellence" will automatically follow, there is little need for a leader. All that is needed is a timekeeper to keep the place on task and a bookkeeper to record the results and the costs. Leadership is only required when the complexities of context require interpretation, adjustment, collaboration, creativity and inspiration. Standardizing leadership is an oxymoron. If leaders can be standardized we don't need them.

We have advocated that the curriculum for preparing school leaders be centered around community organizing and not bureaucratic rule fidelity (Ehrich & English, 2012). This is a decidedly *activist* view of leadership which has one foot in the school and the other foot in the community. It recognizes that real advancement in closing achievement gaps must involve the social safety net as well as relevant learning in the school (Sahlberg, 2011).

The traditional courses found in many curricula at the university level include organizational sociology or "org theory" as it is known; school law, finance and budgeting; personnel management; administrative problem solving or case studies and perhaps group dynamics, labor negotiations, instructional management and curriculum development or design. Other courses might include politics, research, planning, school–community relations, economics, change theory, statistical methods, accountability, history of education and something on cultural differences. In most cases these courses are taught from the perspective of the "inside out," that is, as an administrator would function in a school or school system working inside and looking out. In almost all cases they are taught from the view of maintaining the organization as it is and dealing with conflict as though conflict were a hindrance to smooth bureaucratic functioning. If the allegiance of the educational leader is on always assuming the "inside out" perspective and also of working to maintain harmony at the expense of all else, it is unlikely that radical change will take place. By not taking school leadership outside of the school and into the community, the leader never comes to the "outside in" perspective of school operations.

Pierre Bourdieu (1998) spoke of the logic of practice. By this he meant that all practice contains a logic of its own which makes sense to the people inside the organization but doesn't have to make any sense to those outside of it. By not adopting the "outside in" perspective in preparing school leaders, the internal logic of practice is rarely if ever questioned. We believe that a cosmological shift is required to do this where school leaders need to develop the connoisseur's *discerning eye* but are unlikely to do it unless they are trained to look at schools from the "outside in."

In order for future educational leaders to develop a perspective regarding what constitutes *real organizational change* they must be able to see what schools do and how they work as opposed to the blinkered views even those who work in them have because they have a trained incapacity not to see what they actually do. Courses which can develop the outsider's view would be those that are not primarily centered on existing practices because those rarely, if ever, question the basis of a practice. They simply want to become expert on the doing of practical tasks. These are guaranteed to perpetuate the status quo.

Courses which provide new ways of seeing, that is, of developing *the discerning eye*, would be those that take the student out of immediate practical problems and serve to create a wider vision of considering any and all practices. These courses should provoke the student to engage in *reflexive practice* as opposed to *reflective* practice. The former is concerned with how one is thinking about how one is thinking about practice. Thus, *reflexive practice* is not concerned with the practice per se, but how one is thinking about that practice. *Reflective practice* is about how one is doing the practice and perhaps the results obtained from the doing of it.

We see courses such as the sociology of education in which readers are exposed to different views of schools; theoretical texts which present different lenses to examine schools such as critical theory, critical race theory, feminist critique, forms of postmodern critique; art history; theater and music history; theology; literary criticism; world literature; world religions; cultural anthropology; comparative education; creative thinking; politics and political systems; and forms of governance, ethics and philosophy as providing much merit. In short, these types of courses have the potential to take students out of implementing a practice and just doing it better, to a more metaanalytical plane of analysis.

So much of the criticism of what's wrong with university preparation has been involved with its alleged impracticality, its emphasis on theory and the immediate application that university programs we know have all but abdicated any attempt to provoke a critical response to contemporary practice as it has been understood. The current penchant for "evidence based practice" or "best practice" is an attempt to eliminate context and make decision making easier. In some cases it resembles a search for "the one best way" mentality of Frederick Taylor (1911/1967). As contexts change one type of best practice may not be best in a new situation. One of the downsides is that teachers and administrators are discouraged from "experimenting and trying emerging methods and technologies because they have not been vetted as best practice" (Hewitt, 2015, p. 137). The use of "best practice" is politically charged as neo-liberals tend to pick practices that conform to their ideologies which privilege "market forces, including competition and privatization of social institutions, including education" (Hewitt, 2015, p. 136).

The new cosmology we advocate is re-centering educational leadership away from the neo-liberal ideologies in which the field now swims. This means re-establishing a balance in a curriculum that is lopsided with business and economics concepts and practices that reward student performance on tests to the exclusion of almost everything else. These tests are extremely narrow and parochial slices of the full range of human ability and talent. Clearly a different view and vision of education and schooling are required around which to wrap the task of leadership. The basis of that leadership, as John

Dewey (1958) noted, is communication and "The expressions that constitute art are communication in its pure and undefiled form. Art breaks through barriers that divide human beings, which are impermeable in ordinary association" (p. 244). It is on this platform our advocacy of the connoisseurship of leadership originates. We agree with former Australian Prime Minister Paul Keating (2012) who said, "[the arts are] . . . a massive promoter of imagination."

Key Chapter Ideas

- **A Re-Centered Field of Educational Leadership Must Re-Establish Whole Human Beings as Both Means and Ends Which Include Feelings and Emotions as Legitimate Domains of Practice and Preparation of Educational Leaders**

The dominant model of leadership as expressed in traditional educational leadership textbooks rests on social science models and approaches to the detriment of alternative perspectives that include aspects of leader actions which may be considered non-rational. Current skill lists established for preparation and licensure disembody the whole human being and almost exclusively rest in rational choice theory and business economics. It is as though an educational leader has no heart, emotions, feelings, biases or spiritual presence in a school. Standards for school leaders are therefore lopsided and incomplete. A successful educational leader may be said to be simply "effective," that is, meets a standard or does not meet a standard. Current evaluative methods leave out how well or "beautiful" the actual leading is. Connoisseurship in leadership is a complex, poly-theoretical and polyvalent concept. It elevates a study of leadership into not only the content but the actual performance or the aesthetics of *leading*.

References

A mammoth guilt trip (2014, August 30). *The Economist, 412*(1843), 21–24.
Adler, N.J. (2006). The arts and leadership: Now that we can do anything, what will we do? *Academy of Management Learning and Education, 5*(4), 486–499.
Andrews, E.A. (1854). *Copius and critical Latin-English lexicon.* New York: Harper & Brothers Publishers.
Armstrong, K. (2005). *A short history of myth.* Edinburgh: Canongate.
Atlanta Journal-Constitution (2015, February 12). Continuing coverage, A6.
Barber, J.D. (1983). *The presidential character: Predicting performance in the White House.* Englewood Cliffs, NJ: Prentice-Hall, Inc.
Barnard, C. (1938). *The functions of the executive.* Cambridge, MA: Harvard University Press.
Barnhart, R.K. (1995). *The Barnhart concise dictionary of etymology.* New York: HarperCollins.

Barry, D. & Meisiek, S. (2010). The art of leadership and its fine art shadow. *Leadership*, *6*(3), 331–349.

Baskwill, J. (2008). Stepping out of the shadows and onto the stage: Arts-informed research in educational administration as activist practice. *Journal of Educational Administration and Foundations*, *19*(2), 37–55.

Bathurst, R., Jackson, B. & Statler, M. (2010). Leading aesthetically in uncertain times. *Leadership*, *6*(3), 311–330.

Bennis, W. (1989). *On becoming a leader*. Cambridge, MA: Perseus Books.

Blumberg, A. (1989). *School administration as a craft: Foundations of practice*. Boston: Allyn & Bacon.

Bolton, C. & English, F.W. (2010). De-constructing the logic/emotion binary in educational leadership preparation and practice. *Journal of Educational Administration*, *48*(5), 561–578.

Bourdieu, P. (1998). *Practical reason: On the theory of action*. Stanford, CA: Stanford University Press.

Bourdieu, P. (1999a). *Acts of resistance: Against the tyranny of the market*. New York: The New Press.

Bourdieu, P. (1999b). The abdication of the state. In P. Bourdieu et al. (Eds.), *The weight of the world: Social suffering in contemporary society* (pp. 181–188). Stanford, CA: Stanford University Press.

Burns, J. (1978). *Leadership*. New York: Harper & Row.

Collingwood, R.J. (1938). *The principles of art*. London: Oxford University Press.

Cook, R. (2015, February 12). Prosecution rests; judge weighs some dismissals. *Atlanta Journal-Constitution*, B2.

Cranston, N.C. & Ehrich, L.C. (2007). *What is this thing called leadership?* Brisbane: Australian Academic Press.

Crawford, M. (2009). *Getting to the heart of leadership: Emotion and educational leadership*. London: Sage.

Deal, T.E. & Peterson, K.D. (1994). *The leadership paradox: Balancing logic and artistry in schools*. San Francisco: Jossey-Bass.

Dewey, J. (1958). *Art as experience*. New York: Capricorn Books.

Duke, D.L. (1986, February 1). The aesthetics of leadership. *Educational Administration Quarterly*, *22*(1), 7–25.

Ehrich, L.C. & English, F.W. (2012). What can grassroots leadership teach us about school leadership? *Halduskultuur-Administrative Culture*, *13*(2), 85–108.

Eisner, E. (2002). *The arts and the creation of mind*. New Haven, CT: Yale University Press.

Feyerabend, P. (1995). *Problems of empiricism: Philosophical papers. Vol. 2*. Cambridge: Cambridge University Press.

Fineman, S. (2000). *Emotions in organizations*. London: Sage.

Foster, W. (1986). *Paradigms and promises: New approaches to educational administration*. Buffalo, NY: Prometheus Books.

Greenfield, T.B. (1975). Theory about organization: A new perspective and its implications for schools. In B.M. Hughes (Ed.), *Administering education: International challenges* (pp. 71–99). London: Athlone Press, University of London.

Greenfield, T.B. (1986). The decline and fall of science in educational administration. *Interchange*, *17*(2), 57–80.

Greenfield, T. & Ribbins, P (Eds.). (1993). *Greenfield on educational administration: Towards a humane science*. New York: Routledge.

Gronn, P. (2003). *The new work of educational leaders: Changing leadership practice in an era of school reform.* Thousand Oaks, CA: Sage Publications.

Groopman, J. (2007). *How doctors think.* Boston: Houghton Mifflin.

Hansen, H., Ropo, A. & Sauer, E. (2007). Aesthetic leadership. *The Leadership Quarterly, 18,* 544–560.

Harding, J. & Pribram, D. (2004). Losing our cool? Following Williams and Grossberg on emotion. *Cultural Studies, 18*(6), 863–883.

Harris, C.E. (2006). Collingwood on imagination, expression and action: Advancing an aesthetically critical study of educational administration. In E.A. Samier & R.J. Bates (Eds.), *Aesthetic dimensions of educational administration and leadership* (pp. 45–63). London: Routledge.

Heilbrunn, J. (1996). Can leadership be studied? In P.S. Temes (Ed.), *Teaching leadership: Essays in theory and practice* (pp. 1–12). New York: Peter Lang.

Hepburn, R.W. (2002). Data and theory in aesthetics: Philosophical understanding and misunderstanding. In A. Berleant (Ed.), *Environment and the arts: Perspectives on environmental aesthetics* (pp. 24–38). Aldershot: Ashgate.

Hewitt, K.K. (2015). The continuing search for best practices in classroom instruction. In F. English (Ed.), *The SAGE guide to educational leadership and management* (pp. 135–150). Los Angeles: Sage.

Horton, R. (2007, May 31). What's wrong with doctors. *New York Review of Books.* Retrieved from http://www.nybooks.com/articles/20214.

Ingarden, R. (1975). Phenomenological aesthetics: An attempt at defining its range. *The Journal of Aesthetics and Art Criticism, 33*(3), 257–269.

Jarvie, J. (2015, March 17). Atlanta public school pupils "were robbed." *The Los Angeles Times,* A5.

Jones, M. (2006). *Artful leadership: Awakening the commons of the imagination.* Bloomington, IN: Trafford Publishing.

Keating, P.J. (2011). *After words: The post-prime ministerial speeches.* Sydney: Allen & Unwin.

Keating, P.J. (2012). Interview with Paul Keating. Keating on the arts. *Sky News,* December 18, 2012. Retrieved from https://youtube.com/watch?v=XdY1MthwYzk.

Kelehear, Z. (2008, July 21). Instructional leadership, connoisseurship and critique: Using an arts-based approach to extend conversations about teaching. *International Journal of Leadership in Education: Theory and Practice, 11*(3), 239–256.

Kenneth, R.H., Hamm, R.M., Grassia, J. & Peterson, T. (1997). Direct comparison of the efficiency of intuitive and analytical cognition in expert judgment. In W.M. Goldstein & R.M. Hogarth (Eds.), *Research on judgment and decision making: Currents, connections, and controversies* (pp. 144–180). Cambridge: Cambridge University Press.

Kimber, M. & Ehrich, L.C. (2011). The democratic deficit and school-based management in Australia. *Journal of Educational Administration, 49*(2), 179–199.

Kimber, M. & Ehrich, L.C. (2015, February). Are Australia's universities in deficit? A tale of generic managers, audit culture and casualization. *Journal of Higher Education Policy and Management,* 1–15.

Ladkin, D. (2008). Leading beautifully: How mastery, congruence and purpose create the aesthetic of embodied leadership practice. *The Leadership Quarterly, 19,* 31–41.

Langer, S.K. (1962). *Philosophical sketches.* Baltimore, MD: The Johns Hopkins University Press.

Letzing, J. (2015, February 10). New details emerge on HSBC Swiss unit. *The Wall Street Journal,* C3.

Maxcy, S. (1991). *Educational leadership: A critical pragmatic perspective.* New York: Bergin and Garvey.

McGregor, D. (1960). *The human side of enterprise.* New York: McGraw-Hill, Inc.

McWhirter, C. (2015, April 15). Educators get prison terms. *The Wall Street Journal*, A3.

Menzel, D. (1999). The morally mute manager: Fact or fiction? *Public Personnel Management, 28*(4), 515–527.

North Carolina State Board of Education (2007). *North Carolina standards for superintendents.* Raleigh, NC.

Polanyi, M. (1967). *The tacit dimension.* New York: Doubleday.

Sachs, J. (2000). The activist professional. *Journal of Educational Change, 1*(1), 77–95.

Sahlberg, P. (2011). *Finnish lessons: What can the world learn from educational change in Finland?* New York: Teachers College Press.

Samier, E. (2008). The problem of passive evil in educational administration: Moral implications of doing nothing. *ISEA, 36*(1), 2–21.

Samier, E. (2011). Exploring aesthetic dimensions of leadership. In F. English (Ed.), *The SAGE handbook of educational leadership* (2nd ed.) (pp. 273–286). Thousand Oaks, CA: Sage.

Sergiovanni, T.J. (2000). *The lifeworld of leadership.* San Francisco, CA: Jossey-Bass.

Sinclair, A. (2005). Body possibilities in leadership. *Leadership, 1*(4), 387–406.

Sperville, D.R. (2014, July 9). Major revisions underway for school leaders' standards. *Education Week, 33*(36), 9.

Starratt, R.J. (1993). *The drama of leadership.* London: The Falmer Press.

Strati, A. (2010). Aesthetic understanding of work and organizational life: Approaches and research developments. *Sociology Compass, 4*(10), 880–893.

Tagami, T. & Cook, R. (2015, February 12). APS cheating trial: Possible penalties called into question. *Atlanta Journal-Constitution*, A1 and A6.

Taylor, F.W. (1911/1967). *The principles of scientific management.* New York: W.W. Norton & Company.

Tichy, N.M. & Bennis, W.G. (2007). *Judgment: How winning leaders make great calls.* New York: Portfolio.

Weick, K. (1993). The collapse of sensemaking in organizations. The Mann Gulch disaster. *Administrative Science Quarterly, 38*(4), 628–652.

Wenger, E. (1998). *Communities of practice: Learning, meaning, and identity.* Cambridge: Cambridge University Press.

Zabel, L. (2015, February 12). Six creative ways artists can improve communities. *Guardian.* Retrieved from http://www.theguardian.com/culture-professionals-network/2015/ffeb/12/creative-ways-artists-improve-communities.

Zorn, D. & Boler, M. (2008). Rethinking emotions and educational leadership. *International Journal of Leadership in Education, 10*(2), 137–152.

EPILOGUE

Final Lessons on Connoisseurship

No, you do not have thousands of years to live. Urgency is on you. While you live, while you can, become good.

(Aurelius, 2006, p. 38)

The journey for this book began not as a search for connoisseurship but as a search for new eyes to look at leadership. The authors were convinced that nothing much novel or previously considered in the lexicon of leadership could be discerned using the existing social science models heavily influenced by structural functional behaviorism. This approach's capacity to reveal anything new had long since petered out. We were also deeply suspicious of starting with leaders in schools because of the likely trap of becoming Max Weber's acolytes where leadership is subsumed under management. Thus, our journey was initiated as a venture into different intellectual/conceptual territory to serve as a way to re-sculpt our own vision of leadership and to restore to the leadership equation the full human being, much of what had in the past been labeled too subjective to consider, things like passion, empathy, commitment and morality.

In this quest we were humbled by our respondents, first in the artistic world by their sympathy and understanding for our journey, and secondly by their willingness to reveal their most intimate thoughts and insights into their craft and their own personal lives in the pursuit of competence and understanding of themselves and the times. We felt renewed in listening to their stories and struggles, and we felt that there was indeed something to share with leaders in our world of education and schooling.

Here are the lessons we learned in the journey of this book.

1. Connoisseurship is a Continuum in a Quest to Become More Competent

Connoisseurship is not a condition where in one moment one is not a connoisseur and the next one has arrived as one. It is not a category. Connoisseurship is a unique human phenomenon of living and it represents the human drive to learn and to understand oneself and one's environment. All humans to some extent must come to terms with themselves and their worlds. As their own journey unfolds, some become satisfied or satiated and stop learning. They become convinced that there is nothing more to learn or that efforts to learn it require too much time and trouble. Other human beings keep striving, keep pushing, and stretch themselves to understand more, becoming better and better at their chosen occupation or profession. This passion to learn and to understand goes on until life itself ends. It is perhaps best epitomized by Albert Camus (as cited in Zaretsky, 2010) who said of himself, "I have no wish to lie or to be lied to, I want to keep my lucidity to the last, and gaze upon my death with all the fullness of my jealousy and horror" (p. 159). Connoisseurship is not categorical though it may be allegorical. All human beings have the potential for connoisseurship. There is nothing elite about the concept as we have come to understand the human journey of living and learning. Connoisseurship is a process not an end. It is a continuing process of *becoming* and not a *destination*.

2. Connoisseurship is About Making Limitations and Barriers Into an Advantage

Our work with artists revealed for us that those on a continuum towards connoisseurship view limitations and barriers as part of the process of working in their fields or endeavors. Thus, limitations and barriers are not seen as things to overcome, but rather as things to incorporate into the process of working and leading. In this sense limitations and barriers are integral towards connoisseurship. Here we are reminded of the Japanese concept of *ma* which refers to the space between objects. In the Western mind such spaces are considered "empty" but not so in Japan. The *ma* is a function and it is the underlying concept behind the serenity of the Japanese garden where "Man [sic] and nature are somehow transformed and can be viewed as in harmony" (Hall, 1969, p. 153). The world of artists is one where limitations add to the brilliance of the artistic creation. Creativity is a function of constraint and not overabundance. School leaders tend to see limitations as debilitating and evoking a compromise on what otherwise might be deemed a desired state. Artists rarely see their work in that context. School leaders need to see organizational and bureaucratic constraints as a way to enhance their creative leadership by incorporating them into their leadership practice. Some researchers have called this "creative insubordination" (Morris, Crowson, Porter-Gehrie & Hurwitz, 1984, p. 149). It means one has to know how to break the rules when it is required.

3. Connoisseurship is About Power

Knowledge is neither natural nor neutral. In the human world, knowledge is connected to people and people live within social hierarchies. Knowledge connected to people and to positions of authority are expressions of power. Davidson (1986), quoting Foucault (1980), observed that, "Truth is to be understood as a system of ordered procedures for the production, regulation, distribution, circulation and operation of statements . . . [it] is linked in a circular relation with systems of power which produce and sustain it, and to effects of power which induces it and which extends it" (pp. 221–224).

Not only is connoisseurship connected to performance, it is also linked to power. The drive to become supremely competent is also the drive to hold an opinion or perspective that subsumes all others. It is the power to prevail in an argument. It is not the power to anchor blind subservience. It is the power of expertise, recognized in all forms of human endeavor.

4. The Discerning Eye of Connoisseurship Involves Knowledge and Doing

We have affirmed that the development of the "discerning" or "enlightened" eye of the connoisseur involves knowledge and/or performance. Our research has affirmed that there are those who are on the continuum of connoisseurship as artists or as leaders and there are those who have merely knowledge but who are neither artists nor leaders. In the latter category, our research subjects did not include art or leadership critics. The presence of the pure critic, such as a Vasari with artists, Said with musicians, or Plutarch with leaders, was not included in our study. They do exist, however, as historic exemplars. Our research subjects were nearly all connoisseurs of themselves and leadership performance.

We confess that our interest in connoisseurship for leadership is first to provide a conceptual base to reconsider leadership in the full spectrum of its application in context and not to prepare critics of leadership, though we also recognize that being a critic of one's own performance is central to growth as a leader or as an artist. Arguably an example of the kind of self-analysis that has been described in a way that can be followed is that of Pierre Bourdieu's (2008) *Sketch for a Self-Analysis* in which he set forth to examine his life as a researcher and sociologist and "to subject that experience, set out as honestly as possible, to critical confrontation, as if it were any other object" (p. 1). We found in our artists and school leaders a penchant for self-analysis and a consciousness of craft in a struggle to attain improved performance within the constraints in which they all labored. This is not simply "working hard." And it is also more than "introspection." Rather for us it appeared as a dual thrust of skill acquisition combined with contextual sophistication, that is, that the world becomes more understandable as it became more complex. Enhanced perception and increased understanding leading towards mastery became blended together as an orientation to artistic and educational advanced practice that is distinctive in its genre of living, learning and working.

5. Connoisseurship Involves Csikszentmihalyi's Flow Experience

The joy of becoming more competent, a sense of personal accomplishment and a deep sense of exhilaration accompany the work of the connoisseur. Artists spoke of being so engrossed in their work that they lost all sense of time. Csikszentmihalyi (1990) described this as a *flow experience*. This kind of experience involved being tested to the limits within an altered state of consciousness that was so pleasurable that the respondents would continue to do it even at great cost just for the sake of doing it. Frase (2001) described one example of an educational practice performed by school principals that led to *flow experiences*. Similarly our research also confirmed the presence of flow in the work of artists and school leaders. For the former it was the joy of creativity. For the latter it was the joy of linking administrative practice with improved school climate and the releasing of faculty energy and observing improved student learning (not necessarily better test scores).

References

Aurelius, M. (2006). *Meditations* (M. Hammond, Trans.). New York: Penguin Classics.

Bourdieu, P. (2008). *Sketch for a self-analysis*. Chicago: University of Chicago Press.

Csikszentmihalyi, M. (1990). *Flow: The psychology of optimal experience*. New York: Harper & Row.

Davidson, A. (1986). Archaeology, genealogy, ethics. In D.C. Hoy (Ed.), *Foucault: A critical reader* (pp. 221–234). Oxford: Blackwell.

Foucault, M. (1980). *Power/knowledge*. New York: Pantheon Books.

Frase, L. (2001). *A confirming study of the predictive power of principal classroom visits on efficacy and teacher flow experiences*. Paper presented at the Annual Meeting of the American Educational Research Association. Seattle, Washington.

Hall, E.T. (1969). *The hidden dimension*. New York: Anchor Books.

Morris, V.C., Crowson, R.L., Porter-Gehrie, C. & Hurwitz, Jr. E. (1984). *Principals in action: The reality of management schools*. Columbus, OH: Charles E. Merrill Publishing Company.

Zaretsky, R. (2010). *Albert Camus: Elements of a life*. New York: Cornell University Press.

APPENDIX

Interview Questions

Phase 1: How do artists retain their creativity and resiliency when facing major barriers in their work?

1. How do you decide when to start a project?
2. How do you decide what medium or mode of expression to use to express or shape your work?
3. Do you think about how the medium selected enables and/or inhibits what you are thinking about and what you want to express?
4. Do you ever recognize in doing the work how the tools or materials limit what you can say or express? Do you think about how the limitations can be overcome?
5. Do you ever stop work on a project because you have discovered too many limitations on either the medium you've selected or because you are dissatisfied with its limitations?
6. What do you use to frame your work? Are you aware of the histories of either the expression or the traditions in which your idea has been previously expressed?
7. When do you know a work is finished? Do you work with an eye towards what the final piece or image should contain?
8. What kind of surprises have you encountered in constructing a creative work?
9. How do you deal with ambiguity, either not knowing where a work will take you or what it is going to be like when you decide to quit working on it?
10. How do you know when the way you have framed your work is helping or hindering your work or its mode of expression?
11. What about your work gives you the most satisfaction in doing it?

12. What inspires you to keep working? Do you know what is the source of your inspiration?

13. What do you think makes a work of art last, that is, live beyond its time?

Phase 2: How and under what conditions do artists develop "the discerning eye" and become connoisseurs of their and others' work?
Based on our earlier research with artists, we have developed a model that shows that creative work can be understood in terms of three interactive factors: personal capacities of the artist; a field which consists of a specific institution and its history; and the medium (i.e. dance, painting) in which an artist works. Our questions below are based around these three factors.

1. Would you say that as you matured as an artist and/or as a leader you began to differentiate more clearly your effectiveness and/or your ability to do your work? If so, can you describe in what ways your differentiation of your work or skills happened? Can you indicate any key events or problems that helped you engage in such differentiation?

2. How does your medium and your work in it define your capacity to see it more clearly or begin to notice things you did not notice or see before?

3. In what ways does the place or context or shape of your work or performance and its history define, contain or lead you or help you put your own work and your own performance into a flow of events or a continuum of its development?

4. What metaphors most accurately portray your own development as a leader or an artist?

5. What factors in your work link most directly to your own life story?

6. How do you make meaning of your work? How do you know if it is good or not? What do you use to determine where you want to spend more time creating or working?

7. As you compare yourself to those you admire how do you identify the gaps in your own work or performance? Likewise, those less skilled than you, where do you see their performance not as able as yours?

8. What are the most important shadings of understandings you bring to your work or performance? Over time how have the meanings you give yourself in your work changed?

9. Can you explain any theoretical base for your own work?

10. How important is the public aspect of your work and our ability to understand its public face?

11. What is the interpersonal dimension of your work or performance that you require to continue your work?

12. What are some of the significant interpersonal relationships you had that have influenced your identity and work as an artist? What are your current significant interpersonal relationships and how do they impact upon your work?

Phase 3: How do educational leaders develop a "discerning eye" in their practice? Does this development parallel or imitate the same process with artists?

1. Provide a brief biographical sketch of yourself and how you became an educational leader. In what capacities have you served as a leader and for how long?
2. What factors in your work most directly link to your own life story?
3. How is competence (sometimes we refer to the development of competence as *distinction*) established?
4. How have you matured as an educational leader and can you begin to differentiate more clearly how your skills have developed and been honed with practice?
5. How do you discern outstanding practice in a school leader?
6. Can you describe aspects of outstanding leadership practice in a school leader?
7. Were you on a continuum of development towards becoming or retaining such competence?
8. Can you trace your own understanding of outstanding practice, that is, to insights or incidents which led to that understanding?
9. If your judgment were questioned, to what authorities or sources would you refer to substantiate your judgment?
10. Is there a colleague, educational leader or leader(s) whom you admire as a leader and if so can you indicate what you admire about them?
11. How important is it for a leader to have a role model or a mentor?
12. How do you apprise your own development and competence as a leader?
13. Conversely, if you were visiting a school not your own, what criteria or dimensions would indicate to you the leader was not competent or a poor leader?
14. What metaphors most accurately portray your own development as a leader?
15. Can you explain any theoretical base for your work?
16. How important is the public aspect of your work?
17. How do you make meaning of your work? How do you know if it is good or not? What do you use to determine where you want to spend more time creating or leading?

ABOUT THE AUTHORS

Fenwick W. English (Ph.D., Arizona State University) and **Lisa Catherine Ehrich** (Ph.D., Queensland University of Technology) have undertaken joint research in Australia and the United States on alternative educational leadership perspectives since 2011. Their co-authored conference papers have been presented at the University Council for Educational Administration (UCEA) in Pittsburgh, Pennsylvania; the American Educational Research Association (AERA) in San Francisco, California; and the Athens Institute for Education and Research in Athens, Greece. Both authors have been extensively published in books as authors and editors as well as in academic journals and professional periodicals for over three decades in their respective countries. *Fenwick W. English* is the R. Wendell Eaves Senior Distinguished Professor of Educational Leadership in the School of Education at the University of North Carolina at Chapel Hill, a position he has held since 2001. *Lisa Catherine Ehrich* is Associate Professor in the School of Cultural and Professional Learning at Queensland University of Technology (QUT) in Brisbane, Australia. She began her higher education career at QUT in 1992. *Professors English* and *Ehrich* carry extensive teaching and advising responsibilities for students at the doctoral levels in their respective university programs.

Fenwick W. English has served as president of the UCEA in 2006–2007 and president of the National Council of Professors of Educational Administration (NCPEA) in 2011–2012. In 2013 he received the Living Legend Award from NCPEA for his lifetime contribution to the field of educational leadership.

Lisa Catherine Ehrich has similarly been recognized for her long contribution to Australian leadership education when she was made a Fellow with the Australian Council for Educational Leadership (Queensland Branch) and awarded an Australian Council for Educational Leaders (ACEL) Fellowship in 2014.

INDEX